PIONEER PAINTERS OF INDIANA

George Winter: Portrait of William Digby
Courtesy of the Albert A. Wells Memorial Library, Lafayette

Pioneer Painters
of Indiana

By Wilbur D. Peat

ART ASSOCIATION OF

INDIANAPOLIS, INDIANA · 1954

The Lakeside Press, R. R. Donnelley & Sons Company
Chicago, Illinois, and Crawfordsville, Indiana

Contents

LIST OF ILLUSTRATIONS vii

INTRODUCTION xi

1. FORT WAYNE, VINCENNES, NEW HARMONY, RICHMOND . . 3
   Henry Hamilton, John Whistler, Jonathan Heart, Pierre Le Dru, Samuel
   Seymour, James O. Lewis, Adlard Welby, Basil Hall, Carl Bodmer, Lefevre F.
   Cranstone, William Momberger.

2. VINCENNES, NEW HARMONY 14
   Lewis Peckham, Horace Harding, C. D. Cook, Augustus A. Von Smith,
   William R. Freeman, Peter Tester, Charles A. Lesueur, John Chappelsmith,
   Virginia Poullard Dupalais, David Dale Owen, Peter Duclos, George Warren,
   Miner Kellogg, John Banvard, Jacob Maentel.

3. TERRE HAUTE, EVANSVILLE, ROCKPORT, NEW ALBANY,
   HANOVER, MADISON, VEVAY, LAWRENCEBURG 39
   Sister St. Francis Xavier, Sister Maurice, Sister Mary Albertine, George
   Linen, William R. Freeman, James F. Gookins, Harvey Mitchell, Walter
   Sies, James T. Poindexter, James G. Forbes, Rose O'Byrne, Philip Lang,
   George W. Morrison, Carl P. Fetsch, Ferdinand G. Walker, Christopher
   Harrison, Richard Terrell, James F. Harris, Thomas B. Read, P. C. Wyeth,
   William Henry Hilliard, William McK. Snyder, William Z. Yonge, John
   Gibson Dunn, Wilbur Woodward.

4. SALEM, SEYMOUR, BEDFORD, MITCHELL, SPENCER, BLOOMING-
   TON, MARTINSVILLE, COLUMBUS, FRANKLIN, GREENSBURG,
   RUSHVILLE 69
   James R. New, John Ottis Adams, Patrick H. Davenport, Samuel Richards,
   Cornelius Pering, Theophilus A. Wylie, Marion Blair, John E. Bundy,
   John Nicholson, William M. Chase, Harriet Hillis Tinsley, Edwin Farrer,
   Laura G. Schofield, Retta Mathews, Harry Carey.

5. BROOKVILLE, RICHMOND, CENTERVILLE, DUBLIN, CAMBRIDGE
   CITY, NEW CASTLE, ANDERSON, MUNCIE 85
   John Insco Williams, Samuel S. Walker, Lefevre J. Cranstone, Marcus Mote,
   W. Alden Mote, John E. Bundy, Charles Conner, Solomon Woody, Pliny
   Kersey, Monimia Bunnell Boyd, Peter F. Reed, Flora Stigleman, John H.
   Witt, James M. Dennis, Lewis Cass Lutz, Melvina Hobson Batson, Lucinda
   Bowers McDowell, Mary Ellen Branson, Henry Dousa, Samuel Richards,
   James Whitcomb Riley, John Ottis Adams, Nelson Perry Adams, Linda
   Jenkins Ryan.

6. FORT WAYNE, LOGANSPORT, LAFAYETTE, ATTICA, CRAWFORDS-
VILLE, NOBLESVILLE, GOSHEN, SOUTH BEND, LAPORTE   .   . 109
    Horace Rockwell, R. B. Crafft, Jacob Hegler, R. G. Cosgrove, Edward
    Edmonson, Joseph H. Dille, George Winter, George Adams, John D. Forgy,
    DeScott Evans, Jerome McLean, Robert Swaim, Max Klepper, Mary Carter
    Davis, Wilson R. Berry, Jacob Ackerman, Barton S. Hays, Virginia Wilson
    Todd, William S. Segar, Lew Wallace, John Nicholson, Walter Sies,
    Henry A. Mills, Theodore C. Steele, Daniel Roberts, Granville Bishop,
    Adolphus Van Sickle, J. H. Van Favoren, Curran Swaim, Charles M.
    Heaton, Daniel Kotz, Alexis Comparet, Joseph Mason, Aaron Deane Fletcher.

7. INDIANAPOLIS: 1820–1860   146
    Samuel S. Rooker, Richard Terrell, Michael G. Rogers, J. Insco Williams,
    Ephraim Brown, Jacob Cox, Henry Waugh, James F. Harris, Clark Gordon,
    Thomas Worthington Whittredge, Joseph O. Eaton, Lew Wallace, John
    Gibson Dunn, William S. Unthank, James B. Dunlap, Barton S. Hays,
    Alois Sinks, John H. Niemeyer.

8. INDIANAPOLIS: 1860–1885   171
    Peter F. Reed, Thomas B. Glessing, James M. Dennis, Thomas J. Davies,
    T. Buchanan Read, Ellen M. Ingraham, William M. Chase, John B. Hill,
    James G. Forbes, William R. Freeman, Harry M. Colcord, James F. Gookins,
    John W. Love, Carl P. Fetsch, Theobald Lietz, Alois Sinks, John Antrobus,
    Lotta Guffin, Margaret Rudisill, Mary Hill Culbertson, Henry F. Spread,
    Otto Stark, Dewey Bates, Harry Fowler, Theodore C. Steele, Charles Fiscus,
    Frank Edwin Scott, William Forsyth, Richard Gruelle, Susan Ketcham.

NOTES   211

BIBLIOGRAPHICAL GUIDE   221

ROSTER OF PAINTERS   225

INDEX   243

List of Illustrations

George Winter: Portrait of William Digby .   .   .   *Frontispiece*

PLATE

Henry Hamilton: Ship Rock, Wabash River   1

Basil Hall: Houses on the Banks of the Ohio   2

Carl Bodmer: View of Vincennes, Indiana, 1834   .   .   .   3

Lefevre F. Cranstone: Street Scene in Richmond   .   .   .   4

Lewis Peckham: Miniatures of Paul Peckham and

    Lewis Peckham   5

Lewis Peckham: Portrait of Hyacinthe Lasselle   6

Dexter Harding (attributed to): Portrait of William A. Chatfield .   7

Horace Harding (attributed to): Portrait of Elias McNamee   .   8

C. D. Cook (attributed to): Portrait of George Rogers Clark .   .   9

Augustus A. Von Smith: Portrait of Francis Vigo   .   .   .   10

William R. Freeman: Portrait of Samuel P. Judah   .   .   .   11

Peter Tester: Portrait of Adele Bayard Lacroix   12

Charles Alexandre Lesueur: Major Phillips seated on a box

    of Potatoes   13

Virginia Dupalais: Portrait of Joseph Fauntleroy .   .   .   14

David Dale Owen: Portrait of Richard Owen   15

Miner K. Kellogg: Portrait of Robert Dale Owen   .   .   .   16

Jacob Maentel: Portraits of Jonathan and Rebecca Jaquess .   .   17

George Linen: Portrait of Caleb Mills   18

James F. Gookins: Modisette Ferry on the Wabash   .   .   .   19

James T. Poindexter: Portrait of Mrs. Charles Mason .   .   .   20

Philip Lang: Portrait of Matthias Sharp   21

George W. Morrison: Portrait of Mary Emma and

    Harry Woodward   22

P. C. Wyeth: Sons of Charles L. Shrewsbury   23

PLATE

William McK. Snyder: Madison on the Ohio River . . . 24

William Z. Yonge: Portrait of Lucille Morerod Detraz . . 25

John Gibson Dunn: The Temperance Pledge 26

Wilbur Woodward: Portrait of Adeline Tomlinson McFadden . 27

Patrick H. Davenport: Portrait of Mary Ellen Lemon Hamer . 28

Samuel Richards: Portrait of Harlan Richards 29

Cornelius Pering: The Seminary Campus, Bloomington . . 30

Marion Blair: Portrait of Daily Voss 31

Theophilus A. Wylie: A Political Rally 32

John Elwood Bundy: Summer Landscape 33

Edwin Farrer: Portrait of Leven E. Wallace 34

John Insco Williams: Portrait of Miles Murphy 35

John Insco Williams: Portrait of Susan H. Freeman . . . 36

John Insco Williams: Portrait of Alice Harris Conklin . . . 37

Marcus Mote: Portrait of Elizabeth Chalfont Gilbert . . . 38

Marcus Mote: Indiana Yearly Meeting of Friends . . . 39

Charles Conner: In the Parlor 40

Monimia Bunnell Boyd: The Hoosier's Nest 41

Solomon Woody: Portrait of Paul Way 42

John H. Witt: Portrait of Julia Stanton 43

Melvina Hobson Batson: Portrait of Elizabeth Elliott Peed . . 44

Lucinda Bowers McDowell: Portrait of Samuel Graham . . 45

Henry Dousa: Residence of Thomas Fyffe 46

James Whitcomb Riley: Making Hay While the Sun Shines . 47

John Ottis Adams: Portrait of Sarah Heinsohn 48

Nelson Perry Adams: Landscape with Cows 49

Horace Rockwell: The Samuel Hanna Family 50

R. B. Crafft: Portrait of Robert Filson 51

Joseph H. Dille: Portrait of Thomas W. Swinney . . . 52

George Winter: Portrait of Joseph Barron 53

George Winter: Gathering of Indians 54

David Scott Evans: Portrait of George R. Chitwood . . . 55

PLATE

Wilson R. Berry: Longansport Street Scene 56

Barton S. Hays: Portrait of Lewis D. Lyons 57

Jacob Hegler: Portrait of Mary Alice Lyons 58

Lew Wallace: Portrait of Henry Smith Lane 59

J. H. Van Favoren: Portrait of Alexis Coquillard . . . 60

Curran Swaim: Portrait of Samuel C. Sample 61

Adolphus Van Sickle: Portrait of Frederick C. King . . . 62

Richard Terrell: Portrait of Rebecca Cook Coe 63

Michael G. Rogers: Portrait of Isaac Dunn 64

Jacob Cox: Portrait of David Wallace 65

Jacob Cox: The Morris Morris Farm 66

Jacob Cox: Portrait of Thomas, John, and Eliza Spann . . . 67

Joseph O. Eaton: Portrait of Peninnah Mills Pope . . . 68

William Unthank: Portrait of Harriet Moreland Wishard . . 69

James B. Dunlap: Portrait of Woodville Browning . . . 70

Barton S. Hays: Portrait of Rebecca Raymond Adams . . . 71

Barton S. Hays: Melon and Peaches 72

Thomas B. Glessing: Cold Springs, Riverside Park . . . 73

William M. Chase: Portrait of William Gurley Munson . . 74

James G. Forbes: Portrait of Conrad Baker 75

John W. Love: The Sycamores 76

John W. Love: Portrait of Henry L. Sielkin 77

William R. Freeman: Portrait of Jacob Cox 78

Lotta Guffin: Portrait of Addison C. Harris 79

Dewey Bates: Portrait of Josephine Landis 80

Theodore C. Steele: Portrait of James Whitcomb Riley . . 81

William Forsyth: The Artist's Mother 82

Theodore C. Steele: Pleasant Run 83

Richard B. Gruelle: The Canal, Morning 84

Introduction

THIS IS THE STORY of plain and simple people, who, for the most part, achieved neither fame nor riches, and whose distinction lay in their unusual calling. It tells of picture painters who took their places in our development from a sparsely settled frontier into a strong and fruitful commonwealth. It is the account of all-but-forgotten activities that made up the foundation stones of that structure we regard with no little pride—Indiana art of our day.

The period encompassed is something over a hundred years. It begins with those rugged days of Indians and trappers, soldiers and settlers, who saw the territory being wrenched from Britain's grip, and closes with the mid-1880's when full political, social, and industrial stature had been reached. In the field of painting, the year 1885 marks the end of the formative period in this area and is, therefore, the logical point at which to conclude a history of Indiana's pioneer painters.

As the work is more in the nature of a chronicle than a thesis, dealing with one section of the state at a time and with artists as dissimilar in their methods of painting as they were scattered in places of residence, no plot could be devised to hold the chapters together. If there is an underlying idea it is this: while no celebrated painters worked in the state during the period under consideration, and no breath-taking masterpieces were produced, the fact that a hundred or more men and women seriously and professionally painted here, leaving to posterity numerous portraits and landscapes—many of which are still preserved in local homes, civic buildings, and museums—is reason enough to compile biographical and critical notes on the subject. As factors in our cultural evolution their activities should not be forgotten, and as authors of so large a bulk of our heirlooms their names should not fade completely from our memories.

The number of ancestor portraits (to mention one class of paintings only) to which no artist's name can now be assigned is so large that one cannot help but regret the carelessness or indifference that has allowed this situation to come about. Lack of signatures on most of the canvases is the principal cause, of course, while the failure of original owners to pass along the names of painters has been a contributing factor. The prevailing belief that itinerant limners deserve no better fate than oblivion because of the low caliber of their work has certainly helped in widening this cleft between pictures and their makers.

The stigma that is usually attached to the word "itinerant" was probably deserved in most cases if one judged the product in relation to the performances of highly skilled and celebrated painters in large metropolitan centers. But in the remoter sections of the country the itinerant was not necessarily an incompetent vagabond. One of the characteristic features of frontier regions was the mobility of craftsmen and professional people. Merchants, judges, doctors, preachers, cabinetmakers, and painters were constantly moving, usually on well-defined circuits, to serve the number of clients necessary to keep them in business. The extent of their journeying usually had nothing to do with the quality of their work.

When we realize how limited in number the portrait commissions must have been in newly settled territories, where vanity was suppressed and money hard to come by, it is easy to understand why there were so many transient painters in America in the first half of the nineteenth century. The surprising thing is that they plied their trade so persistently in the face of what must have been very trying and discouraging circumstances. It is also surprising that they could make a living for themselves and their families entirely by painting.

How these migratory artists chose their routes has not been satisfactorily told. Much was undoubtedly left to chance. Reports of thriving business in a certain village would cause them to strike out in that direction; letters of introduction from satisfied clients to friends in other places took them into a new territory; and not infrequently the adventurous ones followed relatives or close friends to new western lands, picking up such jobs as they could along the way.

In most of the towns they entered they rented rooms for a few days and inserted announcements in the local newspapers, if there were any. These printed declarations all followed the same pattern. They boldly displayed the painter's name, invited ladies and gentlemen of the community to come and view specimens of his work, and guaranteed satisfaction at moderate prices. If business was not brisk enough to take care of all expenses the visiting artist usually painted his landlord's portrait—and perhaps that of his wife—in lieu of rent. Prices were seldom given in such advertisements, but from other sources we learn that charges made for portraits ranged from $25 to $100, and many painters were forced by circumstances to take considerably less— not infrequently accepting farm produce as part or full payment for their work.

As this kind of activity offered little reward and a very uncertain future, painters established in the East never cast their lot with the itinerants and seldom were seen west of the Allegheny Mountains, unless engaged to carry out a specific commission. Likewise, the limner with an unusual amount of talent and ambition, who believed that he could go much farther with additional training, was likely to give up his wayfaring habits, move to a metropolitan center for further study, and then either establish himself there or return to a western town where prospects were good. Several of the artists discussed in this book left Indiana in their formative years and became celebrated in eastern cities, never to return to the scene of their early struggles.

Outlets for artistic talent on the frontier were many if a man wanted to turn his hand to a variety of tasks (and he often had to). Equipped with paints, varnishes, and brushes—and a special kind of manual dexterity—he might be called upon to paint signs, glaze or artificially grain wood, stencil ornamental friezes, paint carriages, and put small scenic vignettes on the doors of iron safes. Some went so far afield as to add cabinetmaking to their repertoire.

Sign painting, the most important of these from the standpoint of demand, was far from a menial task. In the first part of the nineteenth century, following the tradition of the preceding era, signs were as ornamental as they were informative, bearing pictorial and emblematic designs in addition to the lettering. This allowed the painter ample opportunity to indulge in figure drawing and composition, and if he displayed unusual talent he doubtless was paid as much for an imposing ornamental signboard as for a portrait.

The evolution of the average frontier painter, who had no formal schooling in art, was from sign painting to portraiture. He would begin as an apprentice in a sign shop, learn how to handle brushes and paint, gradually develop the knack of drawing rudimentary figures in addition to that of hand lettering, and then pick up a few hints about the higher art of capturing likenesses on canvas. Constant practice and close study of portraits by competent painters—and observation of others at work, whenever possible—would finally give him enough assurance to strike out for himself on a professional basis. If, after a few years, he was not entirely satisfied with technical results growing out of his self-tutoring he might enter the studio of a celebrated portraitist as a student or attend an art academy in the East. It was not until 1878 that the first art school was established in this state, and although some painters, like Cox and Hays, held classes in their Indianapolis studios a decade or more earlier, sound instruction in drawing and painting was not to be had in Indiana until long after the Civil War.

Emphasis on portraiture at that time, instead of on landscape or historical painting, is understandable in view of the stage of our artistic development. Few people were interested in pictures as such, and if money was available at all for things as frivolous as art the purchase had to have more than decorative value. Portraits were regarded as something practical and permanent, preserving the features of actual people, and worthy of being handed down as heirlooms for generations.

In spite of the spread of photography in the 1840's and the establishing of daguerreotype studios, portraiture in oil continued to flourish. Cheaper methods of getting a record of one's physiognomy by this new mechanical method drew thousands to the "daguerrean parlors," but had little effect on the portrait business. The family album never entirely replaced hand-painted likenesses in the nineteenth century. However, the camera did exert considerable influence on the portrait painter and his work. First, it led the client to expect greater verisimilitude in a portrait since he now had photographs to prove that an exact likeness was possible and detailed rendering was desirable; second, many a painter turned artist-photographer, combining the two techniques and thereby increasing the popular appeal of his product—not to mention the simplification of getting accurate likenesses. The prevalent method was to make a faint enlargement of a photograph, mount it on linen or cardboard, and then go over it with oil paints. The technique was more than tinting. Paint was applied thickly enough to completely cover the photographic image. While the result pleased the general public it was far from satisfying to those who had an eye for artistic quality and traditional techniques. Fortunately, most painters remained true to their calling, refusing the camera's aid and painting directly upon the canvas while clients sat patiently before them.

The difficulty of obtaining canvas, brushes, and artists' colors in remote places must have forced painters to keep an ample stock on hand, and to carry adequate supplies with them on their trips. Almost any well-stocked frontier store would have had commercial oils and varnishes, but other articles had to be ordered from eastern cities. Firms in Cincinnati supplied most of the painters in Indiana with materials and frames before local art stores were established. Canvas, coming as it does in compact rolls, was easily carried by the itinerant artist, who, with each order for a portrait cut off a piece of the required size and tacked it onto a wooden stretcher.

The prevailing legend that itinerant portraitists painted in advance a number of stock bodies, leaving a blank area where a face could be inserted later, cannot be supported on the basis of existing evidence, nor from the standpoint of practical procedure. One case has been cited in New England where two portraits show women wearing identical dresses and sitting in the same position, suggesting that the heads had been attached to stock bodies. But these instances of exact duplication of costumes are rare, and while poses are often repeated (all painters have personal preferences relative to poses and positions of hands), there is no reason to assume that uniformity in these respects

means advance preparation of the figures. One needs only a casual introduction to the subject of amateurish portrait painting to know that
the unskilled artist feels safer when repeating a pose that has proved
satisfactory; and that it is inept drawing that makes his effigies appear
as if they had been cut out of paper and pasted onto the canvas in sections. The awkward joining of heads and shoulders, arms and hands,
and so forth are not indications of prior painting of those parts, but of
lack of skill.

A stock-body method (if it was actually practiced) could not have
been popular with clients. Few people, particularly women, would
want themselves portrayed in clothes other than their own, and there
are sufficient reports of ladies selecting their dresses and jewelry carefully in advance of posing to convince one that stock bodies would not
have been tolerated.

From the standpoint of the painter himself, the disadvantages of
carrying around a stack of stretched and partially painted canvases
would have been considerable, as against carrying a roll and a bundle
of stretchers. And what was more, he would gain nothing so far as
manual labor was concerned by prior rendering of bodies, because the
head is the most laborious part of a portrait, the costume and background being, in comparison, easily and quickly painted in.

So far as the Indiana area is concerned, no evidence has turned up
to prove, or even to suggest, that itinerants resorted to partially prepared stock canvases.

Degrees of technical competence varied as greatly as individual
mannerisms in this region. In contrast to larger metropolitan centers
where the influence of a highly skilled and successful painter often appeared in the work of a circle of younger men, no "schools" or stylistic
groups can be detected in the state during the period covered by this
history. The reasons for this are clear. Painters who came from the East
brought with them technical manners and methods learned in a variety
of places and altered by personal tastes and idiosyncrasies, while those
growing up in the state got their training and experience under different people in different towns. No strong artistic personality arose
during this period who drew the majority of the young artists to him

and brought about what historians call a school. To be sure, most of the good artists had students, but either the pupils did not attain distinction, or, in reaching technical maturity, quickly shed their teacher's methods for a more personal way of working.

This dissimilarity of styles in scattered points of activity tends to give our chronicle a kaleidoscopic aspect, but that was the nature of midwestern art in the first part of the nineteenth century. A semblance of order has been achieved by presenting the material according to geographical areas of the state. If the reader is disappointed in not finding those circles of stylistic influences that delight the art historian, perhaps he will find compensation in the fact that he is being introduced to a score of painters whom he never knew before.

It may not be out of place to say something about the term "primitive," a word used extensively today in discussing provincial American art. It connotes a stage in an artist's technical development and may be applied to work produced at any time. Primitive pictures were as prevalent in Indiana as in any other section of the country during the time covered by this book, but no stress has been laid on them here in recounting the local story.

While the term is not difficult to define, it is not easy in every case to decide if a picture is primitive in style or merely inept. Nor do all critics agree where the borderline exists between primitive and semi-competent work. A primitive picture is the work of an untutored painter with an innate, if elementary, sense of color and design. His compositions are naïvely devised, lacking linear or aerial perspective, and without foreshortening or normal overlapping of figures. While his drawing may be firm and strong, with emphasis on outlines, he is unable to suggest the graceful articulation of arms, bodies, and heads. His sense of color is childish: subtleties of hues and textures escape his untrained eyes. He is not able to cope with modulations of tones that help to create the illusion of mass or three-dimensional form, so his figures appear flat instead of round.

The same shortcomings characterize the inept dauber, but lacking the primitive painter's natural taste and sensitivity, he produces pictures that are dull and unattractive.

The present interest (one is tempted to call it a fad) in American primitives has done much to focus attention on an important, though somewhat sentimental, aspect of our cultural heritage, and has insured the preservation of many delightfully quaint canvases that might otherwise be lost or destroyed. One regrets, however, that more interest has been shown in acquisition than in scholarship, causing the removal of pictures from their places of origin before research workers have had an opportunity to establish the names of authors and sitters. As a result, the word "primitive" is now synonymous with "anonymous" in the minds of most people. Since the primary purpose of this chronicle of Indiana painting has been to dispel anonymity, no emphasis has been given to the primitives, however delightful such a discussion might be.

No one is more aware of the defects and shortcomings here than the author himself. The large amount of research, stretching over a period of fifteen years, that underlies the narrative has necessitated a "groundbreaking" method—reporting what the spade has turned up rather than evaluating the material. If the unearthing of these facts has brought life again into one aspect of our history, and has reawakened interest in some of America's lost limners, the labor will seem well repaid.

Out of this investigation has grown a large collection of letters, notes, transcripts of newspaper articles, and clippings, which has been deposited in the library of the John Herron Art Museum, and which may be consulted by anyone wanting additional data on the subject. The small photographs, made by the author for record purposes, are included in this miscellany. A second set of photographs, together with the negatives, is in the library of the Indiana Historical Society.

Whoever approaches the subject of Indiana art must turn first to Mary Q. Burnet's book, *Art and Artists of Indiana*. As a pioneer in the field of nineteenth- and early twentieth-century painting in this region, and one of the first books dealing solely with the arts of one state, it holds an important position as regards both the local and national scene. Although subsequent research has brought certain facts to light that alter some of her views, the work is, nevertheless, invaluable, and I want to take this occasion to pay tribute to its author.

To express adequate appreciation of help received in gathering and publishing this material is a difficult task. Hundreds of people, throughout Indiana and in other parts of the country, have had a hand in it. Some owned paintings; some were related, closely or remotely, to the artists; some were curators of historical museums or art galleries; some were librarians; some were historians—not a few of whom had died, but whose writings were found to be helpful; and some were just friends who took an interest in the project and gave encouragement. To all of these I am deeply indebted.

A special expression of appreciation goes to Mrs. Albert M. Cole, Mrs. Paul Robertson, Blanche Stillson, Gayle Thornbrough, and Anton Scherrer for reading the manuscript so painstakingly and making very helpful suggestions. The interest of Caroline Dunn, librarian of the Indiana Historical Society, has been of great help; and the friendly counsel of Eli Lilly throughout the project has been most reassuring. My gratitude also goes to the trustees of the Lilly Endowment for the grant that made the publication of this work possible.

WILBUR D. PEAT

PIONEER PAINTERS OF INDIANA

Chapter 1

FORT WAYNE, VINCENNES
NEW HARMONY, RICHMOND

ON A COLD November day in 1778 Henry Hamilton, lieutenant-governor of Detroit, in charge of transporting a motley army of English, French, and Indian fighters down the Wabash River, paused to admire a scene on the opposite shore. His flotilla had left Detroit for Vincennes almost two months before, and after having ascended with laborious effort the Maumee and crossed over the portage into the shallow waters of the Little Wabash, it had reached more navigable currents four or five miles above the Miami village at the confluence of the Eel and Wabash rivers. A visit would be made on the morrow to the chiefs of the village to enlist their help in Hamilton's campaign against the American rebels who were holding Vincennes.

What drew Hamilton's attention especially that day was an unusual rock formation. It was familiar to French trappers and others who used this water route joining Lake Erie and the Mississippi, and because of its resemblance to a ship it had acquired the name *Le Navire.*

Exigencies of the hour, and probably of the next day, prevented his ferrying across the river immediately to study the rock more closely, but when the opportunity came to examine it he was not disappointed. After a thorough study of the bluff and the adjoining terrain he wrote the following in his journal:

21st [November, 1778]. We had a sharp Frost with high wind, and the difficulty great in getting our boats along—A point of land advances into the River which terminates by a Bluff of rock—This had formerly been called by Travellers Le Navire, *the Ship,* but the last year a considerable

3

part of it having fallen into the river (as I suppose by an earthquake, tho the Indians say 'twas by a stroke of lightning) It has lost its likeness—Chrystals, petrifications of different soils, the coruna ammonis particularly, are found in abundance, the rocks having been lately rent in their fall discover many of them—I had not time to gratify my curiosity fully at this place, but in walking thro' the wood about 300 yards from the shore, and almost abreast of the Ship—We discovered a Rock in the form nearly of a Vessels hull which tho rudely formed attracted our notice—on examining, we found it to contain petrified shells &ca. and to be much of the nature of the Rock formerly called the Ship.[1]

There is reason to think that when Henry Hamilton had finished his stroll around Cedar Island, as it is now called, he selected a spot on the bank of the river that offered a good view of the bluff and, opening his sketchbook, made a freehand drawing of the projecting rock and distant shore. That he made sketches on that 1778–1779 campaign against Vincennes is borne out by notations in his journal and by the existence of two drawings. One, drawn with pencil, bearing the date October, 1778, and the legend "Burying place of the Ottawa Indians," was made on the Maumee River; the other, a rendering in washes of gray water color, from the same sketchbook but without inscription or date, was made, of a certainty, on the Wabash, a few miles above the present city of Logansport (pl. 1). The conclusion that this sketch was made here was reached not only on the evidence of the sketchbook paper, but because it appears to be a pictorial record of the rock described so vividly by Hamilton in his journal.[2]

For the purpose of our chronicle this water color of "Ship Rock" is of more than passing interest. It is the earliest known drawing made within the present boundaries of Indiana, and the forerunner of countless sketches made by subsequent Hoosier artists along Indiana's picturesque waterways.

It would not surprise us to learn that as a soldier Hamilton used his artistic talent for military purposes—making charts, drawing plans of forts, or plotting strategic maneuvers—but for a man in his position to sketch as a pastime, particularly during extremely difficult periods, was unusual. However, as a member of a noble Scottish family, he had received the type of education and training accorded to boys of similar station. He was well versed in history, literature, and geography; had mastered Greek, Latin, and French; and was skilled in the arts of fencing, dancing, and drawing.

What he accomplished in the last pursuit before coming to America we are not informed, but during his travels in Canada and the United States he frequently made small drawings of Indians or sketched subjects that appealed to the artistic side of his nature. Of the forty Hamilton drawings (pen and ink, pencil, and water color) preserved in the Houghton Library, Harvard University, about a dozen are portrait studies on small cards and the others are outdoor scenes, including the Maumee and Wabash sketches alluded to above, two large drawings of Niagara Falls, and one of the falls of the Passaic, New Jersey.

The remainder of the story of Hamilton's Indiana campaign is well known. In spite of low water and inclement weather, his water-borne army (including a gunboat) reached Vincennes on the seventeenth of December, capturing the fort with little resistance. He ruled the community until late February when a surprise attack by George Rogers Clark and his small band of men brought Vincennes again under American control. A prisoner of war, Henry Hamilton was taken to Williamsburg, Virginia (jotting down observations in his journal and occasionally making sketches on the way), where he was imprisoned for almost two years. Following his release he returned to England. A year later he was appointed lieutenant-governor of Quebec; five years later he was made governor of Bermuda; and he finished his diplomatic career as governor of Dominica. He died at Antigua in 1796.

II

If any enterprise of an artistic nature took place along the Wabash River, or anywhere else in this region, during the next two decades, no evidence of it has come down to us. Small settlements sprang up here and there, usually in the shadows of forts or stockades, but continuous fighting between Americans, British, and Indians created an atmosphere that discouraged settlers for many years. It was too arid, culturally speaking, for even the most adventurous itinerant limners.

Fort Wayne, probably the most strategic point on the northern

Indiana rivers from a military and economic standpoint, was apparently the next Indiana community to harbor artistic talent. In 1794, after Anthony Wayne's defeat of the Indians at Fallen Timbers, a new fort was built here and placed under the command of Colonel Hamtramck. One of the officers who helped build the fort was John Whistler, who, in 1814, was made commandant; with him the story of Indiana art resumes.

Although not blessed with abundant artistic talent, Captain Whistler was a capable draughtsman and perhaps a good painter. Reports have come down to us that he was more than a cartographer, and the fact that he was instructor of drawing at West Point Military Academy suggests that he occasionally indulged in the pleasant occupation of painting pictures. If biographers were less silent about this facet of his life, and if more of his artistic endeavors had survived, we could think of him as Indiana's first resident artist. As it is, we have only two drawings upon which to evaluate his ability: one of Fort Dearborn, modest forerunner of the city of Chicago; the other of Fort Wayne—both made as military records, with neither pictorial nor romantic emphasis.[3]

If John Whistler appears to us today as a rather vague artistic personality, his son George Washington, born in the stockade of Fort Wayne on the nineteenth of May, 1800, is seen in a clearer light. Like his father, George chose a military career, attended West Point, majored in art, and developed into a very competent painter. Thus we may claim him as Indiana's first native-born artist, even though he was still a child when he left the state. Although primarily a soldier, he discovered that there was less military activity for men of his generation than there had been two decades before and he began to find an absorbing interest in surveying and engineering, first under military auspices and then for the expanding railroad systems. In 1833 he resigned his commission in the army (he held the rank of major) and entered the field of civil engineering.

His career as an engineer took him from Lowell, Massachusetts, to St. Petersburg, Russia, and though constantly absorbed with problems of building railroads he found many hours of pleasure and relaxation in outdoor sketching. Of greater satisfaction, perhaps, was the privilege of seeing his son rise to the enviable position of one of the leading painters of his generation, placing the name Whistler in the galaxy of the world's supreme artists.

Much as Indiana may like to claim James Abbott McNeill Whistler as a Hoosier by lineage, we can be certain that he would have shown little interest in such an affiliation. If he knew anything about the town or state in which his father was born and in which his grandfather lived for several years he was silent about it. His attitude toward this region was expressed in the condescending statement he made to a man from Chicago: "Chicago, dear me, what a wonderful place! I really ought to visit it some day—for, you know, my grandfather founded the city and my uncle was the last commander of Fort Dearborn!" [4] So far as we know he never made the visit.

A fourth military draughtsman living in Indiana during the trying years of the 1780's was Jonathan Heart. As captain in the First Regiment of United States Infantry he was stationed for a brief period, around 1790, at Fort Finney, where the town of Jeffersonville now stands. What his training or experience in art had been we do not know, but judging by the few existing drawings he aspired to nothing higher than chart and architectural draughting. Three of his original delineations of Fort Finney are owned by the Indiana Historical Society Library: two are perspective views of the fort as seen from opposite directions, and the third is a ground plan. [5]

Jonathan Heart was originally from Connecticut. He served as a volunteer in the American army in 1775 and before 1790 had been commissioned a captain. He died in action on November 4, 1791.

III

The desire to portray the features and customs of the aboriginal American, either for romantic reasons or to ensure a historical record, brought a number of artists from the East to the western frontiers during the first quarter of the nineteenth century. A few passed through Indiana, but none remained until George Winter decided to make this his home in 1837.

The earliest on record, insofar as Indiana is concerned, was a French trader from Quebec by the name of Pierre Le Dru. During a visit to Vincennes in or about the year 1808 he sketched the features of the Indian chief Tecumseh and his brother The Prophet. The drawings appeared as woodcuts, considerably altered as to costume, in Lossing's *Field Book of the War of 1812,*[6] and have been subsequently reproduced in other histories. Lossing stated that the original drawings were in the possession of Le Dru's son in Quebec in 1848, but recent attempts to find them have proved fruitless.

It appears that the earliest artist to visit Indiana for the sole purpose of painting the Indians was Samuel Seymour. According to recent biographers he was the first man with any degree of artistic competence to travel as far west as the Mississippi, making drawings of striking scenic spots and depicting the features of Indian chiefs whom he met. Very little is known about his life. It is believed that he was a native of England and that his early adult years were spent in Philadelphia. There he made some steel engravings and presumably painted a few pictures. The rather inept caliber of his work indicates that he was largely self-tutored.

Seymour's opportunity to depict the Indian in his western environment came in 1819 when Major Stephen H. Long organized an exploring expedition to Yellowstone and felt the need of a staff artist. Evidently Seymour's ability was regarded by Long as entirely satisfactory; he was engaged and, according to the contract drawn up in advance, agreed to "furnish sketches of landscapes, whenever we meet with any distinguished for their beauty and grandeur . . . also paint miniature likenesses, or portraits if required, of distinguished Indians, and exhibit groups of savages engaged in celebrating their festivals, or sitting in council, and in general illustrate any subject that may be deemed appropriate."[7] For this Seymour was to receive $1.50 a day plus traveling expenses.

From 1819 to 1830 Long, Seymour, and other members of the expedition explored the plains and mountains of the West. Their first glimpse of Indiana was from their boat as it descended the Ohio River, but if the artist saw anything of pictorial interest along the shore neither written records nor sketches remain to prove it. However, he did make a drawing of Cave-in-Rock, thirty miles below the confluence of the Wabash and the Ohio.

After returning from the Rockies and taking steps to have his account published, Long set out again in 1823 to explore the country around Fort Snelling, at the junction of the Minnesota and Mississippi rivers, taking Seymour with him again. The party went overland from Pittsburgh to Chicago, pausing at the fork of the St. Mary's and St. Joseph rivers, the site of Fort Wayne. Here Seymour made some drawings of the Indian chiefs of northeastern Indiana. The originals have disappeared, but his portrait of Metea, tribal chief, has been preserved as a lithographic illustration in the published report of Long's expedition written by William Keating.[8]

After returning from the exploratory trip into Minnesota, Seymour lived at Philadelphia for several years, but, eclipsed by skillful and popular painters of the metropolis, he soon faded from sight and left little behind to secure for himself a place in history. The illustrations in Long's books and scattered water colors and pencil drawings are all that remain. Neither the circumstances nor date of his death are now known.

More gifted as an artist than Seymour, and better known as a painter of Indian subjects, was James Otto Lewis. He, too, was a resident of Philadelphia and like his predecessor was engaged as a staff artist on official western tours. Early in his career he became acquainted with General Lewis Cass and was allowed to accompany him and Colonel McKenney in 1819 and 1829 when they went West to make treaties with the Indians. Later, he was employed by the Indian Department of the federal government to paint portraits of prominent chiefs.

Lewis' sketches of Indian ceremonials and customs, as well as likenesses of their leaders, form a valuable artistic and historical collection. Unfortunately, the original paintings were destroyed in the Smithsonian Institution fire of 1865, but the lithographic reproductions in color are preserved in portfolios published in 1835 and 1839.[9] Twenty-two of these represent the chiefs of the Miami, Potowatomi and other tribes living at that time in Indiana, and are from originals drawn during council meetings at Fort Wayne and Mississinewa in 1827. The likenesses are apparently good, and the colorful dress of the aborigines, together with their paraphernalia, give the lithographs considerable charm. One is inclined to agree with a review in the New York *Mirror* of 1835, as quoted in the Lewis portfolio, that "in each of Mr. Lewis' portraits there is an air of reality which impresses us at once with the conviction that the grim gentlemen we are looking at actually lived, moved and had their being, while the accessories, such as scenery, costume, etc. add to the effect."

From this standpoint his portrayal of the famed Chief Francis Godfroy impresses one as being especially successful. Its decorative appeal is heightened by the introduction of a river and cabin in the background.

IV

There was another class of painters who visited Indiana in the early part of the nineteenth century and who should receive consideration in this survey. They were tourists or sight-seers, either traveling alone or accompanying ambitious globe-trotters. In the years preceding the invention of photography it was customary for travelers in foreign countries who contemplated publishing accounts of their voyages to engage the services of artists, whose sketches would serve later as designs for engraved illustrations. When an artist was touring alone he was either gathering material for a proposed album of American views or was satisfying a desire to see and depict the picturesque scenes of the untamed regions west of the Appalachians. He was usually a landscapist, in contrast to the native itinerant portrait painter.

The earliest illustrations to a travel book dealing in part or whole with Indiana appear to be two engravings in Adlard Welby's *A Visit to North America and the English Settlements in Illinois*, published in London in 1821. Welby entered Indiana from Kentucky and crossed the southwestern part of the state on the old road from New Albany to Vincennes and Harmonie (New Harmony). Although he came upon a number of unusual and engaging spots (he found southern Indiana most attractive) he included but two local subjects in his book: a log tavern, perhaps near Hindostan, and the Rappite church at Harmonie. If the author made the drawings himself, which he apparently did, he exhibits a high degree of technical ability. In his panoramic and scenic subjects, sketched in various parts of the Midwest, he combines artistic perception with good draughtsmanship, showing his interest in the pictorial aspects of the subjects as much as in the literal.

As we shall see in a later chapter, the first to sketch extensively the scenes of western Indiana was Charles A. Lesueur. His first glimpse of the state was from the deck of the *Philanthropist* en route to New Harmony in December, 1825. His sketches of towns along the Ohio River at that time, together with drawings made at New Harmony, constitute a rich pictorial heritage, although they were never used by the author in conjunction with books or other publications.

The next tourist-artist to reach this part of the country also got his first impression of Indiana from a boat while floating down the Ohio. He was Basil Hall, an amateur etcher from Edinburgh, Scotland, who traveled in North America in 1827 and 1828 making sketches by means of a contrivance called the camera lucida.[10] Upon returning to Edinburgh he made etchings from his drawings and published them in 1829 under the title, *Forty Etchings from Sketches Made with the Camera Lucida in North America in 1827 and 1828.*[11] While the etchings are important as early pictorial records of American subjects, the fact that the original drawings are now owned by the library of Indiana University is of even greater interest to us. Only two of the subjects, however, relate to Indiana: one inscribed *House on the Banks of the Ohio River in the State of Indiana* (pl. 2), and the other, *Southwest end of Wabash Island,* a view at the confluence of the Wabash and Ohio rivers. The former is dated May 5, 1828.

As might be expected from the hand of an etcher guided by an "artificial eye" the drawings are precise and rather mechanical, with no suggestion of the romantic urge that must have prompted Basil Hall to visit this continent. However, this precision doubtless pleased his patrons as it does those who turn to his etchings today for factual records of disappearing subjects.

Carl Bodmer, the next tourist-painter to visit Indiana, was unquestionably the most eminent of the group. A native of Switzerland, he was instructed in art by an uncle living at Meilen. In 1832, at the age of twenty-three, he joined the expedition of Prince Maximilian von Wied-Neuwied to America, serving as the official artist and producing the drawings that illustrated the prince's published account of his travels.[12] This engagement took him through Indiana twice (Maximilian stayed in America two years), his longest visits being at New Harmony where he enjoyed the companionship of the scientists and artists connected with Owen's community. There he doubtless made many sketches and scientific drawings; but only three Indiana subjects are known through engraved reproductions in the above publication: *New Harmony on the Wabash, Cut-off River: Branch of the Wabash* (near New Harmony), and *Mouth of the Fox River* (its confluence with the Wabash).

In 1953 a collection of his drawings and paintings, owned by Karl Viktor Prince zu Wied, were sent to this country for exhibition; among them were three Indiana subjects: a lynx and white-tailed deer drawn at New Harmony, and a water color of Vincennes made, according to the inscription, June 11, 1834 (pl. 3).

Upon returning to Europe, Bodmer lived in France and Germany. He spent several years at Barbizon, became a close friend of Millet and Rousseau, and exhibited regularly at the Paris Salon. After his second visit to America, in 1843, when he concentrated on drawings of Indians, he lived at Düsseldorf and there earned for himself the name "Indian Painter." Later he returned to France, and his death occurred at Barbizon in 1893.

Two other transient landscapists are known to have sketched in Indiana before the Civil War: Lefevre F. Cranstone, an Englishman, and William Momberger, a German.

Cranstone was recognized in London as a painter of genre and historical subjects, and his work was familiar to visitors at the Royal Academy exhibitions for about twenty years, between 1845 and 1865. Like Basil Hall, he was an etcher as well as a painter, employing a medium he called "fugitive etching." He came to the United States in the late summer of 1859 and from September until June of the next

1. Henry Hamilton: Ship Rock, Wabash River
Courtesy of the Harvard College Library, Harvard University (page 4)

2. Basil Hall: House on the Banks of the Ohio in the State of Indiana
Courtesy of the University Libraries, Indiana University (page 11)

3. Carl Bodmer: View of Vincennes, Indiana, 1834
Courtesy of the heirs of Prince Maximilian zu Wied, Munich, Germany (page 12)

4. Lefevre F. Cranstone: Street Scene in Richmond
Courtesy of the Indiana Historical Society Library, Indianapolis (page 13)

5. Lewis Peckham: Miniatures of Paul Peckham and Lewis Peckham
John Herron Art Museum, Indianapolis (page 17)

6. Lewis Peckham: Portrait of Hyacinthe Lasselle
Courtesy of the Indiana State Library, Indianapolis (page 17)

Wᵐ. A. Chatfield, i, D.H.

7. Dexter Harding (*attributed to*): Portrait of William A. Chatfield

Courtesy of Oscar C. Everhart, Indianapolis (page 19)

8. Horace Harding (*attributed to*): Portrait of Elias McNamee

Courtesy of the Francis Vigo Chapter, D.A.R., Vincennes (page 20)

year he traveled extensively in the eastern and midwestern areas, making sketches of scenes that impressed him. About three hundred of his original drawings were brought to this country recently and acquired by the library of Indiana University; an additional five were added to the collections of the library of the Indiana Historical Society; and thirteen are in the Maxim Karolik collection of American paintings in the Museum of Fine Arts, Boston.

The Indiana University drawings were done in pen and ink, with washes of brownish or bluish water color added. The subjects relate mostly to Wheeling, West Virginia, Washington, D.C., and Niagara Falls. Sixteen are scenes of Richmond, Indiana. Those in the library of the Indiana Historical Society are also of Richmond, painted with water colors, and charmingly depicting the appearance of the town in the winter of 1859–1860 (pl. 4).

William Momberger, a native of Frankfurt am Main, came to America in 1848 at the age of twenty. He apparently remained in this country twelve or fifteen years, during which time he traveled in Wisconsin, Minnesota, Iowa, and Indiana, making drawings of attractive scenic areas which were published as hand-colored engravings in 1869.[13] The Indiana subjects are: *St. Mary, St. Joseph & Maumee Rivers, Near Fort Wayne, Ind., Wabash River near Vincennes, Ind.,* and *Evansville, on the Ohio.* If any of his original drawings are preserved in this country they are not known to the author.

In reviewing the brief visits of these tourist-painters it must be borne in mind that when Momberger and Cranstone were in Indiana the output of landscapes by local resident artists was sizable. As we shall see in subsequent chapters, more than thirty painters were active here in the decade preceding the Civil War, and while most of them specialized in portraiture a number could not resist depicting the natural beauties of the state.

Vincennes
New Harmony

Chapter 2

VINCENNES
NEW HARMONY

THERE ARRIVED AT VINCENNES in the summer of 1815 a young man in his middle twenties who had just completed a long and arduous journey from Newport, Rhode Island. He probably carried with him most if not all of his worldly possessions, as he had decided to make the frontier town his permanent home and base of his operations as a portrait painter. He was Lewis Peckham, artist, musician, and soldier.

As he approached the town from the rolling hills to the east the village must have appeared very pleasant to him. Nestled on the Wabash River and surrounded by lush vegetation, tall virgin timber, and abundant vineyards, Vincennes had made a deep impression on less sensitive travelers; and beyond its physical aspect that day it doubtless held a nostalgic charm for Peckham, because he was returning to the scene of one of his most exciting military exploits and the base of his company's operations during the winter of 1811 following the Battle of Tippecanoe.

It was in July, 1811, that his regiment, under the command of Colonel John P. Boyd, marched west to Pittsburgh and then by river and overland traces to Vincennes to help William Henry Harrison check the Indian uprisings. They arrived in September and took part in the Battle of Tippecanoe on the seventh of November. Peckham's captain, William C. Baen, was killed in action, and Peckham was commissioned first lieutenant two days later.

Following a quiet winter in Vincennes, his regiment, the Fourth U.S. Infantry, was ordered to Dayton and then to the defense of Detroit. After the surrender of Detroit to the British, Peckham was held a prisoner of war in Canada for about two years, and then fought in the campaign against Fort Erie in 1814. With the cessation of hostilities he resigned his commission (he was then a captain) and went home to Newport. After a brief visit he struck out for Vincennes.

By piecing together fragments of information found in letters, parish records, and other documents, we gain a fairly clear picture of his activities during the next seven years in Vincennes, but his early life is obscure to us. He was born at Newport in 1788. The first known reference to his interest in art is preserved in a letter written to his father, telling of the miniatures he was painting of officers stationed with him at Fort Independence, near Boston. This was in 1810. The same letter tells of one of his most significant experiences, his visit to Gilbert Stuart's studio and the friendly reception given him by Boston's eminent citizen. It reads in part: "I enjoy good health at present . . . The fever which had destroyed twenty of our soldiers is much abated, and we have but one that is now dangerously ill. Have fortunately become acquainted with Mr. Stewart[1] of Boston who offers me all the information in the art of painting gratis. Mr. Stewart offers me a seat in his room as often as I shall call on him, he has given me a very fine piece of cloth [canvas] and offers me his pencils and paints, and nothing is wanting on my part but an opportunity to visit Boston, but I flatter myself with some leisure hours which will be improved in this business, have been somewhat surprised in finding a man who appears to be so anxious for my improvement, have offered Mr. S. money for his assistance but it is a fortunate thing for me that he refuses it. I remain your affec't son . . ."[2]

It is reasonable to assume that he missed no opportunity to sketch or paint during his six years of military life, and probably many of the men who served with him became the subject of neatly executed miniature portraits. Arriving in Vincennes in 1815, he had nothing to hamper him in realizing his ambition to become a painter except, possibly, the indifference and poor economic state of the backwoodsmen. By 1816 he had established a studio in partnership with C. D. Cook (regarding whose life our histories are silent), and had begun to insert advertisements in the local newspaper to attract business:

> Co-Partnership. Lewis Peckham & C. D. Cook Begs leave to inform the citizens of Vincennes and its vicinity that they have commenced Portrait, Ornamental, Sign and House Painting, in the chamber over Mr. N. B. Bailey's store where any business in the above line mentioned will be attended to in the shortest notice.[3]

Much of Peckham's time in the years that follow seems to have been spent selecting a tract of land in the New Purchase for the home of his family. Soon after his arrival in Vincennes he had acquired property in the town and did some gardening and fruit cultivation. He was a bachelor, but had applied for a license to marry Elizabeth Gamlin. But something must have happened to their romance because a marginal note on the record states: "the parties name in this Lisence has not been joined in wedlock."[4] A year later, however, he fell in love with Mary Dagenet Shields, joined the Catholic church, and was married by Father Blanch.[5]

Mary Dagenet (also spelled Dageny, Dagne, Dague and Dashnay) was the daughter of Ambrose Dagenet and Mary of the Many Nations, a princess of the Wea tribe. In the Treaty of 1818 between the federal government and the Wea, Mary and her brother Christmas (Noel) were granted a section of land each,[6] but no tract was specified and a good deal of time was spent selecting one in the years that followed. The Wea reservation was north of Fort Harrison, near the present site of Terre Haute, and it appears that Mary Dagenet's claim was finally located there, although Lewis Peckham had made an effort to get some land on Fall Creek north of the present city of Indianapolis. The artist and his family continued to live in Vincennes, presumably gardening, painting, and participating in the town's social life, until his premature death in September, 1822. He was buried there "with all the pomp and honors of war, he being at the time of his death Judge Advocate of his regiment."[7] He was survived by his widow and two children: a son Lewis, born in 1820, and a daughter, Hannah, born in 1822. Both mother and daughter died two years later and the last report of the son indicated that he was living, in 1845, at Montezuma, on or near the Wea reservation.

The only paintings by Peckham now known to us are miniatures of his parents, owned by Mary W. Peckham, of Santa Barbara, California; miniatures of himself and his brother Thomas (pl. 5), in the collection of the John Herron Art Museum; and a portrait in oil of Hyacinthe Lasselle, in the Indiana State Library (pl. 6). A pair of portraits of Lasselle and his wife, formerly owned by Wils Berry of Logansport,[8] has disappeared and is known only through photographs in the historical museum at Logansport. These paintings show that the artist was no better than the average portraitist of his day in technical ability. The likenesses appear to be good and the colors are pleasing, but the work is not distinguished.

The differences in style and execution in the two portraits of General Lasselle pose an involved problem. The miniature, known only through the photograph at Logansport, is unquestionably Peckham's, because, in workmanship, it corresponds to the miniatures that have survived. It shows the same timidity and thinness of line, the same beady eyes and thin lips of the sitter, and the same short brush strokes. The State Library's version of Lasselle, painted with oils on canvas, differs strikingly. This may be partly due to differences in media and scale. But even allowing for these, the traditional attribution to Peckham is puzzling. In the photograph of the lost miniature Lasselle appears as one imagines he looked when Peckham knew him in the years between 1815 and 1822. In the State Library's portrait he appears to be in his early twenties, which would place the painting around 1800. More evidence may come to light in the future to confirm or refute this attribution.[9] In the meantime it will be regarded as the only extant work in oil by Peckham and the earliest portrait made in the state that can be assigned to a known artist.

II

After settling in Vincennes, Lewis Peckham had the field of painting to himself except for a few weeks in 1820, when a competitor by the name of Horace Harding arrived. Harding had wandered into western Indiana from Kentucky, probably by way of Cincinnati, and finding business not to his liking soon returned the way he had come.

The sojourn of Horace Harding in Vincennes presents a number of perplexing problems. In her book, *Art and Artists of Indiana*, Mary Q. Burnet states that "Among the first [in the state] was Chester Harding, who was in Vincennes, Indiana, about 1820 as a painter of portraits and teacher of art." [10] Nothing has been found in early documents to show that Chester Harding ever visited Vincennes; on the other hand, evidence in the form of a newspaper advertisement tells of his brother Horace's visit. In all probability Mary Burnet got her information from a historical sketch of Vincennes or of Knox County in which reference was made to Horace Harding's visit in 1820, and, assuming that a mistake had been made, she substituted the name of Chester, one of the country's leading portrait painters in the pre-Civil War period. Unfortunately, her statement that Chester Harding was in Vincennes has been repeated in later histories and has become so fixed that it is almost indelible.

The assumption is understandable. Actually, Chester Harding did travel west from Kentucky in 1820 with St. Louis as his destination, and unless one reads his autobiography carefully the conclusion might be reached that he passed through Vincennes en route.[11] However, he went by boat from Cincinnati to St. Louis. After a successful year in Missouri, during which he painted the venerable Daniel Boone and accumulated over a thousand dollars, he bought a carriage and a pair of horses and started with his family for eastern New York where his parents were still living. The road generally traveled would have taken him through Vincennes and across southeastern Indiana. In Washington (known then as Liverpool) there is a portrait of John L. Van Trees, owned by Harry V. Hyatt, which reflects Chester Harding's style and may have been painted by him on that trip.

Returning to his brother Horace, we have little information about his life and work. He was born at Conway, Massachusetts, in 1794, the fifth child of Abiel and Olive (Smith) Harding.[12] When he was a boy his family moved to Hatfield, and then to Sullivan, New York. There he learned the trade of chair-making under his elder brothers, and about 1815 he and Chester embarked upon a cabinet- and chair-manufacturing enterprise in Caledonia. From there Horace apparently went to Paris, Kentucky, where he followed the same trade. But soon the urge to paint portraits prompted him to embark upon a new and more fascinating career.

His name appears in Chester Harding's autobiography, *Egotisti-graphy,* when the latter, having decided to be a portrait painter himself, speaks of joining Horace in Paris. That was in 1817. No other references are made to Horace in the *Egotistigraphy,* and if it were not for evidences uncovered in other places one would assume that he remained in Kentucky the rest of his life.

In all probability Horace left Paris early in 1820 with Chester, but instead of going to St. Louis from Cincinnati he came to Vincennes. As his advertisement reveals, he arrived here in February (the announcement ran from February 2 to May 27) by which time he had become a full-fledged portrait painter, though relatively inexperienced. It reads:

PORTRAIT PAINTING

Horace Harding, Begs leave respectfully to inform the citizens of Vincennes and vicinity, that he has taken a room in the mansion of Charles Smith, Esq., where all orders in his profession will be thankfully received and faithfully attended to. Ladies and Gentlemen are invited to call and inspect his performances.

Sign and Ornamental Painting will be neatly executed by his Brother.[13]

While establishing a number of facts about this artist, the announcement poses another query: Who was the brother that accompanied him, equipped to paint signs neatly? There are a few scattered references to younger brothers who also became painters, namely Dexter and Spencer, and either of them would have been in the apprenticeship stage at the time of the advertisement. On the basis of evidence in the form of family traditions, the sign and ornamental painter in this instance appears to have been Dexter, who is known to have accompanied Horace on many of his trips. This supposition is strengthened by the existence of a miniature water-color portrait executed in a precise but amateurish style bearing this inscription: "Wm. A, Chatfield, by D, H," (pl. 7).[14] The work appears to be that of a person more familiar with ornamental painting than with portraiture. It was made, according to the best evidence available, in or near Vincennes, and the date could be 1820, judging by the style of the sitter's costume.

Dexter Harding was two years younger than Horace. He was born at Dedham, Massachusetts, in 1796; he served as a drummer boy in the War of 1812, and may have joined his elder brothers at Paris, Kentucky. In 1821 he married Jane Allen of Hopkinsonville, Kentucky, and lived in Hopkinsonville until 1850 when he moved his family to Pine Bluff, Arkansas, settling on land granted him by the federal government. There he died in 1862. He became a miller by profession, but painted portraits of his family and friends.[15]

Turning again to the Vincennes advertisement, it is of interest to find that this is the earliest document relating to Horace Harding's activity. His name appears later in the Cincinnati city directories, intermittently from 1834 to 1850, during which time he probably traveled a great deal through southern Ohio and northern Kentucky. The lack of references to him after 1850 suggests that he moved to another part of the country. This is confirmed by an inscription on the back of his portrait, painted by his brother Chester, stating that Horace Harding died of cholera (as did his daughter Ophelia) in Woodville, Mississippi, in about the year 1857.[16]

Only four paintings can at present be assigned to him: a portrait of Joseph C. Carter, painted at Lexington, Kentucky, in 1837, signed and dated on the back, now in the home of Mrs. Allen Stanfill, Lexington; a large portrait of Robert Hamilton Bishop, early president of Miami University, Oxford, Ohio, painted about 1830 and traditionally attributed to him; a study of his brother Chester, formerly thought to be Chester's self-portrait, owned by the City Art Museum of St. Louis; and a likeness of his brother Dexter, owned by Captain Chester Harding, Fayetteville, Arkansas.

On the basis of these paintings, as well as on that of date, the portrait of Dr. Elias McNamee (pl. 8), now hanging in the William Henry Harrison Mansion at Vincennes, can be ascribed to Horace Harding with reasonable certainty—the only canvas that can now be associated with his sojourn in Indiana. Unfortunately, the signature and inscription on the back of the canvas are obliterated, the year "1820" being the only legible portion, but the script is enough like that on the back of the Joseph Carter portrait to warrant the conclusion that it is by Horace Harding's hand. The rather inept technique, stiff pose, and flat rendering of forms are such as one would expect from his brush at that time. Its resemblance, stylistically, to the Robert Hamilton Bishop portrait is striking in several ways, although the latter, painted about ten years later, is softer in modeling and less strained in pose.

III

The extreme scarcity of paintings originating in Vincennes in the early 1820's would lead one to conclude that commissions were very few and that only the most adventurous of limners bothered to include the town in their itineraries. But there must have been more production than the few remaining canvases would suggest. This is revealed in an article that appeared in the *Western Sun and General Advertiser* of that community on February 9, 1822, an article decrying the extravagant manners and customs of its citizens:

Let us above all things, avoid the prodigal waste attendant upon evanescent amusements. It is not merely the property expended that makes an inordinate thirst for amusements injurious to the community. Time, lost or squandered, and business neglected are evils equally great . . . But what is this excess of amusement with which we stand charged? . . . Where and when have we expended money and time improperly? We need scarcely glance at our conduct two years ago to find an answer to all these questions. Several thousand dollars were expended by our good citizens in a few months upon a dancing master, a portrait painter, and a theatrical company . . . Instead of paying 12 or $1500 to a portrait painter, why was not that sum appropriated to support a clergyman, whose character, whose interest, and whose hopes were identified with our own?

The questions that naturally rise in our minds have nothing to do with prodigality or conduct. Who was the portrait painter who could earn $1,500 in a frontier community like Vincennes within a few months, in 1820? Could it have been Horace Harding? Where are all the canvases now? Seventy-five dollars would have been a good price for a portrait at that time, and on that basis he would have had to turn out fifteen or twenty paintings. We may, today, be underestimating the production and selling power of the oldtime painter.

Being the oldest permanent settlement in what is now Indiana, and the scene of several incidents significant in American history, Vincennes was the home or temporary residence of a number of illustrious and colorful people. Unfortunately, original portraits of all of her heroes do not exist, but several of more than passing interest have been preserved. In the halls of old Vincennes University there hang two portraits in oil of considerable historical importance. One portrays George Rogers Clark, the other, Francis Vigo. Clark was painted on several occasions during his lifetime, but not while residing in Indiana. The best-known likeness, of which two versions exist, was by John Wesley Jarvis.[17] Another, attributed to Matthew Jouett, now in the Filson Club, Louisville, appears to be a copy of the Jarvis canvas, so will not be counted among those taken from life. However, the Filson Club owns yet another likeness of Clark assigned to Joseph H. Bush, a Kentucky artist, and said to be one of four or five replicas by Bush from an original he made in 1817 or shortly before Clark's death on the thirteenth of February, 1818.

The third life study is that in Vincennes University (pl. 9). Although there has never been any doubt as to the identity of the subject, the anonymity of the painter has brought about much speculation in recent years. In the opinion of the late R. C. Ballard of Louisville, who carefully studied the problems relating to the Clark portraits, it was one of the versions by Bush; but an obvious discrepancy in pose and style precludes such a possibility. What appears now to be the correct information was found in the Draper Manuscripts in the State Historical Society of Wisconsin. A letter written in 1847 by W. B. Gwathmey to L. C. Draper has this to say about the Clark portrait:

With regards to *the portrait* I presented to the His. Soc. at Vincennes I was under the impression that it was drawn by "West" but [during] a late visit from my mother when I showed her my letter to the society she said I was mistaken that it was taken by "*Cook*." My father employed the artist to visit Locust Grove for 80$ for the purpose of taking the likeness at which he was engaged over a month there were occasional contortions of the Muscels of the face which rendered the performance tedious—but when finished I assure you that it was a Master piece.[18]

The writer's use of the term "masterpiece" seems magnanimous when we confront the portrait today. As a work of art it is definitely inferior to many contemporaneous works, and as a depiction of the General's visage and character it leaves with the beholder an uncomfortable feeling. The closely set eyes, peering out angrily from lowering brows, the long thin nose and drooping mouth, and the abnormally high and bald forehead suggest an irascible, spiteful person. In the letter quoted above, Gwathmey expresses the opinion that it was painted in 1810 or 1811, more than thirty years after Clark successfully routed the British from Vincennes. He had retired from military service, and was spending the twilight of his adventurous life near Louisville, Kentucky.

The assignment of the work to Cook is of more than passing interest. Our attention has already been drawn to the C. D. Cook who was in partnership with Lewis Peckham at Vincennes in 1816; and as no other painter bearing that name is known to have worked in the Midwest, it is not unreasonable to assume that the Clark portrait is his work. Where he originated, and whence he came at the time of his visit to Locust Grove, we do not know. Nor is there a record of his activity after painting Clark's likeness. It is tempting to think that he is the same Cook whom Audubon came upon in Natchez late in December, 1820, as succinctly recorded in the latter's diary: "Having Not one Cent when I Landed here I immediately Looked for something to do in the Likeness Way for our Support (unfortunately Naturalists are Obliged to eat and have some sort of Garb) I entered the room of a Portrait Painter Naming himself *Cook* but I assure you he was scarcely fit for a Scullion, Yet the Gentleman had some politeness and procured me the drawing of two Sketches for 5$ each, this was fine sauce to our stomacks . . . Mr. Cook much pleased with My Drawings and quickness of performance, desired to travel with us if suitable Mutual arrangements could be Made. I Asked him to pay me Two Dollars per day Monthly in advance and furnish besides, One Third of the Whole Expenses, providing himself with Whatever Materials might be necessary." [19]

Evidently Cook did not take up the offer because Audubon makes no further reference to him.

The portrait of Colonel Francis Vigo, the second at Vincennes University, has the merit of being pleasant in characterization if no better in execution. Standing with his right hand gripping his cane, the elderly soldier looks out at the observer with a wise and benign expression. Behind him hangs a dark red curtain supported by a classical column, reflecting in composition the grand manner of continental portraiture. A distant view of the Wabash River and its wooded banks appears at the right beyond the drapery (pl. 10).

In this case the artist is known: he was Augustus A. Von Smith, a resident of Vincennes for a few years in the late 1830's and early 40's. It is believed that he painted the portrait in 1835, a year before Colonel Vigo died, and that the canvas remained in his possession until it was sold to the library in 1839.[20] A second version with a plain background, identical in pose and technique, is in the Swope Art Gallery at Terre Haute.

The next report on Von Smith appeared in the Vincennes *Gazette* late in 1842 in the form of a business announcement:

> A. A. Von Smith, Portrait and Miniature Painter Informs all lovers of the Fine Arts that he has taken a room opposite the Post Office, where he would be pleased to execute orders in his profession for anyone who may be disposed to favor him with a call.[21]

Nothing more appeared after that in the local press. Mary Burnet stated that he had a son who also painted and that both were foreign born and largely self-tutored. Besides the two portraits of Francis Vigo, a painting depicting Bishop Robert R. Roberts is thought to be the work of the elder Von Smith. It is at DePauw University, and its damaged condition resulted from its hasty rescue from a fire.

IV

Two more names bring the register of pioneer artists in Vincennes to a close: William R. Freeman and Peter Tester.

Freeman was a typical itinerant, never remaining long in one place. He may be the artist reported as being in Fort Wayne in the 1840's.[22] Mary Burnet spoke of him as working in the southern towns of the state in the early forties where "graphic stories are still extant of his courting the village belles, at times two in the same settlement." [23] He appears more distinctly as a personality after 1849, when he came to Vincennes, rented a studio from Samuel P. Judah, and painted his landlord's portrait for, it is said, the first installment of rent (pl. 11). The painting is now in the home of a descendant, Reynolds Judah, near Vincennes. The same year, or soon after, he painted the two-figure composition of Françoise Cornoyer Van der Burgh with her granddaughter Josephine Somes, now owned by Harry Somes in Vincennes. At about the same time he made the portraits of Charles Andrew Weisert and his wife Eleanor, which hang in the home of Clementine Weisert here.

For a man having so strong a romantic streak and a predilection for feminine charm (if we are to believe Mary Burnet's report) Freeman's paintings are surprisingly prosaic and colorless. Sitters appear rather apathetic, hues are dark and sooty, brush work is ordinary. Later work in Terre Haute and Indianapolis improved only in more natural and photographic effects.

Accounts of his life are not as detailed as they should be for a person whose activity extended over so wide a region and continued for so many years in Indiana. He was born in the state of New York about 1820, came to Indiana early in the 1840's, worked in the eastern (assuming that he was the Freeman reported as being in Fort Wayne), southern, and western sections of the state, and finally in Indianapolis. After leaving Vincennes in 1850 or 1851 he went to Terre Haute, married Jane Douglas in 1851, and lived there until 1873. In 1874 and a part of 1875 he was in Indianapolis; then he went with his family to San Francisco where he probably spent most of the remainder of his life. It is believed that he died in St. Louis in 1906.[24] Further references to his work will be made in discussing the activities of painters in Terre Haute and Indianapolis. While it is recorded that he painted other subjects, all his known canvases are portraits.

Peter Tester, the next artist of Vincennes, was born in Graubünden Canton, now called Grisons Canton, eastern Switzerland, between 1810 and 1819.[25] On the basis of the presumed dates of his paintings—dates calculated on the basis of the sitters' ages—he was working in and around Vincennes in the 1860's. He was probably an adult when he came to America and doubtless was drawn to Freelandville, northeast of Vincennes, by the colony of Swiss and Germans in that area. Old timers recall that he lived on property adjoining the Gus Stoelting farm south of Freelandville, and also remember him as a genial but decidedly shiftless man. His habit was to go off by himself for weeks at a time without disclosing his whereabouts. There are no records to show that he had a family or any close relatives; and it is probable that he lived a solitary and uneventful life, confining his movements to western Knox County. In his latter years he stayed close to his small farm, gradually abandoning his brushes and paint for garden tools. He died in 1882 and was buried at Freelandville.

Tester's work, while not signed, is easily identified by the pose of his models and his method of painting. Figures are placed in a frontal position, facing the observer and looking straight ahead. Expressions are solemn but not pained or glum; the light falls evenly across the face and dress without marked highlights or shadows; technique is precise, lace and jewelry accurately rendered, and colors attractive. His manner of painting does not point to any American influences, leading one to conclude that he got his training, and perhaps some experience as a portraitist, abroad.

Paintings thus far identified as his work are portraits of H. L. Bergeman and his wife Amanda Piety, in the home of Mrs. Earl Robbins, Freelandville; Marcellas Lacroix and Adele Bayard, his wife (pl. 12), owned by Mrs. Thomas Maxwell Shircliff, of Vincennes; Henry S. Cauthorn, in the possession of Clotilde Cauthorn, Vincennes; and Andrew Gardner and his wife, in the home of Fannie H. Hall, of the same city. The eight portraits of members of the Stephen Burnet family of Vincennes, painted in 1869,[26] and preserved as late as 1921, were destroyed by descendants who concluded that they were unsatisfactory likeness.

V

Leaving Vincennes and turning to the communities farther south along the serpentine Wabash, New Harmony and its arts next draw our attention. Unlike Vincennes, which was settled in the 1730's by French fur traders, and whose growth was the natural outcome of economic and geographical conditions, New Harmony, founded early in the nineteenth century, was fashioned from a wilderness into a coherent though small religious colony in relatively few years.

In the summer of 1815 the Rappites moved their entire community of equality from western Pennsylvania to the newly purchased tract of unimproved land, some 30,000 acres, on the east shore of the Wabash River. With ceaseless application of brawn and brain they cleared the land, erected buildings, and organized a self-sustained colony which they named Harmonie. So strenuous was the work that neither time nor energy was left for artistic pursuits, even had the doctrines of George Rapp permitted such frivolities. In 1825 their holdings were purchased by another dreamer of social equality, Robert Owen, and a new Utopian order was launched. He changed the name to New Harmony, little realizing at the time what a misnomer it was.

Whereas the previous colony expressed itself in laborious physical works and strict religious practices, the Owenite brotherhood attempted to attain perfect harmony through broad intellectual and cultural enterprises. Scholars and craftsmen, pedagogues and reformers, were persuaded to leave good positions in the East and cast their lots with Owen and William Maclure on the Indiana frontier.

One of the celebrated members of Owen's staff, and the most important so far as our chronicle is concerned, was Charles Alexandre Lesueur, a Frenchman, born at Le Havre in 1778 and educated in academies abroad. His interest in both drawing and scientific investigation brought him wide renown in Europe as a painter-scientist and led to several early trips of exploration—to Australia and the surrounding islands, then finally to America. Arriving in New York in 1816, he toured the eastern states, then settled in Philadelphia to teach art. Induced by Maclure to join him and Owen at New Harmony, Lesueur accompanied the party of intellectuals that left for Indiana in 1825, arriving at New Harmony on the *Philanthropist,* dubbed the "Boatload of Knowledge," early in 1826. He came West with reluctance, for he liked the artistic atmosphere of Philadelphia and was skeptical about the ultimate success of Owen's venture.

Not only was Lesueur the most eminent artist in the state at the time but he was the only practitioner of painting on anything like a professional scale. Lewis Peckham, of Vincennes, had died; Christopher Harrison was in Salem, but his artistic productions, however meritorious, were pleasant diversions only; Richard Terrell might have been in Madison in 1826, but one would not have thought of him as even approaching Lesueur in technical ability; and Samuel Rooker, a resident of Indianapolis since 1821, was probably painting nothing more glamorous than tavern signs.

Lesueur, it appears, was a tireless worker and a great inspiration to younger men and women in the settlement. In addition to teaching and lecturing on art he sketched continuously for scientific purposes and for his own amusement, participated in archaeological explorations, wrote and published works on natural history, gathered material for a proposed monograph on American fishes, made frequent trips to New Orleans to market the surplus products of New Harmony, and still found time to take part in musical and dramatic performances, even painting scenery for the productions of the New Harmony Thespian Society.[27] He worked without a salary, receiving only living expenses and quarters in addition to a pension from the French government for scientific data and specimens sent back from America—a stipend he was in danger of losing as the years went by and he kept postponing his return to France.

Being primarily a scientist, Lesueur developed a manner of drawing that was precise and factual, and yet when he sketched outdoor scenes for his own pleasure he worked with ease and expressive intent. Unfortunately none of his paintings are around to show how he executed his larger and more ambitious compositions, but a few of his drawings are in the state and reproductions of others have been published.[28] In the Library of the Workingmen's Institute, New Harmony, is a ren-

9. C. D. Cook (*attributed to*):
Portrait of
George Rogers Clark
Courtesy of Vincennes
University (page 22)

10. Augustus A. Von Smith:
Portrait of Francis Vigo
Courtesy of Vincennes
University (page 24)

11. William R. Freeman:
Portrait of Samuel Judah
Courtesy of Reynolds S. Judah,
Vincennes (page 25)

12. Peter Tester: Portrait of
Adele Bayard Lacroix
Courtesy of Martha Bayard
Somes Shircliff, Vincennes
(page 26)

13. Charles Alexandre Lesueur: Major Phillips Seated on a
Box of Potatoes
Courtesy of the Purdue University Libraries, W. Lafayette
(page 29)

14. Virginia Dupalais: Portrait
of Joseph Fauntleroy
Courtesy of the New Harmony
Memorial Commission
(page 30)

15. (left) David Dale Owen:
Portrait of Richard Owen
Courtesy of Kenneth Dale
Owen, Houston, Texas
(page 31)

16. Miner K. Kellogg: Portrait
of Robert Dale Owen
Courtesy of Kenneth Dale
Owen, Houston, Texas
(page 35)

17. (below) Jacob Maentel:
Portraits of Jonathan Ja-
quess and Rebecca Jaquess
Courtesy of Arthur E. Jaquess,
Poseyville (page 37)

dering in pencil and water color of a snipe that shows Lesueur's scientific draughtsmanship, and some pencil sketches in the library of Purdue University show his manner of out-of-doors sketching (pl. 13). Unfortunately the originals of portraits of John Badollet and Francis Vigo, which he is known to have drawn, have disappeared; several small portrait heads in pencil, now in the library of the Indiana Historical Society, are attributed to him. This scarcity of originals is due to the fact that when he left New Harmony most of his drawings and paintings went with him.

When the Owenite structure toppled a couple of years later, as the result of friction and bickering among the leaders and disillusionment among many of the followers, most of the scientists and teachers reorganized under a new name, The School of Industry, and continued their work in a quiet, earnest way under William Maclure's direction. Robert Owen left for the purpose of founding new idealistic communities elsewhere. Lesueur stayed until 1837, ten years beyond Owen's departure, and then went by way of New Orleans to France, where he became curator at the Museum of Natural History at Le Havre. There he died in 1846.

VI

Next to Lesueur the best painter on Owen's staff was John Chappelsmith. Historians refer to him as "a wealthy English artist" who came to New Harmony with his wife on the *Philanthropist* in company with the original contingent of scholars and teachers. Apparently most of his time was spent making scientific drawings, engravings, and maps. According to the federal census, he was still living in New Harmony in 1850, had reached the age of forty-three, and was a practicing artist. This leads one to surmise that with the termination of scientific publications here, Chappelsmith turned his hand to more original creations, but there is no evidence of it now. The few drawings and engravings in the Library of the Workingmen's Institute are of a scientific nature and give us no idea of his powers as a creative or original painter. Following the death of his wife in 1883 he returned to England, where his own death occurred within a few years.

Besides Lesueur and Chappelsmith, the Community's art colony included Cornelius Tiebout, of New York, who supervised the printing and engraving of the schools; the engravers Lyman Lyon and James Walker; Mrs. Samuel Chase, a teacher of music and drawing; and Lucy Sistaire, a talented young lady who married Thomas Say and made the scientific drawings that illustrated her husband's work on conchology. She also taught drawing in the school.

Lesueur's instruction and encouragement developed an interest in art among the younger people that eventually led to a good deal of enterprise and some meritorious results. Among his most talented pupils were his niece Virginia Dupalais, Richard and David Owen, Peter Duclos, and Miner Kellogg.

Virginia Poullard Dupalais was older than the others, being twenty-one when she came to New Harmony and already proficient enough with pencil and brush to assist in making scientific illustrations. She had come under Lesueur's tutelage in Philadelphia and probably acquired from him all her technical knowledge. She was born in Philadelphia in 1804, the fourth daughter of Alexandre du Palais, a captain with the French forces who was sent to help George Washington in the Revolutionary War. Upon the death of her parents Lesueur became her guardian, and when he decided to come to Indiana she accompanied him. In 1828 she married William A. Twigg, and after the dissolution of the Owen enterprise they made New Harmony their permanent home. Here she died in 1864.

Her work consisted mainly of small pencil or pen-and-ink drawings of considerable charm, executed with care and precision, not unlike her uncle's. She was particularly successful with little portrait studies, such as that of Joseph Fauntleroy (pl. 14), in the Fauntleroy House at New Harmony, and of Maximilian, Prince of Wied, in the library of the Indiana Historical Society.

Of the two Owen boys mentioned above, David Dale apparently was the more talented. Unfortunately almost nothing by Richard in the line of drawing or painting is now known, and it may be that he had little interest in art after attaining adulthood. A glimpse of his student days, however, is preserved in a letter written many years later to David Starr Jordan, in which he said: "Lesueur was a magnificent artist, good alike in drawing and color. I have some of his sketches yet, in which, when I was taking drawing lessons from him, he showed me how to outline, for instance, the skeleton of the human figure, and then add the muscular system then the drapery, etc. We usually took views from nature. Although so minute in details of fine paintings he was equally good in large scenery." [29]

David Dale Owen seems to have retained a strong artistic impulse and interest throughout life, and as a geologist he found his technical ability of service in illustrating his publications. Even in the scientific plates there is a suggestion of Lesueur's tutoring and his own sensitive nature. Such a picture, for instance, as the view of the Hot Springs of Arkansas, reproduced in Hendrickson's biography of David Owen, reveals a trained hand and eye as well as a grasp of such technical points as linear and aerial perspective. [30] More important, however, from our standpoint, were his efforts at portrait painting. The oil in the Library of the Workingmen's Institute portraying Joseph Neef, and a water color of his brother Richard seated at a table, in the home of Kenneth Owen at New Harmony, show the range and quality of his work. Unfortunately, the Neef canvas is in very poor condition and has so darkened and deteriorated that it is difficult to get any idea of Owen's technique. It is a half-length study showing the elderly teacher gazing toward the left, his hands clasped at his waist. The attribution to David Owen is based on long tradition and there is no apparent reason to question it.

The water color is well preserved and is a pleasing study of Richard Owen, shown seated in a room, a table at his left and an architectural column behind. It is ably drawn, except for the diminutive feet and hands. The expression and pose are natural, and the rendering of textures agreeable (pl. 15).

The painter-geologist was born in Scotland in 1807, the third son of the social reformer Robert Owen, and was given the name of his maternal grandfather. When his family moved to New Harmony in 1825 he was about eighteen years old. Two years later he went abroad to study, entering schools in Switzerland, Scotland, and London, specializing in geology. In 1833 he returned to New Harmony, made his home here—few of the original community members were still around—and began the scientific studies that led to his appointment as state geologist in 1837. Through this work he continued the impetus that Maclure and other scholars had given to science in the first years of the Community's existence, and his laboratory and museum at New Harmony became the most important of its kind in the state. His brother Richard worked with him for several years before assuming a teaching position at Nashville University. It was probably in that period between 1835 and 1840 that the water-color portrait was made.

To Peter Duclos' ability and attainments we have only the sketchiest of references.[31] He and his brother Victor were nephews of Mme. Marie Duclos Fretageot, one of three Pestalozzian teachers to join the Community and a powerful force in its educational program. The boys accompanied her to New Harmony in 1826. A few years later their father, Jean Duclos, joined them; and then, in 1834, father and sons went to New Orleans. Peter Duclos' apprenticeship under Lesueur has already been noted, and as his interest lay principally in scenic painting he doubtless gained a good deal of practical experience in connection with the scenery that Lesueur was making for the Thespian Society. In New Orleans he decorated the St. Charles Theater, with the assistance of another New Harmony youth, George Warren. It is said that he also painted theatrical scenery in Louisville, Kentucky, and Vevay, Indiana, and then reappeared in New Harmony in 1844. By that time the Thespian Society Players were performing in the Union Hall, the largest theater in the state, and he joined them as official scenery painter, executing, in addition to temporary sets, their permanent drop curtain, which was greatly admired. The latter continued to be used until the theater was converted into a garage.[32]

Duclos remained in New Harmony, where he married Frances Pierce and raised a family of two daughters. In addition to his artistic activity he was town magistrate, postal clerk, and head of the Maclure library. He died in 1869, at the age of fifty-four. His brother Victor also returned to New Harmony, married, and died here in 1905—the last survivor of the original members of Owen's Community.

George Warren, who had assisted Peter Duclos at New Orleans, was also one of the youthful members of the Community. His father, Josiah Warren, a lamp maker, had joined Owen in 1826 even though he was dubious about the workability of the venture. He left when it failed but returned in the thirties, invented a printing press that took a continuous roll of paper, and perfected the stereotyping process. No historical documents refer to his artistic propensity but the existence of one of his pencil drawings, a head of a girl, owned by Mrs. Edd A. Manlove, of Indianapolis, shows that he had more than ordinary ability. His son George evidently inherited some of his father's artistic talent, but if he accomplished much beyond the coloring of maps for David Owen's reports we have no information about it. According to the federal census of 1850 he was living in New Harmony at that time and his profession was given as a painter, which probably meant a house painter. A few years later he moved with his family to Evansville, where he operated a large music store and where he gained wide recognition as a musician and band leader. He painted pictures occasionally but never regarded art as more than a pleasant diversion. He died at Evansville in 1902.

VII

Among the youngest pupils in the Community schools, and the most successful of Lesueur's students, was Miner Kellogg. Although his stay at New Harmony was brief, his early association with Owen's settlement and later contacts with Indiana people justify a biographical summary here. He was born at Manlius Square, New York, in 1814. His parents became converts to the philosophy of Robert Owen and were among the original members of his Community. When the New Harmony venture collapsed they retained their faith in Owen's scheme, and joined the band of disciples that moved to the farm adjoining Jeffersonville near the Ohio River. When this attempt to rejuvenate the plan failed the Kelloggs went to Cincinnati. There Miner received his first sound instruction in painting.

In his manuscript journal, owned by the Indiana Historical Society Library, Kellogg gives an account of his boyhood activities in New

Harmony that is of considerable historical interest. It throws additional light on the art spirit and industry here at the time, and reveals much about the incubation of Kellogg's own talent. It reads in part:

There was a professor of drawing in the Institution [Lesueur] who gave lectures as often as twice a day. These I attended in common with other scholars and gained some of the first rudiments of drawing—the a b c's of painting such as squares, right angles, etc.—which were shown and explained to us on a blackboard.

I was at that time the only scholar who attempted to put in practice the information we had gained. I copied drawings, such as landscape, flowers, birds, etc., from the portfolio of my preceptor, by which I gained certain ideas of Nature, that in a short time I was tempted secretly to copy her— Accordingly on the Sabbath (the only day we were permitted to enjoy out of the precincts of the Boarding School) I took my paper and pencil, and wended my way to the woods, seated myself on a stump, and with my hat turned on my knees, to serve as a table, I conveyed to paper a neighboring bridge and a friendly oak. With these sketches from Nature, I returned with a feeling of self satisfaction and happiness . . .

Robert Owen delivered at times lectures to the members of the *community* (for such the inhabitants of the village were termed) in the great Hall. I attended one of these lectures with the design of taking the likeness of the speaker. I did so, and as the features were somewhat from what I termed an *every day face* the sketch was recognized by all who saw it . . . Mr. Owen hearing I had taken his likeness, on meeting me at the public pump one day, requested me to let him see it. I did so, and it certainly pleased him, for in his kind and even affectionate manner, patting me on the shoulder said, "progress, my son, and you will make a painter one of these days." [33]

One surmises from his journal that Kellogg's art interest while at New Harmony lay in outdoor subjects, but later his training in portrait and life drawing at Cincinnati led to specialization in portraiture. His skill so impressed Martin Van Buren that the President secured for him an appointment to West Point to study art. The following years of his life were crowded with stimulating events, but as they have no direct bearing on our theme they will be reviewed rapidly. Sent as a courier of the Department of State to Europe, he toured the Continent in the early forties and the Near East soon after. He made portraits of potentates, sketched racial types in Asia, associated with diplomats and archaeologists, wrote critical articles about paintings by European old masters, and became a collector of unusual discrimination. His colorful life ended in Toledo, Ohio, in 1889.

The only painting by Kellogg in Indiana of which we have knowledge is the portrait of Robert Dale Owen (pl. 16), painted in 1860, hanging in the New Harmony home of Kenneth Owen. It was made during one of the painter's visits to New Harmony and it serves as a testimonial of boyhood friendship that lasted throughout life. It is a bust-length study, rendered with sound technical knowledge but with no display of dash or virtuosity. Kellogg presents his comrade as a sensitive, idealistic person, looking toward the observer with a calm pensive gaze, his head slightly tilted to one side. Few portraits have stated so sympathetically the understanding that a painter has for the mind and soul of his model.

The story of early art matters in New Harmony may be brought to a close by mentioning two more practitioners whose contributions were effective if not remarkable. They were John Banvard and Jacob Maentel who appeared here in the 1830's.

John Banvard was a panoramist, and the first in the annals of Indiana art, or so it appears.[34] What caused him to come to New Harmony is not known. He was born in New York in 1815, had studied painting and drawing somewhere in the East, and after his father's death went out to Louisville to find some means of support. He was about fifteen years old at the time. From Louisville he went to New Harmony in 1836, and there decided to paint a panorama, or more correctly, some dioramic paintings, with the help of other local young men. When completed, the large canvases were set up for public exhibition on a flatboat, and a tour of towns along the shores of the Wabash, Ohio, and Mississippi rivers began. But Banvard and his companions proved to be less adept as pilots and promoters than as artists, and after many mishaps, both physical and financial, the expedition was abandoned, Banvard continuing his way to New Orleans, the others returning to Indiana. That was the end of panoramic enterprises in New Harmony.

As Banvard never returned to Indiana so far as we know, the remaining adventures of his life as a painter and promoter of panoramas will not be dwelt upon here. In spite of the miscarriage of his New Harmony venture, he did not abandon panoramic work. He made some money in New Orleans and then started out to accomplish a cherished dream, that of making the largest painting in the world based on what to him was the grandest river in the world—the Mississippi. After making hundreds of drawings he chose Louisville as his seat of operations, and from 1840 to 1846 painted 1,200 miles of scenery on what was reported as three miles of canvas. His spectacular enterprise became very popular both in America and abroad, bringing him wealth, fame, and immense satisfaction. Indiana contributed a number of scenic subjects to a section of his *Panorama Royal of the Mississippi and Ohio Rivers,* such as views of the towns of Rising Sun, Vevay, Madison, and New Albany. Unfortunately the huge canvas was later destroyed and nothing remains to reveal the skill with which the subjects were depicted. However, they must have appeared convincing in their reality to audiences everywhere because his press notices were most flattering, and even the London, England, *Morning Chronicle* was enthusiastic: "We are unable to describe this Brobdignagian work of Mr. Banvard with the minuteness which his boldness and skill deserves. He is truly a giant amongst artists, and we can assure the denizens of the metropolis who are determined to make most of the holidays in seeing everything novel, as well as our country cousins who have come up to ransack the modern Babylon for shows and excitement, that Mr. Banvard's Panorama of the Ohio is by no means the least amusing and instructive of the many attractions which London puts forth at this season for both her citizens and her visitors." [35]

The last man to be considered here in connection with New Harmony and Posey County is Jacob Maentel, a person of different mold and background. He was one of the most ingenuous and untutored of the local painters, judging by the artlessness of his water colors, and yet he must have been a well educated and polished gentleman. According to the sparse records now available, he was born at Cassel, Germany, in 1763, was educated as a physician, and served for a time as secretary to Napoleon. What induced him to bring his family to this country has not been revealed, but upon arrival he started for

Texas, was forced to halt in western Indiana due to his childrens' ill-nesses, and found it expedient to remain here. Near Stewartsville, northeast of New Harmony, he settled on a section of land, became a farmer, and undertook portrait painting on a modest scale. This was probably in the 1830's. He remained in Posey County the rest of his life, dying in New Harmony in 1863 as he was approaching his one hundredth birthday.

Since he was an elderly man when he undertook to portray his neighbors, and had had no formal training in art, Maentel's delinea-tions are far from masterly. Examples now known are water colors on paper, about ten by fourteen inches in size, depicting the subjects in rigid, full-length poses. Frequently two members of a family are shown together—father and son, mother and daughter—and the back-grounds carefully reproduce their home environments, either interiors or outdoor settings, the latter including log cabins, trees, and rail fences. In one portrait, that of Jonathan Jaquess, he departed from his usual scheme and showed a harbor with ships in the distance, add-ing the verse:

> There all the ships company meet. Who sailed with their saveor beneath.
> With shouting each other they greet. And triumph oer sorrow and death.

This particular painting has additional documental value in that it is signed, giving the correct spelling of the artist's name (at least three spellings have been used), and bears the date 1841.

The above, and its companion portrait of Rebecca Jaquess (pl. 17), are owned by Arthur E. Jaquess, of Poseyville. In the Library of the Workingmen's Institute of New Harmony there is a study of James Overton with his son Emory, and in the home of Winfield W. Rabb is one of Thomas Rabb with his son James; the last two composi-tions are almost identical. Portraits of seven members of the John Cooper family, mostly in pairs, are in the possession now of Charles Ray, of Terre Haute.

Beyond the work of these men apparently very little was produced in Posey County. New Harmony never became a thriving commercial center and therefore failed to attract the professional itinerant painters who visited other towns in this section of the state. The one exception appears to be James T. Poindexter, successful portraitist of Evansville, who painted Charles Hallett White here in 1877, and James P. Bennett about 1863. These canvases are a part of an impressive collection of portraits and landscapes now in the Library of the Workingmen's Institute at New Harmony. While the collection contains many interesting items, including works by early European artists as well as recent Americans, few of the pictures lie within the scope of this narrative. Probably the most highly esteemed is the portrait of William Maclure, painted in England in 1797 and attributed to James Northcote, renowned British artist, writer, and member of the Royal Academy. It is reported that David Dale Owen made a copy of it for the Academy of Natural Sciences in Philadelphia, thus forging another link in the chain that bound New Harmony so closely to Philadelphia in those years when the little Indiana town was the home of the most important coterie of scientists west of the Alleghenies.

Terre Haute
Lawrenceburg
Madison
New Albany
Evansville

Chapter 3

TERRE HAUTE, EVANSVILLE

ROCKPORT, NEW ALBANY

HANOVER, MADISON

VEVAY, LAWRENCEBURG

THE MOST IMPORTANT SITE on the Wabash River north of New Harmony and Vincennes, with respect to early Indiana history, was Fort Harrison, adjacent to which the town of Terre Haute sprang up. Soldiers stationed at the Post and travelers reaching this region in the first years of the nineteenth century praised it highly, thus influencing many settlers to select it as their future home. Simultaneously with the state's admission into the Union (1816) the town was platted and lots sold; and even though it was still difficult to reach—one had his choice of going by boat up the Wabash or overland from Vincennes— it grew steadily. With the extension of the National Road in 1838, connecting it directly with Indianapolis and communities to the east, its growth was given additional impetus.

If there were painters in the region during the first quarter of the century no information about them has come to light.[1] The oldest portraits now in Terre Haute are those of Richard Blake and his wife Franceska Groverman, owned by Mrs. John C. Ross, painted about 1835 by an unidentified artist. Their superior technique and good characterization suggest that the painter came from an eastern or southern city, perhaps upon invitation from the Blakes, and as no other work of like style has turned up in this area, he probably got no more commissions in Vigo County.

Long before anything like an art colony grew up in Terre Haute, the Catholic girls' school at Saint Mary-of-the-Woods had its sisters who painted and taught classes in drawing and design. The Community, situated on wooded hills a few miles northwest of the city, was founded in 1840 and a year later classes in drawing and painting were added to the curriculum. They were conducted by Sister St. Francis Xavier (nee Irma le Fer de la Motte), a new arrival from France, whose "beautiful, clever, and saintly personality at once commanded respect and admiration."[2] She spent the remaining fifteen years of her life here, teaching, painting, and doing her part in building up a strong religious and educational center. She was followed by Sister Anastasie, an American by birth (Jane Brown) who probably brought to her teaching position better training in art and more experience. Like her predecessor, she worked principally in water colors, several of which are being preserved in the art gallery of the school. Her administrative capacity later brought about her election to the office of Superior General of the Community.

Sister Maurice and Sister Mary Albertine were the other artist-teachers at Saint Mary-of-the-Woods before 1885. Sister Maurice (Madeleine Schnell), a native of Germany, came to the Community when she was about eighteen years old and remained the rest of her life. She was a serious and capable painter, and in addition to this interest in creative work she undertook the formation of a collection of paintings and ceramics that led to the founding of the art gallery at the Community. She worked principally in oils. Her successor, Sister Mary Albertine Sondermann, received her training at the Art Institute of Chicago and at the Cincinnati Art Academy. Later she worked under Bierstadt, Eakins, and Chase, finishing her technical training at the Munich Royal Academy. In addition to the years spent at Saint Mary-of-the-Woods, she taught at St. John's Academy, Indianapolis, from about 1883 to 1887, and in 1883 sent her painting, *Orphan Child* to the loan exhibition held that year by the Art Association of Indianapolis in the English's Hotel block.

The earliest pictures of known authorship made in Terre Haute date from the 1860's, during the town's rapid commercial development. Four painters are reported as having worked here in that decade: George Linen, of New York, William R. Freeman, whom we last met in Vincennes, James D. Wright, an itinerant, and James F. Gookins, a native son.

Identifying George Linen with New York is insufficient. He was a Scotsman, born at Greenlaw in 1802, and a student at the Scottish Royal Academy, Edinburgh. He specialized in portraits of small dimensions, and built up a successful practice in England before coming to America. After 1843 he was in New York, where he gained a high reputation for his precisely executed cabinet-size likenesses. Henry Clay and Daniel Webster were among his illustrious sitters.

What caused Linen to visit Indiana is not known. In all probability he was invited by one of the leading citizens of Terre Haute, perhaps Chauncey Warren, to come here and paint members of his family, which apparently led to other commissions. Judging by the ages of his models, he was here in the early sixties and he doubtless remained only long enough to complete such work as he had on hand. In addition to the portraits of Chauncey Warren and his wife Frances Modisette, Linen painted five members of the Levi Warren family, a double portrait of the Craft sisters—Lucia and Fannie—a portrait of Caleb Mills (pl. 18), and one of Chauncey Rose, founder of the Rose Polytechnic Institute. The latter is owned by the Institute and the others are in the homes of descendants of the sitters. All of the portraits are small, averaging ten by eight inches, and painted with oil colors on cardboard. The technique is meticulous without being fussy; colors are clear and attractive. The portraits are not signed. Their attribution to Linen is based on stylistic comparisons with his recorded work.

After returning East, George Linen continued painting in New York and nearby towns until his death in 1888.[3]

William Freeman was in Terre Haute in the early fifties and again in the seventies. His marriage to Jane Douglas here on March 17, 1851, is the first definite date we have relating to his sojourn in Vigo County, while the appearance of his name in the Terre Haute directory of 1872–1873 is the last. Where he spent the intervening twenty years we do not know.

As was pointed out in the previous chapter, Freeman came from New York and reached Indiana about 1845. He may have received some training in the East but there is no record of his having attended either an art school or a private class. His early work in the state reveals him as a fairly good draughtsman and competent in getting likenesses, but a poor colorist. With the development of the camera he tended more and more to paint with photographic exactitude, and in many cases actually painted with oil pigments over enlarged prints. Preston Hussey, Tousant Campbell Buntin, and Blackford Condit were among Freeman's patrons in Terre Haute, and their portraits, together with those of their wives, are still affectionately kept by descendants. Mary Burnet stated that nearly all the old families here were painted by him,[4] but not more than nine canvases can now be assigned to Freeman with any degree of certainty.

A third painter working in Terre Haute in the 1860's was James D. Wright. Nothing is now known of his life or the quality of his work because neither a biography nor a painting survives. He exhibited some work at the Indiana State Fair in 1857 and his name is listed in Hawes' *Indiana State Gazetteer* for 1860–1861 as a Terre Haute artist, and again in *Chandler's State Directory* for 1868. Doubtless several of the portraits of unknown authorship in this area are by him, but until a picture turns up that is unquestionably from his easel this cloud of obscurity will not be lifted.

II

James Farrington Gookins, the fourth artist mentioned above as a Terre Haute resident, was born here December 30, 1840, the son of Judge Samuel B. Gookins.[5] He began painting in his native city about 1860, having been encouraged to pursue that line of activity by Bayard Taylor, poet and journalist, whom he met in Terre Haute. At twenty, Gookins entered Wabash College, but his studies were interrupted by the war. He enlisted in the Eleventh Indiana Volunteer Infantry under General Lew Wallace, but because of ill health served only a short time. During that period he made some war sketches, two of which were published in *Harper's Weekly* in 1861.[6]

For the next four years he apparently concentrated on problems of painting, dividing his time between Terre Haute and Indianapolis, and studying for a few months in Cincinnati under James H. Beard. In 1865 he decided to live in Chicago, joined the growing colony of artists in that community, opened a studio in the Opera House building, and soon became one of the leaders in local art affairs. With Walter Shirlaw and others he established in 1869 the Academy of Design which later became the Art Institute of Chicago.[7]

His decision to study abroad brought him back to his native city soon after. Here he married Cora Donnelly in June of 1870, and a short time later sailed for Europe with his bride, combining a honeymoon with visits to art galleries and study in the Royal Academy at Munich. During his two years abroad he visited London, Paris, and Vienna (he served as assistant commissioner at the Vienna International Exhibition in 1873) and sketched in the Swiss and Italian Alps, gathering material that served him later in composing many of the large pictures that brought him wide recognition as a painter of mountains.

Upon returning to America in 1873 he re-established himself in Chicago, taught in the Academy, painted landscapes, and wrote poetry. Four years later, in the fall of 1877, he went to Indianapolis to assist in the founding of the Indiana School of Art. The school was short-lived and he returned to Terre Haute where he re-opened his studio. But Chicago drew Gookins away again. From 1881 until his death in 1904 he divided his energies between art and civic enterprises, working with enthusiasm for the development of the city's lake shore and transit facilities while continuing his painting and writing. He returned to Indianapolis for about a year, from the summer of 1887 to the summer of 1888, to serve as secretary of the Commission for the Indiana Soldiers' and Sailors' Monument.

Paintings that came from Gookins' studio were diverse in both subject and treatment. His streak of poetic fantasy and invention found an outlet in decorative floral compositions with fairies playing among leaves and blossoms, a number of which are still in Terre Haute homes. In a more objective vein, but still tinged with romanticism, were the

Alpine subjects mentioned above and a series of mountain scenes made in Colorado. Portraits and figure compositions also occupied his time but, as compared with the other subjects, relatively few are known. Most of the portraits represent members of his family.

His earliest known painting, said to date from the early 1860's, represents the Modisette ferry that crossed the Wabash at Terre Haute (pl. 19). This canvas was long in the possession of the Modisette and Warren families, and was recently added to the collection of the Sheldon Swope Art Gallery in Terre Haute. Its technical quality bears out the supposition that Gookins had had little or no instruction in art at that time. Even before 1860 he had been sending work to the raffles held by the Indianapolis Art Society, indicating his seriousness of purpose and his lack of timidity.

One of his most charming works, and one representing his transitional style, is a portrait of his wife in a white satin dress strolling in a garden, perhaps at Munich, painted soon after they arrived in Europe. It is now in the collection of the John Herron Art Museum. A number of his landscapes painted abroad or in Colorado are in Terre Haute and Indianapolis. The Public Library in the former city has several, and among the Indianapolis owners are Elizabeth Claypool, Mrs. Roscoe Johnson, and Mrs. George Rose.

Although Gookins spent little time in Terre Haute in the seventies, the town was not without the services of painters during that decade. A man by the name of Mitchell was there for a while, as were Henry F. Spread and Walter Sies. None of them was a master technician but each was sufficiently competent to carry out the usual orders.

So little is known of Mitchell that if no work by him remained there would be no point in recording his name. He may have been Harvey Mitchell who, according to historian Fielding, was working in Charleston, South Carolina, in 1830, and doing rather poor work.[8] If so, he did not improve greatly during the intervening years, because such Indiana portraits as have survived reveal him as a mediocre painter using enlarged photographs as the foundations of his pictures, and show that he had no flair for color or pleasing characterization. Among his known works (we may assume that several were destroyed through

18. George Linen: Portrait of Caleb Mills

Courtesy of Helen Condit, Terre Haute (page 41)

19. (below) James F. Gookins: Modisette Ferry on the Wabash

Courtesy of the Sheldon Swope Art Gallery, Terre Haute (page 44)

20. James T. Poindexter:
Portrait of
Mrs. Charles Mason
Courtesy of the Evansville
Museum of Arts and Science,
Evansville (page 48)

21. Philip Lang: Portrait of
Matthias Sharp
Courtesy of Mrs. Samuel I. Hill,
Rockport (page 51)

22. George Morrison: Portrait of Mary Emma and Harry Woodward
Courtesy of Katharine Woodward, Middleburg, Virginia (page 53)

23. P. C. Wyeth:
Sons of Charles L.
Shrewsbury

Courtesy of Eleanor
Shrewsbury Wood,
Indianapolis (page 61)

24. (below) William
McKendree Snyder:
Madison on the Ohio

Courtesy of Paul H.
North, Jr., Columbus,
Ohio (page 64)

cleaning, because the paint was poor in quality and application) are the portraits of Warren Davis and his wife Amelia, and six members of the John H. O'Boyle family, owned by descendants of the sitters. According to tradition, Mitchell was on his way to the West Coast when he painted them, stopping in Indiana only long enough to get such commissions as he could. A contemporary of his in Terre Haute was Henry F. Spread of Indianapolis, regarding whom more will be said in a later chapter. Spread was reported as being in Terre Haute in 1875, but no work by him there has come to our attention.

Walter Sies, for several years a resident of Vigo County in the 1870's and 1890's, made landscape painting a specialty rather than portraiture —although less exalted tasks involving brushes and paint were his principal sources of income. In keeping with the tendencies of the period he was a painter with peripatetic habits, but unlike most of his fellow-artists he preferred the rivers to overland routes. A houseboat constituted his home and studio. How many of the Wabash River towns he visited we do not know but doubtless he was a familiar figure in those within reach of Terre Haute by boat. For a period of time he lived in Paducah, Kentucky, and some years later he turned up in Crawfordsville, which was probably his original home. He returned to Terre Haute in the early 1890's where he is believed to have spent the remaining years of his life.

When and where Sies was born is not known. He was probably a lifelong resident of western Indiana, making a livelihood for his family principally by painting signs and carriages. The only specific dates we have concerning him are 1878 and 1879 when his name appeared in Beesley's *Crawfordsville Directory,* and a few inscribed dates on his late canvases. Landscapes by his hand, in a timid, labored style, are owned by the Swope Art Gallery, by Delphine Bindley, and by the Fairbanks Public Library of Terre Haute. The Fairbanks Library has two: one depicts a steamboat on the Wabash, the other a delineation of Fort Harrison made from an old print.

Another painter who visited Terre Haute late in the 1870's was George W. Morrison, a resident of New Albany, and a more accomplished technician than those we have been discussing. His stay here

seems to have been very brief, and he probably accomplished little beyond the portraits of Edward Bindley and his wife Aimee, now owned
by Delphine Bindley. More will be told later about Morrison's career.

III

The period from 1816 to 1825 was one of steady immigration into
Indiana with most of the new settlers moving into the southern part
of the state, first along the rivers and then inland upon such trails and
roads as were passable. The Ohio and Wabash rivers were to serve for
many more years as the main traffic arteries, and the towns established
on their banks enjoyed increasing commercial activity as the tide of
immigrants moved in from the southern and eastern states.

Evansville, destined to become one of the largest of Indiana's river
towns, was founded in that period, the first advertisements for the sale
of lots appearing in the Vincennes *Western Sun* in the early summer
of 1817. One of the promoters of the sale was Robert M. Evans, for
whom the town was named, and whose portrait is the oldest painting
now in the city (among local productions) and may be regarded as one
of the most important early documents in that region. It was painted
about 1830. According to tradition, it was the outcome of a wager
made on political aspirants: Evans having won the bet was entitled to
have his portrait made by a painter who was visiting Evansville at the
time. Family lore attributes the work to Benjamin West. Obviously
this could not have been the famous American who spent most of his
professional life in England, dying in London in 1820, but it might
have been John Benjamin West, of Kentucky, son of William E. West,
one of the best artists of the bluegrass country in the first quarter of
the nineteenth century.

The portrait, now owned by Knox Corrington, represents Evans as
a man about fifty years of age, robust, and with a ruddy complexion.
He faces the observer with a fixed, analytical gaze, his strong features
revealing a resolute character. The work is that of a well-trained
and experienced hand, competent without being flashy, and is alto-
gether a worthy portrayal of the town's foremost citizen of the time.

If West (or whoever the artist was) made other portraits in or around Evansville none has been found. Nor has the work of any other artist come to light that might have been done before 1850, although the town was large enough to warrant several painters visiting it. But by 1855 the situation had changed. Evansville had by that time a resident painter by the name of James Thomas Poindexter and an itinerant named Gorgas. The latter's connection with the town was as brief as his history is obscure. In fact, it is not certain that he actually stopped at Evansville for our only knowledge of his being in that area is an advertisement inserted in the *Warrick Democrat,* a newspaper published at Newburgh, a few miles above Evansville:

DAGUERREOTYPES, MINIATURES AND PORTRAIT PAINTING

We would respectfully announce to the citizens of Newburgh and vicinity, that we have landed our BOAT at the Ferry Landing, and are prepared to take DAGUERREOTYPES and paint PORTRAITS in Oil or French Pastels, in the finest style, and shortest possible time.

Our boat is fitted up expressly for Daguerreotyping. Our light is of the best kind, which enables us to take the largest sized groups in a few seconds of time.

Call and see us; you will find us capable of producing all work pertaining to the Heliographic art, and on the lowest terms.

Gorgas & Bro.[9]

As was customary, the editor of the paper inserted a brief editorial, calling attention to the advertisement and suggesting that those wanting pictures should call on Messrs. Gorgas & Bro. But no additional light was thrown on their activities there. One of the brothers was doubtless Joseph R. Gorgas, who advertised in the Madison *Daily Courier* during the winter of 1853–1854. Portrait painting was not mentioned, but emphasis was put on his Daguerrean Salon with skylights, enabling the "artist" to take first-rate pictures of his clients "in any weather." The appearance of his name in the city directories as late as 1867 leads to the conclusion that business remained good for him in Madison for several years.

In contrast to the obscurity of the Gorgas brothers, the career of Poindexter stands out in bold relief. Born in Christian County, near Hopkinsville, Kentucky, June 1832, James Thomas Poindexter spent the first twenty years of his life in or near his birthplace. At an early age he had chosen the career of a portrait painter and, having gleaned whatever information he could from itinerants, he undertook to make likenesses in western Kentucky. Later he had an opportunity to study in Cincinnati and, according to certain reports, he even went to New York, Boston, and Italy. If this is so, it must have been much later in his life. It has also been stated that he had studios at New Orleans and Granada, Mississippi, at some time during his professional career. In 1852 he married Nancy Marshall, of Eddyville, and soon after crossed the Ohio River and settled in Evansville. His painting activity was interrupted by the Civil War, in which he served as a telegraph operator for the Confederate Army.

Poindexter's earliest known work in Indiana is a portrait of Sarah Nelson that was made about 1852, now owned by Rev. Samuel Forrest Stitt, of Newburgh. Its relatively flat and simple style reveals him as a rather inexperienced painter, but the firm drawing and pleasing characterization suggest that he had a good deal of natural ability. In the years that followed, his style became more naturalistic as his hand became increasingly proficient. Greater attention was given to the accurate depiction of features and dress, and to the lighting, as one sees in the portraits of Dr. Madison J. Bray and his wife, and Mrs. Charles Mason (pl. 20), in the Evansville Museum, and those of Captain James Bennett and Charles H. White in the Library of the Workingmen's Institute, New Harmony. The latter, dated 1877, shows Poindexter at the height of his career. Many canvases by him have been recorded; there are still others, such as the portraits of Willard Carpenter and his wife in the Willard Library, Evansville, that further study might establish as his.

Poindexter lived in Evansville, confining his activity to the southwestern corner of the state, until 1882, with his studio on Main Street and his residence, after 1872, on Gum Street. After 1882 his name disappears from records here and nothing more is heard of him until his death at Eddyville, Kentucky, in 1891. It was probably during this period that he studied in the East and in Italy. There is no record of his having had any children. When his wife died, the artist's own collection of pictures went to a nephew, Thomas Poindexter Marshall, who in turn willed many of the paintings to Mrs. Maud E. Terrell, of Louisville. In this group is a painting of the Biblical subject *The Tribute Money,* which was one of several religious and historical themes he attempted.

An early resident of Evansville who knew Poindexter described him as one of the noblest characters she ever knew. "His life belied all the impressions of artists," she wrote to a friend, "that is, that they are eccentric, nervous and irascible. His deeply sensitive artist's soul did not make him oblivious to the necessities of those around or dependent upon him. His friends were sacred to him and he grappled them to him with hooks of steel. Is it not too bad that so many noble lives pass away without the slightest record being made of them?"

In this letter from Cornelia Meadows to Mary Catherine Wedding, both of Evansville, written in 1914, the writer mentioned another painter, a Mr. Forbs [Forbes] who spent many winters in that city. She knew very little about him but recalled his saying "that the first president of the Royal Art Academy of London, Wilson, was a pupil of his and he, Mr. Forbs, was instrumental in sending Wilson to Italy to perfect his art education." [10]

As inaccurate as most of that statement turned out to be,[11] it is nevertheless of interest to learn that a British painter of some standing had been a resident of Evansville, Indiana, for several winters. Recent investigation has revealed that the artist was James G. Forbes, a native of Scotland, born about 1800 and a practicing painter there until about 1860 when he came to America. During the 1850's he exhibited his work at the Royal Scottish Academy, Edinburgh, and at the Royal Academy and at the British Institute, London.

After 1860 Forbes was in Chicago, established as a portrait painter with a studio at 88 LaSalle Street. His name appears for the last time in the Chicago directory for 1868, the year he apparently came to Indiana. How he happened to visit Evansville is not known, but probably his acquaintance with H. F. Blount of this city induced him to seek commissions here. The only known canvas in Evansville by his hand is a large one of John B. Baker, mayor of the town, painted in

1868 or 1869, now hanging on the stair landing of the Willard Library. It is an impressive picture, depicting Baker in a full-length pose, standing in a richly decorated room. Through this commission Forbes was introduced to Governor Conrad Baker, brother of the mayor, a meeting that resulted in his being asked to paint a number of the governors of Indiana for the Statehouse collection at Indianapolis. More about that project will be found in a later chapter. Where he went after completing his commissions in Indianapolis has not been discovered.

Most of the other professional painters who worked in Evansville around the Civil War period and during the following decades are no more than names to us today—names found, for the most part, in old city directories. In the sixties, Alex Conn, Lucia A. Eames, James Massalon, and Lewis Evans were listed, the last two being partners; in the seventies, the names of Julius Dietz, Oscar Hakelier, E. L. Morret, and J. A. Holder appeared. Nothing by them has been identified thus far.

Rose O'Byrne, listed as an artist in 1871 and again in the 1880's in local directories, was probably a native of Evansville and, unlike the itinerants mentioned above, was better known to the local citizens. One of her surviving paintings, a view of the Evansville waterfront, reveals her limited technical ability and suggests that she was largely, if not entirely, self-taught. The picture represents river boats in the foreground of the composition with the town in the distance, and while it is not masterly in execution it has decided historical value. It is now in the home of Milford Miller, of Newburgh.

In the eighties there was a marked increase in the number of women painters in Evansville, judging by the directory listings. Outnumbering the men two to one, they must have presented a formidable art front in the small community. Minnie Hallock, Lizzie McQuigg, Eldora Raleigh, Mrs. William R. Barker, Mary E. Hart, Mary Upchurch, Bertha Scantlin, and Grace Tyrrell were some of them.

IV

The next place along the Ohio River that contributed to early art matters was Rockport. James T. Poindexter visited here as early as

1854 and painted the likenesses of Samuel Gibson Brown and his wife Maria Louisa, now owned by Mrs. Edward Simpson. But he was preceded by another painter, one Philip Lang. A resident of Cincinnati for a brief period, Lang came to Rockport in 1852 upon the invitation of Matthias Sharp. In addition to portraits of Sharp (pl. 21) and his wife, owned by Mrs. Samuel I. Hill (the painting in oil of the latter was destroyed but a small water-color study has survived), there are in Rockport half a dozen canvases by Lang, including portraits of James Proctor and his wife, owned by C. W. Halbridge, and of Samuel J. Park and Mary Morgan, now in the home of Mrs. Melba Bullock.

History is silent on the subject of Philip Lang. So far as we know he did not paint elsewhere in the state, and nothing by his hand has been identified in Cincinnati or vicinity. He, or someone by the same name, was listed in the Cincinnati City Directory for 1850–1851, but no profession was given; and at no time during the fifties did his name appear among the artists or portrait painters in the Business Mirrors, the classified section of the directories. Charles F. Goss, in his *Cincinnati, The Queen City* (1912) stated that a Mr. Lang made a specialty of "architectonic painting," that some of his work was in St. Ludwig's Church, and that he afterward went back to Germany. This may or may not be the visitor to Rockport.

The portraits listed above are signed *Ph. Lang,* and in most cases bear the date 1852. They are competent in technique and while the likenesses appear to be good there is little indication of the personality or temperament of the sitters. Their most appealing aspect is color.

Very little of interest to us has come to light in the region between Rockport and New Albany. Tell City and Cannelton doubtless were visited by overland itinerant painters, or artisans traveling by boat, but nothing remains to confirm this. Reports of old portraits having once been in the homes here are current, but the dispersal of families has caused their removal from Indiana. Corydon, the principal town west of New Albany, must have drawn a number of wandering portraitists who hoped to get commissions from the legislators who assembled here when it was the territorial and state capital (1813 to 1825). No local work of that period remains, however. The old capitol building houses a number of portraits, some good and some poor in quality, which have been donated in recent years to decorate barren walls. The most interesting of these depicts Ratliff Boon; it was painted by an unknown hand and probably not in this region.[12] The portrait of Thomas Posey is a dull modern copy, and those of Dennis Pennington, builder of the courthouse, and his wife, are mediocre from a technical standpoint.

V

New Albany, at one time the largest city in Indiana (when Indianapolis was little more than forest and swampland), held a key position on the river and was regarded as the gateway to the Mississippi; as the eastern terminus of the old road or buffalo trace to Vincennes and the western plains, most of the overland traffic passed through it. Three enterprising brothers from New York, Joel, Nathaniel, and Abner Scribner, purchased the tract of land for $8,000 in 1813, platted it, and named the new town for the capital of their native state. Joel and his family lived in half of a double log cabin during their first year here, then built a narrow two-story house on the principal street, commanding a fine view of the Ohio River.

From our standpoint the Scribner house is of particular interest in that it has among its furnishings some of the best of the town's early paintings: portraits of Dr. William A. Scribner (son of Joel), his second wife, Harriet Hale, and her son Charles. They were painted by George W. Morrison about 1852, and are among the artist's earliest productions as well as some of his best. Direct unaffected rendering, firm drawing, and good color give them their charm.

As the town's only resident artist, Morrison painted the likeness of most of its leading citizens, and varied his output from time to time by sketching outdoor scenes. He even undertook a *Garden of Eden* composition. Portrait commissions drew him to other nearby communities, contributing to his reputation as the best painter in southern Indiana in the years preceding and following the Civil War. It is recorded that members of the Bragdon, Montgomery, Nunemacher, and Shields families of New Albany were painted by him.[13] His study of Mary

Stewart Shields, made in 1843, and his self-portrait of the same year (now owned by the New Albany Public Library) are his earliest known works. In addition to the above, portraits of Dr. John Reily, Thomas Collins and his wife Margaret, Jessie Austin as a child, Eliza Reddick Stillson, and a double portrait of Mary Emma Woodward and her younger brother Harry (pl. 22) are known.[14] Probably his most important work is the large portrait of Ashbel P. Willard, painted in 1857, now in the Statehouse, Indianapolis.

George W. Morrison was born at Baltimore, Maryland, in 1820, of Scottish ancestry. He came to New Albany in 1840, where he established himself as a professional painter. What training he had in the East, if any, has not been recorded, but his competent technique leads one to believe that he studied with an able teacher early in his career. He married Lydia Maynard of New Albany and together they enjoyed a twenty-five acre home site in Silver Hills. It is said that in fair weather his favorite studio was a large oak tree on his property. He was described as a handsome, genial person, with long curling hair, and possessing a talent for poetry. After a full and fruitful life he died at New Albany in 1893.

It appears that Morrison had the New Albany region very much to himself for the fifty-three years of his residence here. Only two other painters are known to have worked in the community: Carl P. Fetsch, a native of Germany, and Ferdinand G. Walker. Fetsch's stay was not of long duration, and Walker enters the scene so late in the century that he will be mentioned but briefly in this chronicle.

Fetsch (sometimes spelled Pfetsch) was born in Blankenburg, Germany, about 1817. He probably received his academic education and his training as a painter there before coming to America. He resided in New York for a few years but beyond his affiliation with the German-American Art Club there, nothing is now known of his activities in the East. During the sixties he was in New Albany, where, presumably, he produced some work although nothing by him has been identified. Then, about 1870, he moved to Indianapolis.

While he was recognized as an accomplished painter, working in a tight, meticulous manner and showing a preference for narrative pic-

tures, Fetsch's speciality was oil-tinted photographs, a speciality doubtless forced upon him by necessity. Many of them may still be preserved
in homes at New Albany, but identification of his hand would be
quite impossible where such a mechanical method was employed. One
of the few paintings now assigned to him is a composition of an elderly
woman about to bathe a child, entitled *Grandmother and the Bath,*
which might have been painted in New Albany, although it is now in
Indianapolis. More will be said about his life and work when we turn
to the painters of the capital.

Ferdinand Graham Walker, the third artist associated with the
town, was born at Mitchell, Indiana, in 1859, the son of Rev. Francis
Walker, a Methodist pastor. In his early childhood his family lived in
a number of southern Indiana towns, settling in New Albany in 1874,
by which time the boy had evinced a marked talent for drawing. His
first instruction was received from a local painter; in 1885 he was able
to go to Paris, where he studied painting for two years; after an interval
of about fifteen years, during which time he maintained a studio in
New Albany, he returned to Paris for additional training under
Dagnan-Bouveret and Puvis de Chavannes. A few years after his return to Indiana he moved his studio across the Ohio River to Louisville
where he painted portraits of many eminent citizens of the region.
About twenty years later he re-opened his studio in New Albany where
his death occurred in 1927.

Walker made a specialty of portraiture, and many of his canvases
are in Louisville and vicinity, the majority having been made in the
nineties or after 1900. A portrait of Silas C. Day, painted in New
Albany about 1885, is perhaps the best of his early canvases: a strong
characterization of a forceful personality, painted with firmness and
a competent handling of paint. It is owned by Mary Scribner, of New
Albany. Most of his canvases show the influence of Puvis de Chavannes in their simple compositions and flat rendering of forms, although his colors are usually richer and deeper than those used by the
French master, especially in the latter's mural compositions.

The few additional names that can be added to Floyd County's
artistic coterie come too late in the century for inclusion here.

VI

From New Albany our survey leads northeast along the river to Jefferson County, with Madison as the principal center.

It is generally conceded that the most beautiful area in southern Indiana is the wooded bluff bordering the Ohio River and forming the southern boundary of Jefferson County, and that the spot offering one of the choicest views is at Hanover. Our attention is drawn there in this story not by its picturesque aspect but because it was the setting of a romantic tale relating to the first man with strong artistic inclinations who ventured into this part of the state. He was Christopher Harrison, painter by avocation.

Our best authority on Christopher Harrison's life in Indiana is William Wesley Woollen, who relates how Harrison, presumably disappointed in a love affair, left his home in Maryland and wandered West, hoping that solitude and time would help assuage his grief.[15] He chose a summit commanding a fine view of the river, known as Fair Prospect, later named Hanover, where he built a log cabin and surrounded himself with his favorite books and pictures. Hunting constituted his major activity as it was the principal means of securing food, but much of his time was spent in reading and sketching. This was in 1808 or 1809.

In 1815, he gave up his isolated retreat, moved his few belongings to Salem, about forty miles west, and opened a general store in partnership with Jonathan Lyon. The next year, when Indiana was admitted to the Union, he was elected lieutenant governor, and in 1820 he was appointed one of three commissioners to survey and lay out Indianapolis, the new capital. He returned to Maryland in 1834 where he died in 1863, at the age of eighty-eight.

Unfortunately the report of Harrison's interest in drawing and painting cannot be substantiated by actual examples of work. Nothing by him has been found, and no early chronicler tells of specific pictures and where they might be seen. Several of his sketches in water color were said to be preserved in some old books which were afterward owned by Judge D. D. Banta, of Franklin, but recent efforts to trace them have been fruitless. It is of interest to find again in Harrison's case the classic legend of birds or people being deceived by painted fruit, a tale that goes as far back as the fourth century before Christ to a painting by Apelles. In Harrison's case, a neighbor of his in Salem was mystified by the realism of his work: he had painted a grapevine clinging to his porch so perfectly that she, on seeing it, at once put out her hand, thinking to pluck a bunch of grapes!

Fair Prospect, the site of Harrison's first Indiana home, is now a part of the Hanover College campus. The college had a large collection of paintings, many by early Indiana limners, but the fire that destroyed Classic Hall in 1941 consumed most of them. A small oval portrait of John F. Crowe, founder of the college, was among the pictures which were saved; although its author has not been identified, stylistically it resembles some of Will Snyder's work. Snyder was Madison's leading painter, and Hanover's proximity to that bustling river town would make such an attribution reasonable.

First settled in 1805, and platted four years later, Madison grew swiftly. It was advantageously situated as the nearest river port for interior Indiana, and before the arrival of railroads was an important link with markets in eastern cities and in New Orleans. While its prominence as a commercial and financial center gradually waned with the lessening of river traffic, its reputation as a cultural and artistic community continued. Fine old houses of the forties and fifties became conspicuous, many being furnished with good paintings and family portraits in addition to antique furniture.

In its prosperous years a number of artists and artisans visited Madison hoping to get rewarding commissions—and some succeeded. Being close to southwestern Ohio and northern Kentucky, it was a tempting port of call for painters of those regions long before the town had a resident artist of its own. The brevity of their visits, however, makes it difficult now to identify their work even when their sojourn was noted in the local press. As usual, signatures were the exception rather than the rule.

What appears to be the oldest portrait in Madison is that of Miles Cary Eggleston, believed to date from 1821 when Eggleston was thirty years old. A signature that was fairly legible a few years ago, but which has been obliterated in the process of restoration, appeared to be "T. W. Morgan." The only recorded artist in the Midwest by the name of Morgan was Louis Morgan of Kentucky, but as he was born in 1814 he could not have been the author of the Eggleston portrait. The workmanship is competent and professional, but it lacks recognizable stylistic traits, and cannot at present be assigned to any known painter of that period.

Eggleston, shown with his left shoulder toward the observer, appears to be an amiable, intelligent man. He was neatly dressed in a dark suit and white stock, and has the bearing befitting one of Indiana's most eminent jurists in the first quarter of the nineteenth century. The canvas, formerly owned by Harriet Goode is now in the home of Michael E. Garber.

Sometime in the 1820's Madison was visited by another painter whose identity is more certain, though his craftsmanship leaves something to be desired. He was Richard Terrell, or Terryll, of Kentucky, a conspicuous figure in and around Madison for a number of years, at least until 1828 when he removed to Indianapolis.[16]

Although he was ambitious to paint portraits he was forced by economic exigencies, and perhaps by a limited talent in capturing likenesses, to execute signs and regimental colors, to gild frames, paint architectural ornaments, and do such tasks with his brushes and paint as were in demand. His most ambitious performance, and the only painting in Madison that can now be assigned to him, is a large full-length portrait of the Marquis de Lafayette, that hangs on the upper stair landing of the Masonic Hall. According to an article in the *Indianapolis Star* of June 18, 1921, by Kate Milner Rabb, the portrait has been the subject of not a little discussion and the basis of a number of persistent legends relative to its origin.

We learn from the article that "on LaFayette's journey up the Ohio river, after his stay in Perry county, and the dinner given in his honor at Jeffersonville [April 16, 1825], his boat stopped at a village across the river from Madison, and that he was visited there by a delegation of Madison citizens, among them a number of Masons, of which order he was a member, and that one of the party painted this portrait." The article also states that according to the minutes of the Masonic lodge it is recorded that the portrait was given to the fraternity by Richard Terryll.

It is not unreasonable to assume that artist Terrell was a member of the Madison delegation that paid its respects to the eminent Frenchman, and that he made some kind of a sketch that served as a basis for the portrait. While he may have used engravings, too, in getting Lafayette's features as accurate as possible, the composition and pose do not duplicate any other portraits of the Marquis and therefore tend to confirm the report that the Madison canvas is an original work. Someone thought, according to the article quoted above, that it was a copy of the large portrait in the Statehouse at Frankfort, Kentucky, but this is not so. The latter shows the General walking beside a river, and in a different pose and attire.

The Terrell portrait represents Lafayette standing in a room, a bare wall behind and a curtained window at the extreme left. He is dressed in a heavy overcoat that comes down to his ankles, a hat in his left hand, his right hand extended in a gesture denoting serious conversation or debate.

Although the canvas is not in good condition and not well lighted where it now hangs, it resembles in manner of execution the few portraits by Terrell that are known. It is far from being the performance of a virtuoso. The drawing is stiff and blunt, colors are dark and murky, and the face lacks expression. However, if its history is reliable it has the merit of being one of the few likenesses of Lafayette painted in this country from life, and the only one by an artist associated with the state of Indiana.

More will be told of Terrell's career when we turn to the Indianapolis scene.

During the next two decades art activities were at low ebb in Madison, judging by the paucity of references to such events, but by the middle of the 1840's the situation had changed. A number of wandering brushwielders found their way into town. Some, like William Hanbeck and James F. Harris, used the medium of the local newspaper to announce their presence; others, like Thomas Buchanan Read and William R. Freeman, probably had connections that enabled them to get orders from the leading citizens. Tradition and existing canvases confirm their sojourn even though the press ignored them.

"William Hanbeck, *Portrait Painter*, begs leave to announce to the citizens of Madison and vicinity," reads the *Republican Banner* of April 1, 1846, "that he has located in Madison for the purpose of practicing his Profession. His room is on Main Cross street, in the brick building immediately west of the Post-Office and nearly opposite the Methodist Church, where the citizens generally are invited to call and see him, and examine his specimens. His prices shall be moderate, and likenesses warranted in all cases where proper attention is given."

With so gracious and reassuring an invitation one would expect nothing but great success for Hanbeck, but evidence points in the opposite direction. No work by him can now be identified.

In September of the same year another business card appeared in the *Republican Banner* with a similar message, inserted by a Mr. Harris. He announced himself as a portrait painter, staying at the Franklin House, and able to supply oilcloth window shades in addition to facsimiles of people's faces.

Like Hanbeck, Harris gives no clue to his previous activities or future plans. But research has revealed more about his life, even though none of his work in Madison has been discovered. He was James F. Harris, who appeared in Indianapolis in 1853 where he painted a panorama called the *Mirror of Intemperance* that brought him a good deal of fame.

VII

Probably the best artist in Madison before the Civil War was Thomas Buchanan Read. Although he was not a prominent figure when he first visited here (about 1840) he was soon to attain considerable distinction as a poet as well as a painter. "Sheridan's Ride" was one of several poems by him that people read with enthusiasm, and his large literary pictures, such as *Milton Dictating Paradise Lost to his Daughters*, were renowned. His unusual artistic and intellectual capacity and cultivated manners placed him high in the estimation of his colleagues wherever he lived: Cincinnati, New York, or Rome. He was born in Chester County, Pennsylvania, in 1822; he was in Cincinnati in 1836, and opened a studio in New York in 1841. In 1850 he went to Europe and resided in Rome, but made frequent visits to America. He died at New York in 1872.

The tradition that James F. D. Lanier brought Read to Madison to paint portraits of members of his family has persisted among descendants. Some have pointed to the oval portrait of Mrs. Lanier hanging in the fine old Lanier Home as his work, but both date and style of painting seem to preclude such a possibility. However, recent examination of a full-length study of Lanier himself, now owned by Mrs. Charles Davidson, of Madison, has revealed Buchanan Read's signature on the newspaper lying upon the table near the left edge of the composition. Lanier stands in a proud, self-sufficient pose, a cane in his right hand, his left hand resting on his hip. His small size, in relation to the large canvas and the expansive room, makes him appear dwarfed and somewhat unimportant in spite of his bumptious stance. As a very early product of the artist's brush, it lacks fluency of execution and attractive color. Nevertheless, its historical associations are of interest, and as the earliest known painting by Read it assumes importance in an understanding of the painter's development.

Visitors to the historic Lanier Home (Francis Costigan's masterpiece) have seen the large portrait of James F. D. Lanier hanging in the hall. Although not a local production, its presence in so attractive a shrine justifies a word about its origin. It is a copy made by Leslie Emmet of New York of the original painted by Waldo and Jewett. Lanier left Madison in 1848, taking up his residence in New York, and he probably had the artist-partners paint him early in the fifties. The copy was commissioned in 1926 by Charles Lanier, son of the subject, soon after the Home was acquired by the state.

Another portrait of interest in the Lanier Home and possessing unusual charm is that of the youngest son, James, who was drowned in the Ohio River at the age of seven. If it was made from life—and it doubtless was—the date was about 1835. The boy is portrayed stand-

27. Wilbur Woodward:
Portrait of Adeline
Tomlinson McFadden
Courtesy of Mrs. Everett F.
McCoy, Indianapolis
(page 68)

28. Patrick H. Davenport: Portrait of
Mary Ellen Lemon Hamer
Courtesy of the Division of State
Parks, Indiana Department of
Conservation (page 71)

25. William Z. Yonge: Portrait of
Lucille Morerod Detraz
    Courtesy of Julie LeClerc Knox, Vevay
    (page 65)

26. John Gibson Dunn:
The Temperance
Pledge
    John Herron Art
    Museum, Indianapolis
    (page 67)

31. Marion Blair: Portrait of Daily Voss

Courtesy of Edgar R. Strong, Bloomington (page 77)

32. (below) Theophilus A. Wylie: A Political Rally

Courtesy of the University Libraries, Indiana University (page 76)

29. Samuel Richards: Portrait
of Harlan Richards
Courtesy of Harlan Richards
Logan, Tampa, Florida
(page 72)

30. (below) Cornelius
Pering: The Seminary
Campus, Bloomington
Courtesy of the University
Libraries, Indiana University,
Bloomington (page 75)

ing in the parlor, beside a chair, his legs crossed, wearing a plaid frock and a sailor hat with ribbons. It is painted with considerable skill, is pleasing in composition and unusually colorful. The unidentified artist may have been a resident of Cincinnati.

The next painter to appear in Madison, so far as we know, was P. C. Wyeth, an itinerant who obtained, in 1851, the coveted commission to paint the children of Charles L. Shrewsbury. The five sons, John, William, Lewis, Samuel, and Culver, ranging in ages from two to twelve, are portrayed on a large canvas, grouped around a sofa (pl. 23). The daughter, Mary Louise, on her mother's lap, is portrayed on a second canvas.

After completing the work, Wyeth wrote in large Spencerian script on the backs of the pictures the names of his youthful models, their ages, the date, and his signature. It is one of the rare instances of fully documented paintings originating in that period. Still hanging in their original positions in the Shrewsbury parlor, the two portraits constitute the only known work by Wyeth. They reveal him as an earnest but only moderately able painter, equipped with native talent but little if any academic training. His inability to draw in a masterly way is offset by a strong, direct manner of applying paint to canvas. The formal pose of the brothers, standing in a row behind the sofa and staring self-consciously at the observer, and the pompous background of columns, arches, and panoramic view of the Ohio River, give the picture a theatrical effect that contrasts strangely with the little elfin faces of the boys.

Unfortunately we know very little about Wyeth. He lived in New York in 1846 and sent work to the National Academy of Design that year and again in 1858. He was in Cincinnati from 1849 to 1851, occupying a studio in the Art Union Building, according to the *Williams' Cincinnati Directory*. After his visit to Madison in 1851 he probably returned to Cincinnati and later to New York. His last recorded place of residence was Brooklyn, where he was living in 1858.[17]

During Wyeth's brief visit to Madison other painters may have been here, although we do not hear of any until the following year. An article in the *Indiana Journal* published in Indianapolis, October 18, 1852, reported the marriage of Edgar P. Gillet to Mary Lizzie Bennett of Brattleboro, Vermont, adding that he had a "striking propensity for art," and that he was destined to "become one of the state's best artists." Although the article links Gillet with Indianapolis and the capital's leading artist, Jacob Cox, the reader is led to believe that Gillet was at the time a resident of Madison and that he had already embarked upon the career of a painter. If this was so, the reporter's prophecy was not fulfilled, for Gillet is not only missing from the roll of the state's recognized artists but nothing more is heard of him.

Ten years after the announcement of Gillet's marriage we learn of another young artist coming to Madison. Harry Hilliard was about twenty years old when, for reasons unrevealed, he quit his home at Auburn, New York, for the southern Indiana town. He remained in Madison about ten years then left for Indianapolis, where he attracted considerable attention by his work. From there he went to Boston and then to Europe. On the occasion of one of Hilliard's visits to Indianapolis, after his return from Europe, the *Indianapolis Journal* reported that he had achieved an enviable reputation in America and abroad, that he had been honored by the Salle d' Heur of the Paris Salon (1884), and that the French government had bought one of his pictures for the Luxembourg Gallery.[18]

While in Madison and Indianapolis Hilliard showed in his work considerable versatility in choice of subjects and a fair amount of talent. His earliest known Madison picture is a composition of two stags with locked horns, dated 1862. A small oval portrait of Anna Webber Dold, that appears to have been painted over an enlarged photograph, is also attributed to him. Its style is that of the average commercial photographer-painter of the period, and if it is the work of Hilliard it bears no resemblance to his more creative productions. In 1862 he sent a number of pictures to the Indiana State Fair at Indianapolis, among them a composition after Landseer (probably the picture of stags mentioned above), a dramatic portrayal of a prairie fire, as well as floral and fruit pieces. One of his most charming flower studies now known is a small oil painting of Italian roses, in the collection of Carl B. Shafer, Indianapolis.

Several landscapes in oils and water colors by Hilliard may still be seen in Indianapolis homes. His most important work in this category is a large mountain scene with a river in the foreground, owned by James W. Carr. Both subject and technique suggest its origin somewhere in the East, and it was probably painted after Hilliard had left Indianapolis. It is romantic in style and has something of that "quality of dreamy elegance" which, according to early critics, was characteristic of his work.

Harry Hilliard, or more correctly, William Henry Hilliard, was born at Auburn, New York, in 1836. After his Indiana sojourn, and following his trip to Europe, he settled in Boston, returning to Indianapolis occasionally to visit relatives. His death occurred at Washington, D. C., in 1905.

Madison's best-known painter during the latter part of the century was William McKendree Snyder, better known as Will Snyder. Most of his life was spent in the attractive river town where he came to be regarded as its chief mentor in artistic affairs.

The son of a Methodist preacher, W. W. Snyder, Will was born at Liberty, Indiana, in 1849. When a small boy his family lived for a time at Vevay, and then moved to Madison. At the age of twelve he volunteered as a drummer boy in the Union army, later going to Cincinnati to study art in the studio of J. Insco Williams. Sometime later, he studied in the East under the eminent landscapists Bierstadt, Wyant, and Inness. At another time he received some instruction from William M. Hunt in Boston.

Returning to Madison, he applied himself seriously to painting. In 1875 he married Allena Belle Rodocker and, except for brief trips to Cincinnati, remained in Indiana. Early in his career he painted a number of portraits, but gained nothing more than a local reputation in that line. Most of them are artistically dull, lacking color and character. What appears to be one of his more successful performances is the likeness of his mother-in-law, now in the home of Mrs. Daniel A. Farley at Madison. Portraits of his parents, of equal merit, are owned by his nephew, Frank R. Snyder, of Oxford, Ohio.

Figure compositions, literary in theme and frequently including nudes, were at one time regarded as his forte, but they now appear tedious and uninspired, not unlike the typical salon pictures of the Victorian era. Among the recorded canvases in this vein are *Pythias at the Block, The Battle of Shiloh, The Nymph of the Lillies* (that hung in the Gibson House), and *Ophelia* (owned by Mrs. Hilda Weaser, of Madison).

Eventually, outdoor compositions became his major interest and to the average person the name Snyder is synonymous with autumnal beechwoods. Largely because of the popularity of these subjects he earned his livelihood and established a reputation for himself in both Cincinnati and southern Indiana. Crowded with details to the point of fussiness and rich in fall coloring, the many canvases that came from his studio late in his life repeated with little variation his favorite theme of silvery-gray tree trunks seen against russet and orange leaves. His early landscapes are less repetitious in subject and more interesting as depictions of local scenes, some of the better ones being views of Madison as seen from the bluff northwest of town (pl. 24).

Not only did he know the best sketching spots in southern Indiana, but he was one of the earliest, if not the first, to paint in Brown County. This is of interest in view of the popularity the county has since achieved among painters. It is reported that he went there as early as 1870 from Columbus, Indiana, where he was in the photographic business with his brother, R. W. Snyder.[19] He was at Columbus until 1872 when he left for the East, presumably to study under some of the painters mentioned above. Not long afterward he was back in Madison, where, except for occasional sketching trips and visits to Cincinnati, he spent the remainder of his life. His death occurred there in 1930, as he approached his eighty-first birthday.

VIII

Continuing up the Ohio River our survey leads next to Vevay, about fifteen miles distant, and then to Aurora and Lawrenceburg.

Vevay, as the name implies, was established by Swiss immigrants who found the hilly terrain not unlike what they had left behind. The county was called Switzerland, and in keeping with Old World tradition the region became famous for its fine wines. But in later years vineyards were replaced by potato patches because it was found that a bushel of potatoes would bring as much as a gallon of wine and was far easier to produce.

Into this thrifty community few artists ventured—or perhaps it is more accurate to say that few were able to persuade the early settlers to sit for their portraits. One of the earliest paintings in Vevay is the likeness of Antoinette Dufour Morerod, a charming study made about 1830 by an itinerant artist, perhaps working out of Cincinnati. It is owned by the local historical society.

Nothing else seems to have been done here in that line until William Zebulon Yonge attained maturity and began to portray the local citizens. Yonge was born in 1851 at Aurora, the town his parents selected as their home when they arrived from Holland. When about twenty years of age, he moved to Vevay where he met Will Snyder, from whom he received his first and perhaps only instruction in art. He lived in Vevay until 1907 when he went to Chicago and entered the field of commercial art. He died at Vevay in 1939.

A number of portraits by Yonge may still be seen in Switzerland County, some in homes, others in the possession of its historical society. The most successful of his canvases in the society's collection is the portrait of Lucille Morerod, wife of Benjamin Detraz (pl. 25). His study of Mrs. Julia Morerod Le Clerc was duplicated seven times by Yonge so that each of the daughters could have one. Two are now in the home of Julie Le Clerc Knox, who also owns a portrait of John E. Williams by the same artist.

From these and other paintings we see that William Yonge was a strong draughtsman, but he lacked the finer graces of the art of portraiture. His style is rather hard and blunt, colors are quite harsh, and the features of his sitters are without expression. Nothing is added to the compositions to relieve the plainness of faces set against unadorned backgrounds.

Aurora, named in honor of the goddess of dawn and the birthplace of artist Yonge, claims no other native son in the field of the visual arts, nor are there records of itinerant painters having worked here. Its stately old houses overlooking the river can boast of many romantic and historic events of bygone days, but they treasure no canvases that might add interest to this story.

Lawrenceburg, a few miles to the northeast, and the last community on the river west of the state line, can take pride in its artistic heritage, even though little of significance can be found here today. Its proximity to Cincinnati may have induced a number of limners to visit it in the early years of its history, and one wonders if the charming portrait of Catherine Eliza Tate, painted about 1840,[20] was not by the hand of a journeyman artist from the larger city. About the time it was made Lawrenceburg's talented son John Gibson Dunn was in Indianapolis receiving some instruction in art from Jacob Cox. Because most of his kaleidoscopic career was spent away from Lawrenceburg none of his work can be found there today.

Dunn was born in Lawrenceburg about 1826, the son of George H. Dunn, a well-known state official. He was educated at College Hill, near Cincinnati, and at South Hanover, Indiana. When about seventeen years old he decided to become an artist and entered the studio of Jacob Cox in Indianapolis; as his father was state treasurer at that time, the Dunn family was living in the capital. After becoming fairly proficient in drawing he decided to take up medicine, and enrolled in a college at Cincinnati (probably at the Medical College of Ohio) where he received his degree. He was about to start his professional practice in 1846 when the Mexican War started; he accepted appointment as assistant surgeon of Company K, Third Regiment of Indiana Volunteers, and performed his duties with ability.

To what extent he practiced medicine is not known. He was listed among the painters of Indianapolis in the spring of 1851; he was back in Lawrenceburg that fall, dividing his time between medicine, mechanical inventions, painting, and poetry; and practically nothing is now known about the last years of his life. It is reported that he left Indiana for Louisiana after 1855 and that he died in New Orleans in the spring of 1858.[21]

Only two of Dunn's paintings are mentioned in early reports: *The Temperance Pledge* and *Christ's Descent from the Cross*, the latter having been described in the *Madison Daily Courier* of September 1, 1851, as "perhaps the largest painting ever produced in Indiana, being 11½ x 8½ feet." The report went on to say that it was to be exhibited throughout the state. Apparently no one today knows what happened to it. *The Temperance Pledge* (pl. 26), painted in 1851, is in the permanent collection of the John Herron Art Museum.

Our best appraisal of Dunn's character comes from the pen of Jacob Cox: "He was genius with more ill-jointed, badly directed talent than any man I ever saw. His ideas on color were admirable—exquisite; his invention was wonderful, but he never carried a picture to completion. He was somewhat of a poet, too, but wild and erratic to the last degree: His death, I fear, was the result of dissipation, as he was given to terrible sprees." [22]

Contrasting sharply with the eccentric and rather capricious performances of Dunn, is the rational and diligent activity of Wilbur Woodward, whose home for a short time was at Lawrenceburg. He was born at St. Omer, Indiana, in 1851. At about ten years of age he served as a drummer boy in the regiment in which his father had enlisted. His first art training was received at the McMicken School of Design at Cincinnati; then in 1871, at the age of twenty, he went to Antwerp, where he enrolled in the Royal Academy; two years later he went to Paris, where he entered the studio of Gérôme and studied in the Ecole des Beaux-Arts. His paintings were accepted for exhibition in the Paris Salon on several occasions. Returning to America after seven years abroad, he came to Lawrenceburg where his parents were then living, but soon afterward he was in Cincinnati teaching at the McMicken School. In less than a year his promising career was cut short by death.

Judging by critics' comments and obituary notices, Woodward was an extraordinary person. Being an incessant worker he had acquired an unusual fund of knowledge about the craft of painting and had produced a large amount of work; he could speak and write six languages fluently, and possessed a refined taste and noble character. According to the *Cincinnati Commercial*, "He had a wide range of style and painted a great variety of pictures, landscapes and figure pieces, portraits and original compositions . . . In some of his pictures there was a use of deep shadows and bright rays of light that had in it something suggestive of Rembrandt; more and more his thoughts turned to representation of the grand and terrible in the passions and life of great men." [23]

Among his canvases which were lauded in contemporaneous reviews were *Ossian* (the Fenian hero, harp in hand, singing to the widow of Toscar), and *America* (the nude figure of an Indian girl seated on a mountain peak). At the time of his death about fifty of his paintings and sketches were shown at Indianapolis in the home of Mary Dean, art critic of the *Indianapolis Journal*. A good example of his work in the field of portraiture is the painting of Adeline Tomlinson McFadden (pl. 27), wife of James B. McFadden, owned by Mrs. Everett F. McCoy, of Indianapolis—signed and dated 1868. His study of a nude girl in an outdoor setting, entitled *Springtime*, is in the John Herron Art Museum's collection.

It is apparent that Woodward was one of the most gifted and best trained among the state's native painters of the period, and it is to be regretted that he died before he had an opportunity to go farther in his chosen field.

Columbus Greensburg
Bloomington Seymour
Mitchell

Chapter 4

SALEM, SEYMOUR, BEDFORD

MITCHELL, SPENCER

BLOOMINGTON, MARTINSVILLE

COLUMBUS, FRANKLIN

GREENSBURG, RUSHVILLE

TURNING OUR ATTENTION inland from the Ohio River, we find in the south-central portion of the state an extension of the art activities already reported, and come upon the work of several additional painters. Most of the larger communities of the region—Salem, Seymour, Bedford, Mitchell, Spencer, Bloomington, Martinsville, Columbus, and Franklin—were visited by the typical itinerants; some of the towns could also boast of native sons who were destined to attain eminence in the field of painting.

Salem, most southern of the places listed above, has already been mentioned in connection with Christopher Harrison's career. It was here that he established a small general store in partnership with Jonathan Lyon in 1815, which he presumably gave up when he was elected lieutenant governor of the state. His small two-room brick house with its attractive garden was a popular gathering place for the youngsters of the neighborhood, and he was always ready to entertain them with stories and sketches.

One cannot help wondering if among Harrison's youthful admirers there was a boy named Jimmy New, whose home was at Salem. One may assume that Harrison gave the boy his first and perhaps only instruction in painting. The only work by James R. New on record is a

69

portrait of Joseph Bartholomew, noted soldier and statesman. It is said to have been painted in 1826 when New was still an art student, and given many years later to Bartholomew County Courthouse, Columbus, by J. Thompson New.[1] So far, little information has been ferreted out concerning the career of James R. New. Even his span of life is unknown. Presumably he was a young man when he made this portrait, and as he died before 1830, he had insufficient time to perfect his skill and make a name for himself as a painter—assuming that that was his ambition.

The likeness of Bartholomew is concise and simple in technique. Flat and poster-like, the head and shoulders are silhouetted against a plain background. Its resemblance to the McCoy portraits hanging in the historical museum at Salem makes one wonder if New also painted the McCoys. If not, their unknown itinerant author was at the same stage of technical development.

One other early painter is associated with Salem: E. P. Newman. Judging by his landscape in the historical museum here, he, too, was a novice. The scene, painted about 1860, represents the home of John H. Farnum and is more interesting as a record of a place than as a work of art.

Seymour, about twenty-five miles northeast of Salem, has more to add to the chronicle of early Indiana art. It was in 1875 that the first recorded painter worked here, although it is not improbable that others had already come and gone. He was John Ottis Adams, who, in the last decades of the century, became one of the state's best-known artists. A native of Amity, Indiana, where he was born in 1851, Adams received his elementary schooling at Franklin and Shelbyville, and his high-school work at Martinsville, after which he attended Wabash College for a couple of years. Finding it financially possible to study abroad, he went to England and entered the South Kensington School of Art in London. Two years later he was back in America and had joined his parents at Seymour, where he had a studio during the winter of 1874–1875. The next year he went to Martinsville, and about a year later had settled in Muncie for a four-year stay. The sequel to this biographical sketch appears in the section dealing with that town.

After the sound training Adams had received in London, one would surmise that his work at Seymour and Martinsville was far more competent than the output of the average portrait painter of that region, but as nothing by him can now be found in these communities we have no way of determining this. A portrait he made of Hazel Anderson is remembered by some of the citizens of Seymour, but it was probably removed from the town many years ago. Several other portraits made by Adams in Muncie have been traced and will be discussed in the next chapter.

Mitchell, known to most people as the gateway to Spring Mill State Park, was the principal point of activity of an artist named Patrick Henry Davenport. Although a native of Kentucky, Davenport painted rather extensively in Indiana, methodically moving from one town to another. At Mitchell in 1857 he painted at least six canvases portraying Henry T. and Mary Ellen (Lemon) Hamer (pl. 28), their sons George Volney and William Francis, and Dr. Jacob and Mary A. Lemon. They now hang in the reconstructed log cabins in Spring Mill State Park.

Davenport was one of the few painters who signed and dated his work (on the backs of the canvases), thus enabling one to chart without difficulty his meanderings through the state. In 1850 he was at Algiers, Pike County, where he made the likenesses of Robert and Elizabeth White Logan recently in the home of the late C. E. Logan. At that time the painter was living at Sumner, Illinois, and the Logan portraits may have resulted from his first trip into Indiana. In all probability he obtained other commissions in the southwestern sector of the state on the same journey.

By 1857 he had penetrated deeper into Indiana. Around the time he painted the Hamer and Lemon families at Mitchell he was asked to paint George Dunn, of Bedford; three versions of this portrait are known. Two years later Davenport was at Spencer (he doubtless returned to his home in Illinois between his Indiana excursions) where he painted canvases depicting William and Mary Ritter Franklin, dated 1859, now in the home of Mrs. George Moore of that city. Subsequently, he was in Fort Wayne where he painted Abner Alexander;

in 1873 he was working in Indianapolis, as confirmed by his portraits of Thomas H. Jameson and his wife Anna Rhoades—the latter painted from a photograph after her death—owned by Mrs. James Drummond, of Indianapolis.

Davenport's manner of painting was terse and harsh. His taut, rigid drawing plus stern expressions on the faces of the subjects, particularly in his earlier productions, give the impression that all his sitters were grave and sullen people.

While much of his early work is in Indiana, Patrick Henry Davenport did not begin his career in this state. His earliest known portrait is that of Brutus J. Clay, painted near Paris, Kentucky, in 1829, when he was about twenty-six years old. He was born at Danville, Kentucky, in 1803, son of Brigadier General Richard Davenport. In 1827, after his marriage to Eliza Bohennen, he embarked upon a painting career with little or no formal instruction; he may have had some lessons from Asa Park, of Kentucky. From Danville he moved to Crab Orchard Springs, and then to Illinois, settling in Sumner, where he doubtless painted many portraits, and from which point he made repeated excursions into Indiana. He died at Sumner in April, 1890, leaving a widow and eight children.

When Davenport was at Spencer in 1859 he had no competitors, so far as we know, but his attention may have been called to a talented boy by the name of Sammy Richards, whose home was here. Richards was born at Spencer in 1853, the eldest of four sons of Harlan Richards. His marked artistic interests and aptitudes were revealed very early in life—taking the forms of poetry, music, and painting—and in each he was largely self-taught in the initial stage of his development.

When about eighteen years old, he opened a studio in Spencer and began painting portraits. A likeness of his father (pl. 29), dated 1871, is the only canvas of that period that seems to have survived. In June of that year, realizing his technical inadequacy, he went to Indianapolis to get some instruction from Theobald Lietz, painter and photographer. As Lietz possessed more talent for factual representation than for artistic rendering, young Richards probably gained little of value besides accuracy of drawing. However, Lietz was able to transmit to his pupil his enthusiasm for the art centers of Europe, as well as teach him the German language, both of which acquirements were to stand Richards in good stead in later years when the opportunity came for him to study in Munich.

Richards' stay in Indianapolis was brief. He returned to Spencer, then went to Bloomington, where he enrolled at Indiana University. Evidently academic pursuits did not appeal to him, for the following year he was painting portraits again, this time at Franklin. He remained in Franklin about four years, where he painted, among others, John Fothergill and his son; the pictures are owned by Mary M. Hunt. Richards' "serious pursuit of his art won the prompt approval of the city's elders while his genial charm and amazing mimicry captured immediately the younger crowd."[2] Evidently his personality and talents also won the admiration and affection of a young lady named Louise Parks, because he married her there in 1875.

Having exhausted all possible portrait commissions at Franklin, Samuel Richards and his wife moved to Anderson, probably late in 1877, where he remained until 1880, at which time the opportunity came for him to go abroad to study. In Anderson he completed a number of portraits, and painted some of his first landscapes—a discussion of which will appear in the section devoted to Anderson artists and art activities.

There are doubtless many portraits painted by Richards in Spencer and Franklin which have not come to light or which await identification. He was evidently a popular painter of children because several portraits are known: one of Guy Robinson as a baby, painted in 1871 or 1872, owned by Jesse Robinson, of Spencer; and two similar portrayals of children, in the possession of Mrs. Perry Cooper, Vincennes.

In addition to the Fothergill portraits, he painted during his Franklin sojourn a portrait of James L. Mitchell (signed "Sam'l G. Richards," the only evidence of his having a middle initial, and dated 1873), which hangs in the library of Indiana University; and four years later he made a likeness of Silas Bailey, an early president of Franklin College, which is now owned by the college. None of these early performances has merit beyond faithful portrayals, hardly suggesting the artistic powers that the artist developed in the studios of the Royal Academy at Munich.

When Richards was finishing his year in the studio of Lietz at Indianapolis there appeared in Spencer another painter, an itinerant by the name of W. R. Davis. Our only knowledge of the man comes from the *Gosport Independent* of May 16, 1872, which announced: "W. R. Davis, the great Cincinnati artist and portrait painter left our town last Sunday for Spencer where he expects to make his home for some time. A tip-top gentleman and a first-class painter."

One would think that so eminent a person would have made his presence deeply felt in Spencer, and that some evidence of his visit would have survived in the form of a painting or two—but such is not the case. And what is equally disappointing, no references have been found to his activity in Cincinnati. He could not have been as prominent in art circles there as the editor of the *Independent* would lead us to believe, because no list or roster of painters working in Cincinnati between 1870 and 1875 carries his name.

II

Bloomington, the seat of Monroe County and of Indiana University, has always had two distinct classes of citizens: one made up of farmers, merchants, and small industrialists; the other of professors and students. Villagers and farmers chatting on the courthouse square today have no more in common with the student body and faculty than their ancestors had with the academic family when the state seminary opened in 1824.

It is significant that the first artist in Bloomington whose name is now known was a pedagogue—an Englishman by the name of Cornelius Pering, who had arrived in the town in 1832 to establish a female seminary. In spite of the competition that the state college must have given him, Pering's venture was successful, and it gained strength three years later when it was combined with the Monroe County Seminary here.[3]

Pering, his wife and six children, continued to live at Bloomington until 1846, when they moved to Louisville, Kentucky; there he founded a new school for girls, with a curriculum devoted to the arts. An announcement in the *Republican Courier* of Madison, Indiana, that year spoke of it as a Female Institute specializing in music, drawing, and painting, adding that "from the experience Mr. Pering acquired under members of the Royal Academy in London . . . he hopes to obtain the encouragement thus respectfully solicited."[4]

The enterprise was successfully carried on in a fine old house on West Walnut Street, Louisville, during Pering's lifetime, and after his death in 1881 his daughter Cornelia continued to manage its affairs. An article in the *Louisville Herald* in 1923, written at the time of Cornelia's death, spoke glowingly of the talent of father and daughter, and of the recognition they had received in art circles in this country and abroad. It referred particularly to miniatures by them "which the world recognizes as masterpieces."[5] Unfortunately, none of their work in this line can now be identified.

During his residence in Bloomington, Pering painted a large scene in oil, representing his campus: a wide stretch of landscape, a section of the town in the background, the seminary building at the left, and his own family (including himself) lined up in the foreground (pl. 30). Its charm lies principally in the unsophisticated and simple manner in which it was painted. The canvas, now in the library of Indiana University, is the only work that can be assigned to Pering with certainty. It is reported that he painted the portrait of Andrew Wylie, first president of the university, and that he gave it to Dr. Dodds, a Bloomington physician, but its present whereabouts is unknown to local historians.[6]

The close relationship of academic and artistic pursuits in Bloomington appears again in the activity of Theophilus A. Wylie, professor of natural sciences at Indiana University from 1837 to 1886. He came to Bloomington when he was twenty-seven years old, remaining there until his death in 1895, except for two years and a half spent at Miami University in the early fifties. Wylie made no pretense of being an accomplished artist, and it is doubtful if he did very much painting after his first years at the university. His only known oil painting is a large canvas representing a political gathering at Bloomington, made about 1838 (pl. 32). It is a forceful composition, successfully conveying the spirit of the occasion in spite of amateurish drawing. It gives the impression that Wylie was largely self-taught as a painter, but that he possessed a good deal of ability and not a little courage.

Richard Dennis Wylie, son of Theophilus, had an equally strong artistic inclination and hoped to become a portrait painter. He was born at Bloomington in 1841, and received his education here in public schools and at the university. When about nineteen years of age he enlisted in the Union Army; he died in the fall of 1861.

His portrait of Andrew Wylie, owned by Mrs. Thana L. Wylie, of Bloomington, is dated on the back March 1, 1861; as President Wylie died in 1851, this work must have been made from another portrait or from a photograph.

The man who made the strongest mark as a portrait painter in the village of Bloomington during the Civil War period was Marion Blair. A native of the town, he attended the university, married a local girl, and gradually came to be recognized as the community's resident painter. It appears that he was unschooled in the finer points of painting; if he received any instruction it was probably from itinerants passing through Bloomington or in the studio of one of the artists established in Indianapolis.

Blair was born in 1824, the son of Enos and Rachel Blair. When a young man he moved a few miles south of town to a spot called Blair Hollow. His strong inclination toward art, literature, and natural history, coupled with his antipathy for farming or manual labor of any kind, did not make him a good provider for his growing family. His wife, unable to cope with his dilatory habits, finally left him and moved to Kansas, taking their children with her.

Continuing to live at the Hollow, and pursuing his favorite subjects, Blair came to be regarded as the sage of that region. His advice was sought in all kinds of matters, including legal transactions. He read and wrote letters for his less literate neighbors, patched up lovers' quarrels, and painted pictures when inspired to do so. He got a number of portrait commissions in Bloomington and apparently had some success in the same line at Indianapolis.

33. John Elwood Bundy: Summer Landscape
Courtesy of Jo C. Johnston, Greensburg (page 78)

34. Edwin Farrer: Portrait of Leven E. Wallace
Courtesy of the Rush County Historical Society, Rushville (page 82)

35. (above) J. Insco
Williams:
Portrait of
Miles Murphy
Courtesy of Helen
M. Goodwin, New
Castle (page 87)

36. (above left) J.
Insco Williams:
Portrait of Susan
H. Freeman
Courtesy of Mrs.
William E. Gavin,
Indianapolis
(page 150)

37. J. Insco
Williams:
Portrait of Alice
Harris Conklin
Courtesy of Pauline
Woodward Mont-
gomery, Cambridge
City (page 89)

38. Marcus Mote: Portrait of
Elizabeth Chalfont Gilbert

Courtesy of Harry W. Gilbert,
Richmond (page 93)

39. (below) Marcus Mote:
Indiana Yearly Meeting of
Friends

Courtesy of Earlham College,
Richmond (page 93)

With the outbreak of the Civil War, Blair raised a company of Monroe County volunteers and was stationed for sometime in Indianapolis. He held the rank of captain.

Most of Blair's paintings appear to have been made in the fifties and early sixties. His earliest is probably that of Daily Voss (pl. 31), a boy in a red coat, painted about 1846, now owned by Edgar R. Strong, Bloomington. His last is said to be a portrait of Abraham Lincoln, painted after viewing the martyred President as his body lay in state in the capitol building at Indianapolis.[7] It is reported that Lincoln's death so depressed Blair that he never took up his brushes again. However, knowing his inclination to shy away from work, one wonders if other factors might not have contributed more to his decision to give up painting. For one thing, competition among painters in central Indiana became increasingly acute after the Civil War, and he may not have had the will to participate in the struggle. Just what he did with his time for the remaining thirty-five years of his life we are not informed (he died in 1901); he doubtless continued to enjoy the position he held as the pundit of Blair's Hollow.

Blair received his most important commission from the Indiana General Assembly—a full-length portrait of Oliver P. Morton, the state's war governor. The canvas, now in the Indiana State Library, represents the chief executive as a stern, uncompromising man, rendered in brown, murky colors and fairly competent technique. Unfortunately, the canvas is badly damaged, and the paint has turned so dark that the model is difficult to identify.

Other portraits by Blair are in the homes of S. Edwin Smith, Mrs. L. R. Oaks, and W. Austin Seward, of Bloomington. In the last, portraying Austin Seward and his wife Janet, candid description combined with hardness of execution produce an austere effect.

Martinsville, already referred to as the early home of J. Ottis Adams, became later the residence of another gifted artist, John Elwood Bundy. When Adams was here he might have known Bundy, a young man about his own age, who was living at Monrovia, about ten miles north of Martinsville. Bundy, ambitious but with little formal training, had undertaken portrait painting on a professional basis at Monrovia, and in all probability visited Martinsville from time to time, seeking orders among the wealthier residents.

Bundy's name has long been associated in the public's mind with pictures of beechwoods painted in the vicinity of Richmond, and few people know that he lived and worked at other places. Not only were his first and perhaps only portrait studies made in Morgan County, but here he also painted his first landscapes (pl. 33). They are rather ordinary performances to be sure, but being the artist's first steps in that direction they are of more than passing interest.

John Elwood Bundy was born in Guilford County, North Carolina, in 1853. When he was about five years of age his parents, John and Mary (Moore) Bundy, moved to a farm near Monrovia. There the boy grew up, was educated in the public schools, and began to attract attention by his drawings and sketches. Determined to become a painter, he went to Indianapolis when about twenty years old and took some lessons from Barton S. Hays, one of the leading figures in art circles at the capital. He remained there only about two weeks, but he learned how to mix colors and had an opportunity to see the work of painters living in Indianapolis at the time. For the next twelve years he worked in and around Monrovia, painting both portraits and landscapes, but concentrating more and more on the latter.

Sometime during that period he went to New York, where he received additional instruction and studied the paintings in the Metropolitan Museum of Art. In 1875 he married Mary A. Marlatt at Monrovia; ten years later he moved his family and studio to Martinsville, where he remained a year; and then in 1887, he moved to Richmond, where he built a house and studio on the edge of the woods. In addition to painting, he taught art at Earlham College from 1887 to 1895. Except for short visits to California and northern Michigan, he spent the rest of his life in Wayne County, growing steadily in his power to interpret the moods of the Indiana countryside. His death occurred at Cincinnati in 1933.

Bundy's earliest known oil painting is a portrait of his mother, made in 1876, presumably at Monrovia, now owned by Paul Conner, of Long Beach, California; a few years later he painted the likeness of

Thompson Hendricks, of Martinsville, now in the possession of Mrs. Edith Smith, of Indianapolis; and, perhaps his most ambitious effort, the double portrait of Rachel Marker Johnson and her daughter, owned by C. B. Showalter, of Indianapolis, was painted in 1884.

All of these canvases possess the same stylistic traits: hard and taut rendering of forms, deep shadows under cheek bones and within eye sockets, and dull, somber colors. They give the impression of having been painted from photographs—the blank, stony faces suggesting that the problem of getting accurate likenesses so plagued the painter that he gave little thought to characterization or expression. With so little talent for portraiture it is not surprising that Bundy soon turned to a much more sympathetic field, that of landscape.

III

Columbus, the seat of Bartholomew County, has long had a reputation for progressive agricultural and industrial enterprises, and its prosperity must have attracted a number of itinerant painters in the past. However, there is little evidence now of their visits; existing records and pictures pertaining to the decades covered by this history are few. Attention has already been called to the canvas portraying Joseph Bartholomew painted by James R. New, of Salem, but as it was not made in this county it adds nothing to the story of local productions. A second portrait of Bartholomew, also owned by the county, is said to have been painted in Louisville in 1826 and is believed to have served as the model for New's canvas.

The earliest painter recorded as working in Columbus was John Nicholson, who came here in 1845 from southern Indiana to embark upon the career of a sign and portrait painter. Nicholson was something of a jack-of-all-trades and a roving one at that. He was born on a farm in Jefferson County in 1825, the son of Jesse C. Nicholson, a carpenter; while still in his teens he was in St. Louis and Louisville, and then in the southern Indiana towns of Jeffersonville, New Albany, and Salem. At that time he made Windsor chairs, but was beginning to pick up some information about painting. When twenty years old he went to Columbus, remaining there three or four years; in May of

1850, after a brief sojourn in Tennessee, he removed to Franklin, where he combined the arts of fruit culture, painting, and photography. He was probably successful in his ventures because he remained in and near Franklin for twenty years. At the end of that period he moved to Kokomo, then to Crawfordsville, where he made a specialty of oil-tinted photographs. There his roving life came to an end in 1893.[8]

As might be expected, Nicholson's work, after the perfection of the camera, reflected more and more the characteristics of photographic precision, and his later productions—oil glazes applied to enlarged prints—have no individual characteristics, so far as the artist's hand is concerned, even though the likenesses must have pleased his customers. One of the few identifiable early portraits by him is that of Royal S. Hicks, owned by Mrs. Bess Ehrmann, of Rockport. It was painted in 1854, when Hicks was about thirty years of age and Nicholson was a resident of Franklin. In workmanship it has that sharp incisive character that comes from observing photographs more than living models. The drawing is inflexible, and the strong lighting from the right throws dark shadows across the far side of the subject's face.

A number of other portraits in Franklin and Columbus might be assigned to Nicholson on the basis of those stylistic characteristics, among them that of Benjamin Peter Irwin, made about 1860, owned by Howard Irwin, of Columbus. Also, some of the portraits of early members of the faculty of Franklin College might, with further study, be found to have come from his studio.

The next painter known to have worked in Columbus was Will Snyder, whose removal here from Madison in 1870 to open a sign shop with his brother has already been noted. His enthusiasm for the scenery to the west of Columbus induced him to make many sketching trips into Brown County, which he described as "a charming and varied bit of landscape beauty, consisting of hills and various heights with much primeval forest growth. Beautiful valleys with small flowing streams and cozy farm houses, all of which combine to suggest restful peace and happiness." [9]

The stimulation of this experience probably had much to do with

Snyder's eventual specialization in landscape painting. His companion on some of the treks was Peter Fishe Reed, regarding whom we will have more to say later, and it is reasonable to assume that Snyder learned much, technically, from that more experienced painter.

The city's best-known artist, Orrin Pentzer, arrived here too late for inclusion in this survey. Much of his life was spent in Illinois, although during his formative years he lived at Lafayette, Indiana, where he got his first instruction in painting from George Winter. He taught school at Hartsville, Indiana, from 1888 to 1899, and in 1900 transferred his residence to Columbus.

The town of Franklin has already been mentioned in connection with the work of Samuel Richards and John Nicholson. A third painter whose name was associated with it was the eminent William M. Chase. Some biographies list the town as his birthplace, but he was born ten miles to the south in the village of Williamsburg, now Nineveh. Chase was doubtless in Franklin many times during his youth and early manhood, and two of his rudimentary portraits, those of Benjamin Love and James B. McFadden, are said to have been painted here. The former is now owned by Mrs. Prudence Douglas, of Shelbyville, and the latter has not been located. They were done by Chase after he had received some instruction in Indianapolis from Barton S. Hays. More will be said about the man and his work in the chapter dealing with Indianapolis.

The communities lying between Franklin and the Whitewater Valley to the east—Greensburg, Shelbyville, and Rushville—lie in Indiana's rich corn belt and have enjoyed steady, if modest, prosperity since their founding. Because of its accessibility to Cincinnati, Greensburg was visited in its formative years by artists from southwestern Ohio, or its citizens went to Cincinnati to have their portraits painted. A romantic portrayal of Mary Ewing, for instance, was done by a Cincinnatian named Isaac Quick; the likeness of Marie Louise Chitwood, poetess, is attributed to George White, of Hamilton, Ohio; and portraits owned by Arthur Donnell and Bert Fee, of Clarksburg, are said to be the work of Cincinnati painters whose names have been forgotten by the owners of the paintings.

A canvas portraying David Hollis is believed to be the work of Harriet Hillis Tinsley, sister of Lotta Hillis Guffin. Little is known of Harriet Tinsley's life, but her sister became well known as an artist in Indianapolis. The girls were daughters of William Hillis, whose family lived near Greensburg, in Decatur County.

Greensburg apparently had no resident painter, but Rushville, her neighbor to the north, had. He was Edwin Farrer, an Englishman, who decided to make Rushville his home. He was one of three orphaned brothers who came to America in 1861; his elder brother Henry remained in New York, becoming a prominent painter and etcher; the oldest of the three, Thomas, also an artist, returned to London. When Edwin reached New York he was about ten years of age and he probably received some instruction in painting in the East, in addition to his general schooling, before coming to Indiana. His earliest artistic efforts were in the field of scenery painting for theaters, an occupation that apparently took him to several cities, including Cleveland, early in his career. In 1870 he arrived in Rushville, decided to stay here, married Sarah Jane Broadhead, and soon identified himself with the community's civic activities. He held a county office in Rushville for a number of years and was highly respected by his fellow townsmen as a citizen and artist. His declining years were spent with a brother-in-law at Indianapolis, where he died in 1921.

Among Farrer's paintings in Rushville is a portrait of Ebenezer Smith, owned by Mrs. Wendell Willkie; studies of his wife and himself are in the Odd Fellow's Lodge; a portrait of youthful Leven E. Wallace (pl. 34), posed with his rocking horse, is in the Rush County Historical Museum; and several of his landscapes are owned by Mrs. Howard Ewbank.

Farrer's work has the deficiencies that generally accompany inadequate technical training. While his portraits appear to be good likenesses of the subjects, they lack those refinements of color, tonal values, and brush work found in highly accomplished performances. His portrait of Leven Wallace has undeniable charm, however; due to its simple, direct painting and pleasing color—not to mention the artist's characterization of the winsome lad—it makes a strong appeal.

Several women painters were active in Rush County in the latter half of the nineteenth century. The most accomplished were Laura Gifford Schofield and Retta Mathews. Laura Schofield evidently developed her talents by working out technical problems by herself, becoming in time both a painter and a teacher. A child's portrait by her in the historical museum of Rushville, representing Jesse Peters, is not the work of a mature, experienced hand, but its provincial style and colorful composition produce a pleasing effect. It was painted about 1876 when the subject was two years old.

Retta Mathews, whose home was at Arlington, a few miles northwest of Rushville, had more instruction than Laura Schofield and attained more eminence in her speciality. She was born in 1856, the daughter of William and Mary Mathews. Her training included work in art schools at Cincinnati, New York, and Paris, where she received instruction in both painting and sculpture. She was forced to work with her left hand as her right side was paralyzed. For many years she taught art in the public schools at San Antonio, Texas; but her last years were spent in her original home at Arlington, where she died in February, 1899.

Retta Mathews' work was shown in exhibitions in the East and in Paris, giving her wider recognition than most other painters in Indiana. She was commissioned by a group of women of the state to make a statue of the typical Indiana woman, which was exhibited at the Chicago World's Fair of 1893. In recent years her name has been all but forgotten and few people know anything about her paintings or the position she once held in art circles. Some of her paintings and drawings are owned by Clark Offutt, of Arlington, who reports that "many fine pieces of Miss Mathews' art were placed in the backyards of neighbors here in Arlington unprotected, and were soon destroyed by the elements." A still life by her is in the Rush County Historical Museum's collection.

Another artist associated with Rushville's early cultural history was Harry Carey. James Wilson, famous horse-breeder in Noble Township, Rush County, brought him out from Philadelphia to paint portraits of members of his family. According to reports, Carey came with his wife and a number of dogs, and settled down for a visit of several months in Wilson's home.

Portraits of the senior Wilson and his wife are now in the Rush County Historical Museum, and those of the children are owned by descendants. Judging by these canvases, Carey was a second-rate professional painter, intent upon pleasing his clients by producing accurate likenesses and sharp definition of features. The lack of more artistic qualities of design, color, and paint handling probably was of no concern to James Wilson; knowing that the artist came from the East presumably satisfied him that the pictures were of superior workmanship.

Unfortunately nothing has turned up regarding Harry Carey's life. If he was actually from Philadelphia, his place in art circles there was not a prominent one. His visit to Rushville was in 1877.

Anderson Muncie
Richmond
Cambridge City

Chapter 5

BROOKVILLE, RICHMOND

CENTERVILLE, DUBLIN

CAMBRIDGE CITY, NEW CASTLE

ANDERSON, MUNCIE

THE SOUTHEASTERN EDGE of the state, drained by the meandering Whitewater River, is a picturesque region. It was here in the latter part of the nineteenth century that Indiana's landscape school was born, when artists returning from European academies found their most inspiring subjects around Vernon, Brookville, and Metamora.

Years before, as the tide of immigration followed the valley and its serpentine roads up from the Ohio River, journeying painters, mostly from Cincinnati and northern Kentucky, sought commissions in the small villages. Unfortunately very few pictures remain today as records of their enterprise and those that are still around cannot be assigned to known painters. Most descendants of the first settlers have moved away, taking their heirlooms with them.

Only two names of early Brookville painters have been found in old newspapers: George W. Ryan, a house and sign painter, who probably never aspired to be a portraitist; and J. B. Goodwin. Ryan announced his presence in the Brookville *Indiana American* on August 29, 1834, and, as he was stopping at the Brookville Hotel instead of setting up his equipment in an office building, his visit was probably very brief.

All we know about Goodwin is contained in the advertisement he ran in the same paper from May 22 to August 30, 1844, and in the announcement written by the editor on May 24. The advertisement, typical of nineteenth-century business cards, reads:

85

PORTRAIT PAINTING

The undersigned has taken a room in the Court House and is pursuing the line of his profession. He invites the public to call and see his portraits he has on hand, believing that he will be patronized when his reasonable terms become known and his likenesses have been examined.

J. B. Goodwin

The editor's remarks add no information about the painter's past performances or place of origin. He stated that Goodwin had on hand some good specimens of portraits of citizens of that place (none of which can now be found) and made the following sagacious observation: "When our friends are dead, we always regret that we have not their portraits. Yet all our friends will die and unless we obtain whilst living the best copy of their form and features, we will have no memorial left, except their dim and fading impression upon our minds."

Richmond, the largest community on the Whitewater River, is the most rewarding to persons in quest of old pictures in this region. After its founding in 1806 a staunch and hardy community of Quakers settled here, contributing much to the town's economic and intellectual life. In spite of their tendency to frown upon so frivolous and questionable a pursuit as art, a number of those embracing the faith became successful painters, and not a few of the others posed, self-consciously perhaps, before the easels and scrutinizing eyes of migratory or resident painters.

Probably the first man to open a studio in Richmond was a native of Ohio by the name of John Insco Williams. One chronicler stated that in his youth he was apprenticed to an uncle here, a house and carriage painter. So far as we know his first professional visit was in 1832, when he was nineteen.

Williams was born in a log cabin at Oldtown, Ohio, north of Xenia, in 1813. Most biographies give his birthplace as Dayton, but he was not actually a resident of that city until late in life. After a brief apprenticeship in Richmond, he returned to Ohio and lived for a while at Miamisburg. Then, with very little experience but fortified by some instruction received in Cincinnati, he entered the highly competitive field of portrait painting. Presumably feeling inadequate, technically, to compete with established artists in Cincinnati and Dayton, he decided to try his luck in smaller and more remote places. His trek westward led him first to Richmond.

Williams' earliest known paintings are small profile studies in pencil and water color of Rev. Joseph Tarkington and his wife Maria Slauson (Slawson), said to have been made in 1832, about a year after their marriage.[1] The portraits are only about twelve by eight inches in size, the heads of the subjects almost filling the paper. The work is competent, the drawing being both descriptive and sensitive. As the Tarkingtons were living in Centerville that year, the young preacher having just been appointed to the Wayne Circuit, the portraits were doubtless made there.

About that time Williams probably made other portraits in Richmond, but none has been identified. A profile study of Josiah White (attributed to Marcus Mote) owned here by Esther Griffin White, and a similar, but larger, likeness of John Finley, now in the Indiana State Library, have stylistic resemblances to the Tarkington portraits. In 1835 Williams traveled northwest from Richmond to New Castle, where he made similar sketches, delicate in line and charming in color, of Colonel Miles Murphy (pl. 35), his wife Elizabeth, and of the children, Maria and Clinton. The portraits are owned by Helen Goodwin. In the late summer of that year he followed the National Road west to Indianapolis, rented a room at the Mansion House Hotel, and remained about a month.

After this exploratory journey into the heart of the state, regarding which more will be said later, Williams returned to Ohio, and then went East. Three years were spent at Philadelphia, where he enrolled in the Pennsylvania Academy of Fine Arts and also studied with Russell Smith and Thomas Sully.[2] When he returned to his profession, he gave up the pencil and water-color method, having acquired technical proficiency in the use of oil colors.

We do not know when he made his next visit to Indiana, but in the summer of 1840 he was back in the state and had traveled north to Logansport. Several references to his having studied with George

Winter have appeared in articles from time to time, but neither the date nor the place could be fixed. Fortunately a letter has come to our attention to clarify this point. It was written by Samuel S. Walker, a fellow artist of Ohio, to his wife. Walker was visiting Richmond at the time and had just met J. Insco Williams:

He [Williams] is a first rate clever fellow as ever lived and his supereour as an artist is not to be found in the city of Cincinnati . . . He painted pictures in Philadelphia at 100 dollars apiece, until he laid up 3000 dollars —which he has loaned out at 10 per ct interest and holds mortgages on real estate for security . . . [he] lived all last summer and fall with Mrs. Dodd at Logansport—He knows Winter too.[3]

As this letter was written in June 1841, Williams' visit to Logansport must have been made in 1840, the previous summer. However, the importance attached by some writers to his tutelage under George Winter is an exaggeration, because after studying in Philadelphia for three years—to say nothing of having advanced far enough to get one hundred dollars for his portraits—he could not have profited much from such technical advice as Winter might have offered. It is of interest to know, however, that Winter was sufficiently well known beyond the borders of the state in 1840 for an Ohio artist to make the above reference to him in a personal letter.

The date of the letter coincides, oddly enough, with an editorial that appeared in the Richmond *Palladium* extolling the merits of the two Ohio painters who had but recently found themselves friendly competitors in the Indiana village. As one of the first of its kind to appear in any newspaper of the state it deserves to be quoted in full:

THE FINE ARTS

We have had the pleasure of viewing a finely executed portrait on ivory, the work of S. S. Walker, portrait painter, now in this city, which, in our humble opinion, may be considered good. As we have not been favored, heretofore, with a visit from artists of this character, our ladies and gentlemen of taste and fashion should by all means contribute to the encouragement of this gentleman. He will remain probably for a few days: rooms with Mr. Williams. Here permit us to say, notwithstanding the scarcity of money, those who feel able should by no means neglect to encourage real merit in the arts. As it is for the indulgence of the finer feelings of our nature, we should strive—more than for the acquirement of pecuniary gain; and what does more to promote such feelings, than to relax our tight drawn purse strings to contemplate the wonderful imitative faculties that man is endowed with? Would that we could portray by the pen what Messrs Walker and Williams can by the pencil! One word for the latter gentleman [J. I. Williams]; he is a native of our soil; has spent some time in the Eastern cities, with a view of perfecting himself in the art; how far he has succeeded we cannot say, but from his earlier efforts, and the high estimation in which he is held where he has sojourned, have good reason to recommend him to a liberal public. He will be found at William A. Cammack's, on 5th st.[4]

Happily, two pairs of portraits by J. Insco Williams dating from that period are known: George McCullough and his wife Eliza Jane (signed J.I.W.), owned by Mrs. Demus S. Coe, of Richmond; and those of Benjamin Conklin and his wife (pl. 37), still hanging in the old Conklin house at Cambridge City. Not only had Williams switched to the oil medium in these, but his manner of working had changed considerably since the execution of his first commissions in the state in the middle thirties. Flat profiles gave way to well-modeled heads and figures, and compositions became rich in color and strong in tonal contrasts.

At a later date, perhaps 1847, he painted, or is believed to have painted, the family of William Buford, of Delphi: three canvases portraying the husband, wife, and daughter Frances holding a doll on her lap. They are owned by Mrs. Charles C. Crampton there. If these are by his hand, and stylistically they appear to be, they are the last of Williams' works in Indiana so far as we know.

Soon after 1840 Williams had established his residence and studio in Cincinnati. He is not listed in the city directories there until 1846, nor are there any references to his activity in the Cincinnati newspapers, but a letter written by him from Cincinnati to his friend S. S. Walker informs us that he was in that city in 1842. The note reveals Williams' opinion of Cincinnati, but most strikingly exposes his inability to spell and punctuate. It reads in part:

"I have painted Sully's Country girl and you should see it, for the loaffers of this city say that it is the prettyst thing that they ever have seen from my pencyl they have told me so often that I have got to believing it almost, I am trying to finish up my pictures in this place as soon as I get them don and get paid for them then I will Slope from here ... this place is a poor place for Bread." [5]

Another letter to Walker in 1845 stated that he, Williams, had spent the summer at Louisville, where he had found plenty to do, painting portraits at a hundred dollars per head.

On his trip to Indiana in 1847 he again visited Richmond. During that visit he met Mary Forman, a child of fourteen, with whom he fell in love. She was living with foster parents whose harsh treatment of the girl so incensed Williams that he took her to his parents' home near Dayton. There she remained until she was sixteen when they were married. Although the painter was twenty years older than his bride, the marriage was a happy one; they made their home in Cincinnati for the next twenty years; the last months of his life were spent in the home of a son in Dayton, where he died in 1873.

In addition to carrying on a brisk career as a portraitist, Williams caught the panorama fever that swept this part of the country in the 1840's. He chose to depict Biblical history from the creation of the world to the fall of Babylon, completing the herculean task in 1849. It was first shown at Cincinnati, and then, during the summer months of that year, in Dayton. In 1850 it was destroyed by fire in Independence Hall, Philadelphia.[6] There is no record that it was displayed in Indiana, but a second panorama of the same subject, exhibited in various parts of the country between 1856 and 1871, was shown at Richmond and nearby towns in 1866. Its presentation at Bethel that year was announced by the following advertisement that appeared in the Richmond *Humming Bird* of May 26:

J. INSCO WILLIAMS
GRAND MOVING PANORAMA OF THE BIBLE
will open at
BETHEL
on Tuesday evening, May 29th
and continue a few nights

It is reported that in the end this panorama sold so well that it made the artist comfortable for the rest of his life.

Toward the end of the nineteenth century three other painters named Williams lived and worked in Richmond. John N. Williams, a cousin of John Insco Williams, and his wife Margaret, were well known in this region for their landscapes. Harry D. Fluhart, having lived many years with the Williams family, adopted the name; according to William Forsyth, he was a stepson of John N. Williams;[7] he was born at Kokomo in 1861, and was one of several Indiana artists to study in Munich. He taught art at Earlham College, Richmond, lived in several places in this country, and spent his last years in Florida. There he resumed his father's name, Fluhart.

Returning to Samuel S. Walker, whose association with J. Insco Williams was referred to above, it is regrettable that none of his work produced in Richmond can now be traced. On the evidence of his sketches and letters, he painted miniatures of several people here, but no descendants of the sitters can now be found in the city. Two portraits in oil of Josephine and Elizabeth Rohrer as children, owned by Elizabeth Comstock, Richmond, are attributed to a painter named Walker and may be his work, but they were painted in eastern Ohio, perhaps at Germantown, and taken recently to Richmond by relatives of the subjects.

Although Walker was well on his way to becoming a recognized portrait painter when he appeared in eastern Indiana in 1841, he was actually a physician by training. He gave up medical practice to become an artist in 1836, and apparently undertook the painting of miniatures with no academic or formal training. Having met Williams in Richmond, Walker took lessons from him in oil painting and later shared his studio at Cincinnati. So far as we know he did not visit Indiana again. His death occurred at Cincinnati in 1848 when he was forty-two years old.

The next artist known to have visited Richmond was the roving Englishman Lefevre J. Cranstone, whose American tour was mentioned in Chapter 1. His drawings and water colors of Richmond made in December, 1859, and January, 1860, are interesting records of the appearance of the town at that time and, like the rest of his work, are very competent in draughtsmanship and attractive as pictorial compositions. Many of them were reproduced in the Richmond *Palladium* in April, 1947.

II

For about three years after Cranstone's visit there was no production of art in Richmond worthy of mention. With the outbreak of the Civil War and the accompanying political broils, not much attention would have been given to cultural matters even if something noteworthy had happened. Then in 1863 Marcus Mote arrived. He was in his middle forties and had been successful as a painter and teacher in Ohio for several years before taking up residence at Richmond.

Mote's original home was near West Milton, Ohio, where he was born on a farm in 1817, the third of five sons of David and Miriam M. Mote. One of his ancestors, W. H. Mote, was a successful copper-plate engraver in England, and it is believed that Marcus' interest in art can be traced back to him. As his parents were strict orthodox Friends he got no encouragement from them when at an early age he showed a keen interest in drawing. As paints were not easy to obtain, he made, according to family tradition, his first colors from plants and organic matter, and indigo from his mother's laundry supplies (the same story as told of Benjamin West's boyhood efforts to get painting materials).[8]

Mote was self-trained, acquiring as time went on such technical information as he could from other painters in the region. His career as a professional artist started in the early 1830's with his removal to Waynesville, Ohio, and then to Lebanon. He began by painting stage-coaches, then gradually got a few people to sit for portraits. By the time he decided to transfer his activity to Richmond, Indiana, he was regarded as one of the leading portrait painters in western Ohio.

In Richmond, Marcus Mote opened a studio with Samantha Ann Hankins as partner, specializing in portraits—oils on canvas and tinted and untinted photographs. Before long he was also conducting an art school, which was so successful that at one time, according to reports, he had 541 pupils.[9] His enterprises were advertised repeatedly in the

40. Charles Conner:
In the Parlor

John Herron Art Museum,
Indianapolis (page 95)

41. (Below) Monimia Bunnell
Boyd: The Hoosier's Nest

Courtesy of Mrs. V. A. Bunnell,
Hagerstown (page 96)

42. Solomon Woody: Portrait of
Paul Way
Courtesy of the Wayne County
Historical Society, Richmond
(page 95)

43. John H. Witt: Portrait of
Julia Stanton
Courtesy of H. Edgar French,
New Castle (page 100)

44. Melvina Hobson Batson:
Portrait of
Elizabeth Elliott Peed
Courtesy of the Henry County
Historical Society, New Castle
(page 102)

45. Lucinda Bowers
McDowell: Portrait of
Samuel Graham
Courtesy of the Henry County
Historical Society, New Castle
(page 103)

Residence of Thomas Fyffe Bainbridge Putn. Co. Ind. 1878.

H. Dousa Del.

Making Hay while the Sun Shines

46. (above) Henry Dousa:
Residence of Thomas
Fyffe
Courtesy of the Indiana
Historical Society Library,
Indianapolis (page 104)

47. James Whitcomb Riley:
Making Hay While the
Sun Shines
Courtesy of the Miami County
Historical Society, Peru
(page 105)

local press, the following announcement from *The Indiana True Republican,* of July 5, 1866, being typical:

M. MOTE & CO.
Richmond Academy of Design
Paint Portraits, Color Photographs, and draw plans.
Rooms No. 104 Main St., upstairs.

M. Mote
S. A. Hankins

Portraits by Mote in Richmond and eastern Indiana are numerous. Among his better canvases are likenesses of Jonathan Roberts and his wife Mary, and of Lavinia Hunt Morris, now in the Wayne County Historical Museum; of Elizabeth Chalfont Gilbert (pl. 38) and James Garr, owned by Harry Gilbert, Richmond; and of John Shroyer, Jehu T. Elliott, and Hannah Branson Elliott, hanging in the Henry County Historical Museum, New Castle. Miniatures of himself and wife, and other portraits, are in Earlham College.

Like J. Insco Williams, Mote began portraiture by making small profile studies in pencil or ink. The earliest of the kind in Indiana is a small water-color likeness on paper of John Smith made somewhere in western Ohio twenty years before the artist came to Richmond. A miniature self-portrait of about 1835, and the above, are owned by Elmer Porter. Mote's early work is attractive in its directness and simplicity of expression, qualities that gradually disappeared as he strove to approach the effect of photographic images. His last works are little better than large tinted photographs even when painted directly from the model, and his rather dry and timid style continued to the end.

A different phase of Mote's output is seen in his pictorial commentaries or cartoons dealing with theological controversies within the Quaker church. Their artistic quality is not high in most instances but the intensity of their message, coupled with a naïve approach, is appealing. Two are preserved in the Wayne County Historical Museum. Of a more factual nature, and lacking the flavor of parody, is the oil painting *Indiana Yearly Meeting,* owned by Earlham College, one of Mote's few known canvases dealing with contemporary scenes (pl. 39). In addition to these subjects he made Sunday-school and Biblical

illustrations, some of which are now preserved in the library of Earlham College, where a number of his sketchbooks are also kept. In 1854
he painted, with the help of others, a large panorama depicting the
Geological History of the Course of Creation, and, spurred on by the
public interest shown in it, made three more panoramas, one based on
Uncle Tom's Cabin, another titled *Paradise Lost and Regained,* and a
third dealing with the evils of intemperance.[10] What has become of
them no one knows.

Mote spent the remainder of his life at Richmond, dying here in
1898 at the age of eighty. He reared a family of four children, none of
whom showed any marked ability in art. But the tradition of artistic
endeavor in the family was continued after his death by a nephew,
Alden, who, though less talented, was equally enterprising.

William Alden Mote was also from West Milton, Ohio, where he
was born in 1840, the son of Luke Smith Mote, brother of Marcus.
He moved to Richmond about the year 1870, studied under his uncle,
and received instruction from Harry Hilliard and Barton Hays, of Indianapolis. Like his uncle, Alden specialized in portrait painting,
adopting the method so popular at that time of glazing over enlarged
photographs. He went into partnership with his brother Elisha, conducting business under the name Mote Brothers, Artists and Photog-
raphers. In the early 1890's he opened an art school in his studio at
828 Main Street, which was moderately successful. He died in 1917
in Richmond, leaving behind a number of canvases, the best ones
being a portrait of Daniel Reid, now in the Reid Memorial Hospital,
and that of James M. Starr, in the historical museum, Richmond. A
large portrait of Edna Stubbs Cathell, at Earlham College, is also believed to be his work.

In the eighties and nineties of the last century there had grown up
in and around Richmond a notable group of artists, most of whom
painted landscapes in the impressionistic manner or an adaptation of
it. John E. Bundy, previously discussed, had, during the late 1880's,
developed from a commendable painter to a highly competent and
popular landscapist, adroitly capturing on canvas the different aspects
of Wayne County's wooded areas.

Before Bundy moved to Richmond (1887), a young man by the name of Charles Conner was already attaining a certain amount of local prominence. He was Richmond's first native son possessing marked artistic ability. Born in 1857, Conner had from childhood shown a strong desire to draw and sketch subjects around him, and, although trained as a pattern maker, he soon turned to painting as his major pursuit. It is reported that he was self-tutored, and while his early work confirms this by its amateurish execution his mature work has a very professional appearance.

One of his first oils depicts a young lady, his fiancée, seated on a sofa in her home at Fountain City, playing a mandolin (pl. 40). It was painted in 1885, and its appeal lies chiefly in its anecdotal and descriptive character. Later he painted landscapes only, and painted them with breadth and surety. Many of them are in public and private collections in the state, the largest number being in the possession of John Nixon, Centerville. In 1887 he went to California with his brother Albert, who was also an artist, and spent many years painting the scenery of the Pacific coast. He died at Richmond in 1905, not long after his return. The year after his death, one of his paintings, *A Wet Night in February,* was shown at the St. Louis Exposition.

Among the many portraits by various artists in the Wayne County Historical Museum, Richmond, two of moderate technical quality make a special appeal. They are rather artless, but nevertheless strong, portrayals of Paul Way (pl. 42) and his wife Achsa Moorman, and were painted by Solomon Woody. A resident of Fountain City for many years, artist Woody was born of Quaker parentage on a Wayne County farm in 1828. Left an orphan early in life, he was brought up by his grandfather who evidently did not oppose the boy's desire to follow an artistic trade. When about twenty years of age he went to Cincinnati, became a successful salesman of men's clothing, and gathered what information he could from local artists about the technicalities of painting, working at it in his spare time. If he had any formal academic training no reports of it have come down to us. His self-portrait, painted there when he was twenty-one, now owned by Mrs. Earl T. Smith, of Fountain City, is surprisingly good.

When the gold rush was at its height, Woody left for California with some of his friends; his financial gain was very modest but the experience was probably of some value to him. Returning to Fountain City, he opened a general store, but continued to devote spare hours to the painting of portraits, landscapes, and other subjects. He died here in 1901, survived by his wife, Rhoda Huff, and four children.

Another artist who lived at Richmond for a few years was Pliny Kersey. He was not a professional painter but, having a talent for drawing and an eye for picturesque views, he made sketches of the town and its environs. In spite of his limited technical ability his drawings and water colors, made in 1868, have a certain charm; they will become increasingly important as historical documents as time goes on and the old landmarks disappear.[11]

Pliny Earle Kersey was born in North Carolina in January, 1850, the son of Dr. Vierling Kersey. His family moved to Richmond in 1861, where his father became active in county medical circles. The son became a schoolteacher at Newport, near Fountain City but, failing in health, removed to California where he died in 1873.

Other painters constituting the Richmond and Wayne County group appear too late in the century to be included in this survey. Some like Henry Mosler and Charles Clawson attained prominence in Cincinnati; Edgar Forkner was best known for his work in the East and later in California; Frank J. Girardin, a native of Kentucky but a resident of Richmond many years, is remembered for his work done at the turn of the century. And the followers of Bundy—George Baker and William Eyden—so popular in recent years, were not recognized until the first quarter of the twentieth century.

III

One of the most romantic stories relating to early Indiana art has to do with a picture painted in Wayne County, titled *The Hoosier's Nest* (pl. 41).

Monimia Bunnell, daughter of a physician living at Green Fork, was a talented and ambitious young lady. As a child she displayed unusual ability, according to family lore, and in her teens had begun to attract attention as a landscape and portrait painter, even though she had had little or no formal training. This deficiency was corrected when, after her marriage to Samuel S. Boyd, a medical student, she had an opportunity to study in Cincinnati.

Not long after her marriage, the husband, enamored of John Finley's poem "The Hoosier's Nest," which had appeared in the Richmond *Palladium,* suggested to his wife that the episode of the stranger arriving at the humble log cabin would make an effective picture:

> I'm told in riding somewhere West
> A stranger found a Hoosier's nest—
> In other words, a buckeye cabin,
> Just big enough to hold Queen Mab in;
> Its situation low, but airy
> Was on the borders of a prairie . . .

Monimia concurred. She selected a very large canvas and after several months of hard work completed the painting to her satisfaction. Greatly admired by her friends, its fame so spread that it attracted the attention of state officials; as a result a call was made upon her by a committee from the legislature for the purpose of soliciting the picture for the State Library. Evidently flattered by the request, Mrs. Boyd presented her masterpiece to the state. It was formally accepted, the General Assembly officially acknowledging the gift in a rhetorical resolution—one of the few instances in which our legislative body has recognized the work of a local artist.[12] The large canvas was hung in the library, at that time in the Statehouse.

But the amiable relationship between artist and state did not last many months. A critic on one of the Indianapolis newspapers regarded the work as an inferior technical performance and allowed his appraisal to appear in print. When it was brought to the attention of the artist she was heartbroken. Unable to endure the thought of her masterpiece remaining in Indianapolis, surrounded by unsympathetic and even hostile people, she pleaded with her husband to go immediately to the Statehouse and bring it back to her. In spite of his conviction that this would be impossible, now that the picture was the property of the state, he submitted to her entreaties, saddled his horse, and set off for

Indianapolis. As he expected, the librarian refused to release the picture. However, concern for his wife's health made him courageous. He waited for an opportune moment, and when the librarian was out of the room he cut the canvas from the frame and hurried away with it.

The purloined painting remained in the artist's home until her death in 1862; then it was placed by Dr. Boyd in the high school at Dublin, Indiana, when he enlisted in the Civil War. There it remained for about sixty years, forgotten, except for the people who noticed it in the high-school library; if state officials tried to regain it in the meantime no report of their action is on record. When the old school building was demolished, the large canvas was stored in the home of a descendant of the artist, and then it became the possession of Mrs. Minnie Bunnell, who proudly cares for it in her home at Hagerstown, Indiana.

Although the exact statement made by the critic in 1850 is not known (it has not yet been recovered from old newspaper files), we can concur in his opinion, as indirectly reported,[13] that the painting is not a great technical achievement. But intervening years and events have surrounded it with a romantic veil that adds greatly to its appeal. And it is unquestionably the most ambitious anecdotal painting attempted by any local artist, exclusive of panoramas or murals.

In addition to this imposing canvas, Monimia Bunnell Boyd painted a few narrative subjects, including *The Lord's Supper*, and a number of portraits. The former is in the home of Mrs. Belle Barnard, of Hagerstown, and the portrait of her father, Dr. William Bunnell, is now owned by Mrs. Minnie Bunnell. It is recorded that she also painted the likeness of U. S. Senator George W. Julian, of Centerville (later of Irvington), but the picture's whereabouts is unknown.

Centerville, the first town west of Richmond, was the home of several men prominent in the state's early annals, and it reflects today the tastes of some of its former inhabitants in the fine old residences that still stand. Situated as it is on the National Road it was doubtless visited by a number of itinerant painters and artisans, but few canvases are now known to have originated here. Those portraying Judge Jacob Julian and Rebecca Hoover Julian, by two different painters (neither as yet identified), are among the most interesting of the local productions. Formerly owned by the late Mrs. Christopher B. Coleman, they are now in the home of Mrs. E. C. Bray, St. Paul, Minnesota.

The first painter of note who is known to have worked in Centerville was Peter Fishe Reed. He was a native of Boston, Massachusetts, had begun his professional work, like many others, as a sign painter in Cincinnati, moved to Vernon, Indiana, where he painted and wrote articles on art subjects, and went to Centerville to teach at Whitewater College in 1861. He remained here a year, after which he went to Indianapolis and then to Chicago. It is reasonable to assume that some of his paintings (he made both portraits and landscapes but preferred the latter) found their way into Centerville homes, but as nothing has come to light bearing his signature it is impossible to assign anything to him at this time.

The town's only native artist was Flora Stigleman, who was born here in 1858, later moving to Olive Hill, Wayne County. She studied with Marcus Mote, of Richmond, and also with painters in the East, but she did not attain more than a modest local reputation. The only paintings by her that are now known are portraits in oil of her parents, Henry and Caroline Stigleman, painted about 1880, and the likeness of Paul O. Jones as a child, made about five years later. The latter is owned by Mrs. Addie Jones, Indianapolis.

Dublin and Cambridge City, lying west of Centerville on the National Road, probably had their quota of wayfaring artists, too. Although names of most of them have long been forgotten, Dublin recalls two of her sons who attained more than local fame: John H. Witt and James M. Dennis.

Witt was born in Dublin in 1840. Little is now known of his early years. When a young man he worked as a machinist and wagon painter in a small factory owned by his uncle; then, deciding to become an artist, he undertook to develop his technique by diligent practice with brushes and paint, later going to Cincinnati where he received instruction from Joseph O. Eaton. By 1860 he had embarked upon portrait painting as a profession in his native town.

Two portraits made about that time mark the beginning of a career that led eventually to considerable success in Ohio and New York. They represent Samuel Dillon and Julia Stanton, later Mrs. John Crumin; the former is owned by Mrs. Florence Stewart, of Dublin, the latter by H. Edgar French, of New Castle. The canvas of Julia Stanton (pl. 43), in some ways the more competent of the two, suggests the influence of Eaton and was probably painted after Witt had been at Cincinnati.

Around 1863 Witt left Dublin for Ohio, and when next heard of he was in Columbus, where he received commissions to paint a number of the Ohio governors for the statehouse. He remained there fifteen or sixteen years, progressing steadily in his chosen field and varying his output by painting an occasional landscape. One of these he sent to an exhibition held at Indianapolis in 1875, and it received the following appraisal from the pen of a local reporter: "We must allude to a landscape . . . painted by Mr. Witt of Columbus. It is called 'The Old Crossing,' and, with the exception of the woolly trees in the middle distance, it is a magnificent landscape."[14]

From Columbus John Witt went to New York, where he spent the remainder of his life. In recognition of his achievement as a painter he was elected an associate member of the National Academy of Design. He died in New York in 1901.

As James M. Dennis was born at Dublin the same year as Witt, and as both grew up there, it is reasonable to assume that their mutual interest drew them together in their youth. Like Witt, Dennis picked up the rudiments of painting in whatever way he could and then, when about eighteen years of age, he, too, went to Cincinnati, studying under Eaton and Alexander Wyant. This apprenticeship under both a portrait and landscape painter enabled Dennis to become proficient in both branches, and throughout his life he turned from one subject to the other.

In 1865, not long after Witt had gone to Ohio, Dennis went to Indianapolis. There he soon established himself, enjoying a fair degree of success in spite of the competition of more experienced painters. Eight years later he went to New York, entering again the studios of Eaton and Wyant, both of whom had by that time gone East. After a year or so he was back in Indianapolis for a second period of residence, regarding which more will be said in our discussion of Indianapolis and its art affairs. In 1883 he moved to Detroit, remaining there until his death in 1918.

Up to this time no work produced by Dennis at Dublin, his native town, has been found. What he accomplished here we do not know, but it is not unreasonable to assume that he painted some family portraits and an occasional landscape.

A third painter whose name is associated with Dublin is J. Dodds, but he is so shadowy a figure that neither his life nor artistic endeavors are known. Mary Burnet states that he lived here around the year 1869, later going to New York, but there are no records in Indiana nor in the East that throw any light on his activities.

Cambridge City has already been referred to in connection with the activities of J. Insco Williams. Here he painted, around 1841, the canvases portraying Benjamin Conklin and his wife (pl. 37).[15] How many other painters preceded or followed Williams we do not know; so little remains now in the line of old pictures that it is impossible to reconstruct the story. The town's most famous son in the field of art was Lewis Cass Lutz. He was born here in 1855, the son of John C. Lutz, a forceful political writer and founder of the *Western Mirror*. When about nineteen years of age, Lewis was enabled through the aid of a friend to attend the McMicken School of Design at Cincinnati, and his progress was so remarkable that three years after entering the academy he was made an instructor of one of the preparatory classes.

In 1881 Lutz went to Munich, where he remained for three years. Upon his return to America he decided to take up his residence again in Cincinnati, having been offered a position on the faculty of the McMicken School, which had become by that time the Art Academy of Cincinnati. He held that position until his death in 1893. As his mature years were spent away from his native town, and as none of his professional work was apparently done in the state, there are no paintings by him in or around Cambridge City today. A portrait of Lutz, painted by Thomas S. Noble, a Cincinnati colleague, hangs in the town's public library.

IV

New Castle, where J. Insco Williams painted Miles Murphy and members of his family, could not have been much of a town when the artist visited here in 1835, for it had been founded only some twelve years before. Being north of the National Road and less accessible to journeying artists—particularly those headed toward the capital from western Ohio—it probably lured few painters in the years preceding the Civil War. But judging by the number of old family portraits in the Henry County Historical Museum (one of the largest collections in the state) considerable activity of an artistic nature took place here in the years that followed.

Most of the walls of the museum are covered from ceiling to floor with painted or photographed visages that look down at the observer with a variety of expressions: complacence, severity, ardor, and sullenness. The majority of them have no place in a survey like this because they have little merit beyond preserving facial features of the various subjects. Some, however, have more than average artistic worth, while others have a justifiable claim to our attention by virtue of having been painted by local artists who can be identified.

Among those that might first attract the visitor's attention are likenesses of John and Elizabeth Shroyer, painted by Marcus Mote in 1867, and those of Jehu Elliott and his wife Hannah Branson, which may be by the same hand, although tradition assigns them to a Cincinnati artist. Portraits of Abraham Elliott (father of Jehu) and his wife Keturah are the works of Melvina Hobson Batson, one of three local women painters. By the same hand is the pleasing unsophisticated study of Elizabeth Elliott Peed (pl. 44).

Melvina Hobson, daughter of Evan and Elizabeth Elliott Hobson, was born at New Castle in 1826. She was largely self-taught, but a year's study in Cincinnati helped to improve her technique. However, this tutoring was of little avail as she died soon after of typhoid fever (1853), survived by her husband, Dr. Andrew Batson, and two children. It is reported that most of her portraits were painted before she was twenty years of age.

In addition to the canvases mentioned above, Melvina Hobson Batson painted the portrait of Amanda Elliott Bundy, wife of Judge Martin L. Bundy, owned by Mrs. Cicero Bailey, of New Castle; and it is also understood that she was the author of the portrait of Abraham Elliott that hangs in the library of the courthouse. Judging by its simple artless style it was probably one of her earliest efforts.

A second woman who attained local recognition in the same line of endeavor was Lucinda Bowers McDowell, wife of Joseph McDowell. She was born at New Castle in 1827, received her first lessons in painting at Yellow Springs Seminary, Ohio, and then studied with John Love at Indianapolis and Marcus Mote at Richmond. She taught art at New Castle and exerted considerable influence upon young men and women with artistic talent.[16] She died here in 1909.

There are a number of paintings in New Castle that attest to her ability. One of the best is the portrait of Samuel Graham (pl. 45), an early coverlet weaver of Henry County, now in the historical museum here. The museum also owns a small water color of a family gathered around a tombstone, under the drooping branches of a willow—a typical early American funeral or memorial piece—which is so amateurish in execution that it must be one of the painter's first efforts.

Four portraits of members of the Hinshaw family hanging on the crowded walls of the historical museum call our attention to a third local woman painter, Mary Ellen Branson. She was born at Greensboro, Indiana, in 1826, the daughter of Seth and Abigail Hinshaw. She received instruction in painting from J. Insco Williams and Marcus Mote, becoming so proficient that after her marriage to Elisha Branson she was able to support her growing family during times of financial stress by selling her paintings. Her price for portraits was twenty-five dollars each.

Although her name appears here in connection with the artists of New Castle, most of Mary Branson's life was spent at Knightstown, in the southwest corner of the county, and there she did most of her painting. The last years of her life were passed in the home of a daughter in Milton, Indiana, where she died in 1911. Many of her paintings are now in the possession of a grandson, H. W. Lindsay.

Of minor technical distinction, but nevertheless of interest, are the portraits in New Castle by Henry Dousa, the sixth painter known to have worked here. According to some reports Dousa was previously in Lafayette, where he began his career as a painter of cattle and horses—that is, recording the likenesses of prize-winning animals for their proud owners. From the painting of livestock he turned to the portraying of people, as he felt more secure in his calling and more skillful with his brushes.

It is possible that Dousa came originally from New York, but nothing is known of his early life. He was in Lafayette in the 1870's, but by 1879 he had moved to New Castle where his first patrons were Thomas Wilhoit and Simon T. Powell. His physical appearance and name led some people to regard him as a Frenchman, although others thought he was German or Italian. In Lafayette he had married Lena Icenoggle, many years younger than himself, whom he took to New Castle to share his successes and failures. Not long afterward they returned to Lafayette, where he died obscure and indigent.

One early chronicle speaks of the admiration Dousa had for Lucinda McDowell's ability to paint horses and riders. After seeing some of his paintings of cattle, such as the large one in the Henry County Historical Museum, that is easy to understand. Dousa's compositions of cows in a pasture give the impression of brown and black silhouettes having been fixed to a green background, with practically no variation in their positions. His representations of farms and farmhouses are not more adroit in draughtsmanship and perspective. A water color in the Library of the Indiana Historical Society, depicting the home of Thomas Fyffe in Putnam County, is typical (pl. 46).

In the field of portraiture he is well represented in the museum at New Castle: Solomon Denius and his wife Elizabeth Thornburg, Cyrus Pence and his wife Catherine, and Mrs. Kate Elliott, are the subjects. Frontal poses, chartlike in the delineation of features and devoid of shading or tonal values, the depictions show only too well that Dousa had little or no formal training in the craft he was pursuing.

Another artist known to have lived in Henry County was Hiram B. Vanneman. He held the rank of captain during the Civil War, and while in service he put his talent to good use by making maps and sketches. He was a friend of Marcus Mote and may have received some instruction in drawing from him.

V

Anderson and Muncie, lying north of the communities considered above, have been referred to earlier in discussing the lives of Samuel Richards and J. Ottis Adams. Little more can be added with respect to the former's life in Anderson. He moved here in 1877, after exhausting all possibilities in Franklin, and he stayed on until 1880, the year he and his wife sailed for Munich. It was during those years that Richards met James Whitcomb Riley, a young reporter on the Anderson *Democrat*. Riley, not yet recognized as a poet, also aspired to be a painter, and it is tempting to surmise that whatever instruction he received in the manipulation of brushes and paint was from Richards. Many references have been made to Riley's painting of signs for patent medicines, but the only known picture assigned to him is an oil painting on cardboard that depicts a boy and girl who have chosen a haystack as their rendezvous, bearing the title *Making Hay while the Sun Shines* (pl. 47). It is now in the Miami County Historical Museum at Peru. The attribution of the work to Riley is based on sound tradition, and as nothing else by his hand exists, except two signboards for McGrillus' Tonic Blood Purifier,[17] it is impossible to confirm it on the basis of style.

There is no certainty that any of Samuel Richards' work in the field of portraiture done between 1877 and 1880 survives in Anderson. And yet he must have had several clients. Of some interest to the historian are the large landscapes he painted sometime during that period that hang in some of the local homes. As his first work in that field they are timid and labored, revealing the hand of a novice.

His study and travel abroad, made possible by financial aid from some businessmen in Spencer in the form of prepayment for pictures, and by help from his father-in-law, extended over a period of nearly eleven years. As that phase of his life is beyond the scope of this survey—and because it has been fully reported elsewhere—there is no need for dwelling upon it here.[18] His second Anderson period was too short and his health too poor for him to accomplish anything of note. He returned to Indiana in 1891, but within a few months he was advised to go to Denver, where he died of tuberculosis in 1893.

While in Munich he produced his masterpiece, *Evangeline*, which was exhibited at Munich, Paris, and London. Later, it was brought to America where it received glowing appraisals on the part of critics. The *Indianapolis Sentinel* referred to it as "one of the most famous pictures ever done by an American artist."[19] A collector in Detroit, Bela Hubbard, bought and gave it to the Detroit Institute of Arts.

A number of the artist's portrait studies made at the Munich Royal Academy about 1885 are in the John Herron Art Museum. As might be expected they show a great technical advance over the portraits he made in Indiana a decade or more before, and confirm the report that Richards was one of the best draughtsmen among the Indiana artists of the nineteenth century.

As was pointed out previously, John Ottis Adams went to Muncie in 1876, having already embarked upon his career as a portrait painter at Martinsville. He rented a studio at Muncie and, while getting established, worked for a photographer named Gamble, presumably tinting photographs. Unlike most of the photographer-painters we have discussed, Adams apparently resisted the temptation to reproduce in his paintings the effects of a camera-made image. He retained in his work an artistic perception and individuality of style.

A number of his canvases of the 1876–1880 period are known. Mrs. Robert H. Hartley has a charming study of a girl in an outdoor winter costume, seen against a snow-covered landscape (pl. 48). The subject was Sarah Heinsohn, later Mrs. J. J. Hartley. A portrait of the girl's father, Julius A. Heinsohn, was also painted by Adams but it belongs in his next Muncie period, following his return to America in 1887 from a second trip to Europe.

One of Adams' best patrons in Muncie was Dr. W. C. Willard. Although Willard had his own portrait painted by Barton S. Hays, of Indianapolis (it is now in the Ball Memorial Hospital), he engaged Adams to paint his wife and children. At least four canvases are known, but all have been taken to other states by members of the family.

Due to the superior training Adams had received in London, portraits painted by him in the late 1870's were among the best turned out in the state during that period. Their closest rivals, technically, were being produced at Indianapolis by Steele, Hays, and Cox. But Adams felt the need of additional training. Learning that several Indiana painters were making plans to study at the Munich Royal Academy, he joined them when they sailed for Europe in the summer of 1880.

Upon Adams' return to Indiana in 1887 he came back to Muncie, re-opened his studio, painted portraits and landscapes, and held classes in art. He taught at Union City and helped establish the art schools at Fort Wayne and Indianapolis, becoming the head instructor in the latter, the school of the John Herron Art Institute, from 1904 to 1909.

The phase of his life and work that is best known today centered in Brookville. When he and the other artists returned from abroad and began to take frequent sketching trips into different parts of the state, they found much of their pictorial material in the Whitewater Valley near Brookville and Metamora. Adams and his wife, Winifred Brady, (also an artist) made their home at Brookville in 1897, having bought an old house on the river that came to be known as the "Hermitage." There Adams lived and painted most of the time until his death in January, 1927.

By coincidence, a second painter by the name of Adams was in Delaware County and Muncie when J. Ottis Adams was there. He was Nelson Perry Adams, a stock farmer with a predilection for drawing pictures. As a young man he had little time to indulge in so impractical a pursuit as painting, but late in life he had a studio in his home and turned out pictures of limited technical caliber. They were usually based upon, if not actually copied from, color prints, and, although he attempted various subjects, his specialty was animals. Two of his large landscapes with cows in the foreground are owned by Ball State Teachers College (pl. 49). He offered instruction in painting, and attracted a number of students, the most talented one being his son Wayman Adams, who later became his assistant; townspeople referred to him as the "boy artist of Muncie."

Nelson Adams was born on a farm between New Castle and

Muncie, in northern Henry County, in 1861, the son of Alvis and Aseneth Baldwin Adams. Father and son operated a successful stock farm until the former's death; then the son turned to painting, removing to the town of Muncie. He painted a few portraits of members of his family (those of his parents made about 1880 are now owned by his widow), but he preferred landscapes and animal subjects. He died at Muncie in 1917.

A few more artists worked at Muncie in the latter half of the nineteenth century. Mrs. N. M. Suffrins, a professional portrait painter of Indianapolis, was here in 1868. None of her work, in either Indianapolis or Muncie, has been traced, so neither her clients nor her artistic capabilities can be commented upon. Better known to us today is the work of Linda Jenkins Ryan (Mrs. L. F. Ryan). She was not a professional artist but painted for her own pleasure, usually deriving her ideas and subjects from other pictures. A period of instruction under Theobald Lietz of Indianapolis gave her some confidence in painting portraits, and the likeness of her daughter, Susan Ryan, as a child, shows distinctly the influence of her teacher.

Gradually the art colony of Muncie grew but it did not become prominent until the twentieth century, and its best-known artists came too late in point of time for inclusion in this story.

Chapter 6

FORT WAYNE, LOGANSPORT

LAFAYETTE, ATTICA

CRAWFORDSVILLE, NOBLESVILLE

GOSHEN, SOUTH BEND

LA PORTE

THE TOWNS AND CITIES in the belt across northern Indiana lie in a region rich in historic lore as well as abundantly supplied with agricultural and industrial enterprises. From Fort Wayne southwest to Attica, following the upper reaches of the Wabash River, and northwest to Michigan City, a triangle is formed that encompassed some of the most significant events in the state's history. It is also important with respect to the theme being developed here.

Fort Wayne was referred to in the first chapter as the town of the Miami Indians which was visited by Henry Hamilton in the fall of 1778 and where his water-borne army portaged from the Maumee River to the Wabash. One may assume that Hamilton made some sketches here but no evidence remains today. It was also the temporary home of Captain John Whistler and the birthplace of his son George Washington. The earliest existing drawing made here is John Whistler's map of the fort and environs, which has already been discussed. We have also spoken about Fort Wayne in connection with the visits of Samuel Seymour and James O. Lewis.

The first painter to reach Fort Wayne with the intention of making it the center of his professional activity was Horace Rockwell. The place of his origin is not known, but he was referred to by early chroniclers as being "of Philadelphia," and the catalogue of an exhibition held by the Artists Fund Society of that city in 1835 lists a portrait by him. He is also listed as being from New York,[1] so he doubtless practiced there, too, before coming West.

Be that as it may, he settled in Fort Wayne about 1836 and found a number of clients among the pioneers. Portraits of Edward Stopelford and his wife Susan, painted in 1836, and a third canvas portraying Charlotte Griffith Ewing, of about the same date, are now in the Fort Wayne–Allen County Museum. A more imposing work is the large group portrait of ten members of the Samuel Hanna family gathered around a parlor table (pl. 50), now in the Fort Wayne Art Museum. It is composed in the manner of the early English "conversation piece" and is one of the most ambitious works executed by any of the state's early painters.

On the basis of these canvases it seems safe to assign to Rockwell the portrait of Francis Comparet and his wife, painted about 1845, owned by Clifford Matson, of Fort Wayne.

In spite of Rockwell's previous experience in eastern centers and the acceptance of his work by the committee in charge of the Artists Fund Society exhibition, he was by no means a master technician. While there is a certain firmness in his drawing and a suggestion of solidity in the modeling of heads, the figures in his compositions appear stodgy and without expression. A feature that is peculiar to his work is the drawing of hands (the fingers are held together and the thumb usually points away from the hand), and cuffs are frequently drawn with sharp, angular edges.

The first reference to Horace Rockwell in the press was an article that appeared in the Indianapolis *Journal* in 1852, commenting upon a display of his "scriptural" paintings and stating that "the Resurrection of Christ and the Virgin Mary, executed by Mr. Rockwell of Fort Wayne will be exhibited at the lecture room of Wesley Chapel."[2] How the citizens of Indianapolis responded to the announcement, and what their reaction was to his work, we do not know, but doubtless it satisfied Rockwell to have his masterpiece shown in the capital.

A few years later, the artist left Fort Wayne and made his home in the neighboring town of Roanoke. Frank Bash, in his *History of Huntington County,* alludes to him as "an artist of far more than ordinary ability," [3] and states that he lived a secluded life at Roanoke while his wife and daughter were prominent in social circles. The author said that Rockwell would quietly steal away to New York or Cincinnati "where he would exhibit his oil paintings, win prizes in competition with other artists, and dispose of his pictures at good prices."

E. M. Wasmuth's book, *The Saga of a Hoosier Village,* discloses another facet of the "eccentric's" life. After speaking of a canvas that he recalled seeing in the painter's home (a representation of Jacob's Ladder) he said: "But Rockwell, the artist, had other talents. He was an inventive genius and long before the Wright brothers gave humanity wings, he conceived a flying machine. Like many another genius with like intent he failed to perfect his instrument and his efforts met with the derision of his neighbors." [4] His forced landing, after taking off from the roof of a barn, destroyed both machine and his faith in the possibility of air travel. Rockwell died at Roanoke in 1877. His tombstone, standing in the abandoned cemetery west of town, gives his age at the time of death as "65 Yrs. 6 Mos. 3 Days."

About three years after Rockwell settled at Fort Wayne another artist, R. B. Crafft, arrived who probably gave him serious competition. Unlike Rockwell, Crafft was a native of the state, probably of Clinton. [5] His portraits of Robert Filson (pl. 51) and his wife Eliza, in the historical museum here, are his earliest known productions, and the date they bear (1839) is the earliest record we have relating to Crafft's career. How old he was at the time we do not know.

The next reference to him is in the *Fort Wayne Sentinel,* where his announcement as a portrait painter appeared February 3, 1844:

> The subscriber informs the public that he is now ready to take in a superior style the likeness of all who will favor him with their custom. All likenesses are warranted correct and satisfactory or no charge will be made. Ladies and gentlemen are respectfully asked to call and examine specimens. R. B. Crafft.

Nothing more appeared in the local press regarding him.

About that time he succeeded in getting orders to paint the Indian chief Francis La Fontaine and three members of his family: his wife Catherine Richardville, his son John, and his father-in-law Jean Baptiste Richardville. The canvases are now owned by Howard Owen, of Huntington, Indiana.

Crafft's manner of painting shows that he had had a good deal of experience by the time he reached Fort Wayne, but there is no suggestion in his technique of formal academic training. He painted in a firm, direct way, strongly marking the differences in facial characteristics if not revealing much of the inner life of his sitters. His subjects pose in rigid frontal positions, their heads turned slightly to left or right, looking at the observer with steady gaze.

What eventually happened to Crafft and his later work we do not know. Judged on the basis of style, portraits of E. H. Shirk and his wife Mary, and those of Lucien L. Davenport and his wife Mary Lauer, may be by his hand.[6] They were painted in central Indiana more than a decade after the Filson portraits; although they reveal a marked technical advance it is not unreasonable to assume that he was competent enough by that time to have made them.

A third artist of Fort Wayne, contemporaneous with Rockwell and Crafft, was John Jacob Hegler. He arrived here in 1845, if we are to accept an advertisement in the Fort Wayne newspaper of that year as his initial announcement.[7] He had come to Indiana from Switzerland, stopping off in one or more eastern cities en route. He was in his middle thirties when he reached Indiana and he remained in the state the rest of his life.

Born at Bretzwil, Switzerland, near Basel, in 1812, Hegler perhaps received training in drawing and painting in Switzerland before coming to America in 1831. For several years he followed his father's trade, that of a miller. He lived in Ohio for a brief period, where he took his initial steps as a portrait painter, and where he met his future wife Julia Ann Richards. From Fort Wayne he moved to Lafayette and then to Attica. He died at Attica in 1856, survived by his wife and their two sons.

From the standpoint of style, Hegler was a more pleasing painter than Rockwell or Crafft. His pictures have a decided charm in both composition and color; and though he never became a facile performer, his figure drawing is good and his technique more than adequate. He painted with firmness if not with dash.

The only canvas that can now be attributed to his Fort Wayne period is a portrait of Charles A. Munson as a boy, posed with his pet dog. It is in the historical museum here, and the attribution to Hegler has been made on the basis of his known work in Lafayette and Attica, regarding which we will have occasion to speak later.

A fourth painter working at Fort Wayne before 1850 was B. G. Cosgrove. He is no more than a name in the annals of Indiana art as neither his work nor life history is known. His presence in this community was noted by Slocum and Robertson in their *History of the Maumee River Basin.*[8] It is possible that he is the creator of several portraits in and around Fort Wayne now awaiting identification.

In the 1850's and 1860's a number of painters made Fort Wayne their home, some for a brief period, others for several years. Edward Edmondson, of Dayton, visited here in 1863 and painted the attractive portrait of Alice Belknap Torrence, wife of George Torrence, now in the possession of Dr. C. R. Dancer. He also made the portrait of George W. Wood, first mayor of Fort Wayne, which is in the historical museum, and a landscape owned by Mrs. Warren Sweet.

Edmondson, one of Dayton's most successful artists in the second half of the century, is a person whose biography is as yet unwritten. His name appeared in early Dayton directories, and a sketch of his life is included in Crew's *History of Dayton.*[9] He was born at Dayton of Quaker parentage; he had no aptitude for tinsmithing (his father's trade), so he turned to art; it is said that he was self-taught, but his work suggests that he had some training in a professional school or under a competent painter. First he specialized in still-life subjects but soon switched to portraits, in which line he enjoyed considerable success; his death occurred in California where he had gone for his health. Fort Wayne was apparently the only Indiana town in which he worked.

In the decade from 1855 to 1865 at least two women painters visited

Fort Wayne: Emily Jenison, whose name appeared in the city directories from 1858 to 1861 as a portrait painter, and Mrs. E. L. Burr, who inserted her name in the 1864–65 directory as an artist. No work by them has come to our attention to throw light on their capabilities or accomplishments.

From 1867 to 1871 the *Allen County Gazetteer* and Fort Wayne directories list one artist only: Joseph H. Dille. Because of his extended stay here and his large output of work he came to be regarded as the town's leading artist, and today he is looked upon by many as Fort Wayne's "old master." He painted landscapes, still lifes, and portraits, and as a partner of Augustus C. Crane, photographer, he tinted photographs and painted with oil colors over photographic prints.

Dille was born near Cleveland in 1832. His family had arrived in this country from Alsace-Lorraine not long before, settling in northern Ohio, where Joseph grew up. The next one hears of the young artist he was in Fort Wayne; here, in 1854, he married Carrie I. Hedges. After his wife's tragic death in childbirth, Dille removed to Goshen, Indiana, where he embarked seriously upon his career as a painter and where he met Libby Crane, who became his second wife. In 1865 he returned to Fort Wayne with his family, which now included a son; here most of Dille's work was done, and here his son Ralph grew up to become a painter, too. Toward the end of his life Joseph Dille lived at Amelia, Ohio, where he died in 1918.

Working in a neat meticulous technique bordering on fussiness, Dille produced pictures that appealed to his patrons in Allen and Elkhart counties. One of his best Fort Wayne portraits is that of Thomas W. Swinney (pl. 52), painted in water colors in 1887 and preserved in the historical museum; another, in oils, is the canvas bearing the likeness of Mrs. John G. Olds, dated 1869, in the same collection, a work of comparable merit.

But it was by means of small fruit and flower studies and landscapes that he made his living, selling many of them through dealers in Fort Wayne and Cincinnati, as revealed in a letter written by him, from Amelia, to his son: "I think I could sell a good many of the little and cheaper ones here and in Cincinnati . . . Just received a 16.00 check from Mr. Schenz [Fort Wayne] for a little 6½ x 14 Apple piece, one dollar more than the price I put on it. Comes good. 6.00 coal takes money. What do you pay for coal now?" [10]

Although the career of his son Ralph Dille is too late in the century to occupy a place in this chronicle, it should be reported that his work is to be found in the historical museum at Fort Wayne and in several local homes. His speciality was apparently landscape painting, and he worked in a laborious, amateurish way. Presumably his entire training was gotten from his father, and he had little or no opportunity to get technical hints from skilled painters or inspiration from notable works of art in large eastern cities. His span of life was from 1860 to 1937.

II

Leaving Fort Wayne and turning our attention toward the west, following the course of the Wabash River, we find the next center of early art activity at Logansport. The first professional painter to arrive here was George Winter, who chose it because it was in the heart of the Indian country.

So much has been written about Winter that only a cursory biography will be necessary here.[11] He was born at Portsea, England, in 1810, the youngest of twelve children. He obtained a good general education there, was given encouragement by his parents in his early artistic endeavors, and, when about sixteen years of age, he went to London to study art. He actually got little training in drawing and painting at the time, but he visited exhibitions, studied paintings in museums, and made the acquaintance of many people in art circles. When he was about to enroll in the schools of the Royal Academy he decided to come to America.

He arrived at New York in 1830, spent three years in the school of the National Academy of Design, occasionally exhibited his work in eastern shows, and presumably intended making the metropolis his home. But after five or six years, "led by a touch of romantic feeling to see and sketch the Indians of the Wabash," he came west, remained for a year at Cincinnati and in the spring of 1837 moved on to the little settlement of Logansport.

Such instruction as Winter received in England was principally in miniature painting, but subsequent study in New York gave him confidence in executing portraits in oil. Both techniques are found in his Indiana output. Most of his studies of the aborigines and their customs are small water colors on paper, rendered with a neat hand, while his portraits of the frontiersmen are usually oils on canvas, painted with breadth and directness.

Winter happened on the scene at a time when federal authorities were investigating irregularities in the business practices of Indian traders. Soon after his arrival a number of councils were held by federal agents for the purpose of hastening the removal of the Indians from the state. Both activities gave the artist an unusual opportunity to see and study the red man, in ceremonial as well as casual attire (pl. 54), and to capture on paper and canvas the likenesses of their leaders. Even more romantic, if less spectacular, was his participation in the incidents following the unexpected discovery of Frances Slocum, "White Rose of the Miamis," and his commission to paint her portrait for her brothers when she refused to return with them to Pennsylvania.

After the departure of the Indians for regions west of the Mississippi, Winter devoted himself to portraits of local settlers and to landscapes. The latter were based on sketches he made along the Wabash, frequently incorporating groups of redskins gathered on the shores. Tinged with an air of romanticism in both composition and color, and planned to bring out the most picturesque aspects of the region, they became very popular, finding their way into many local homes.

Among the best-known portraits dating from his Logansport period are those of Joseph Barron, Indian interpreter (pl. 53), and Chief Francis Godfroy, now in the Tippecanoe County Historical Museum, Lafayette; those of David D. Pratt and George Proffit, in private collections; and the brothers Jordan and Cyrus Vigus, in the Cass County Historical Museum, Logansport.

In Peru, sixteen miles east, he found other patrons: Albert Cole and his wife Mary Galpin, Daniel and Emma Cole Bearss, and Simon Wilkinson and his wife. The last pair of portraits is in the Miami County Historical Museum.

The importance of George Winter's work in the annals of the state is gaining wider recognition. Not only has he left a pictorial record of people and events connected with our early history but in his various journals he recorded both personal and historical data of much interest and value. All things considered, he may well be regarded as the most significant of Indiana's pioneer painters.

In 1840 Winter married Mary Squier of Dayton, Ohio, and they had two children, George and Annette. In 1851 they moved to Lafayette, a larger and more active town farther down the Wabash. He continued painting (his only means of livelihood) and, in spite of a very limited clientele, succeeded in making a reasonably good living. More about his life at Lafayette is told in a later section of this chapter.

About the time Winter arrived at Logansport another painter by the name of J. R. Richards came, according to historian Powell.[12] His period of residence here was from 1837 to 1845, and as he was referred to as a "painter of some reputation," he must have obtained some orders but nothing by him has been found. In 1844 he was at La Porte, as will be noted later; and he was probably the same Richards who was working in the settlements on the Wabash in the decade between 1850 and 1860.

Another painter at Logansport was George Adams, a friend and pupil of Winter. He came to Logansport from his home at Harpers Ferry, Virginia (where he was born in 1814), a year before Winter arrived. He opened a sign-painting shop, but ambitious to get into a finer, and perhaps more lucrative, branch of art, he took instruction from Winter and developed into a fairly good painter. Only one portrait by him is now known—a self-study owned by Mrs. Sara D. Reed—but a number of his landscapes have been preserved. Sign painting and commercial art, however, proved to be better sources of income; he gave up portrait painting but continued to make outdoor sketching an avocation. At one time he thought of moving to Chicago, but after a brief visit he returned to Logansport, reporting that Chicago was a backward place made up principally of Indian wigwams.

A fourth painter, a man named Stephens, may have been at Logansport during that period, too. A portrait of John P. Dillon, owned by the Indiana State Library, was assigned to him many years after it was painted, by Wils Berry, a local artist, but nothing is recorded concerning Stephens' life or work. In the Logansport city directory of 1874 Josiah W. Stephens is listed as a house and sign painter, and although the Dillon portrait was painted twenty-five or more years before that date (judging by its style) it may possibly be his work. As with many of his contemporaries throughout the state, the oblivion into which Stephens has fallen makes him an intriguing subject for the research student or art historian.

Apparently nothing of importance happened at Logansport along the line of painting during and immediately following the Civil War, but in the seventies activity was resumed, for in that decade half-a-dozen artists were here: John D. Forgy, David Scott Evans, Jerome McLean, Jacob Ackerman, Robert Swaim, and William J. Potter; following them came Max Klepper, Wils Berry, and others.

Forgy, who made a specialty of landscapes, was a native of Logansport and apparently spent most of his life here. He studied in Cincinnati, both at the Academy of Design and with Albert Bierstadt. Upon his return to his native town he opened a studio and inserted his announcement in the 1868 edition of H. C. Chandler & Co.'s *Business Directory of Indiana:*

LANDSCAPE PAINTING
John D. Forgy

Late of the Academy of Design, Cincinnati, Ohio, will give thorough instruction in Landscape Painting at his studio, Fetter's Photographic Studio, McTaggert's New Block, corner of Broadway and Fourth Streets, Logansport, Ind. Semi-annual distribution of Pictures, January 1st and July 1st.

There are doubtless a number of his landscapes in Logansport homes today, and probably several of the young artistically inclined men and women took advantage of the courses he offered. Not long after this, however, Forgy moved to Des Moines, Iowa, where he spent his remaining years.

D. Scott Evans was in Logansport from 1872 to 1875 as a teacher of music and art at Smithson College. He came from Boston, Wayne

County, Indiana, where he was born in 1847, the son of Dr. David S. Evans and his wife Nancy. One of his earliest artistic efforts was the painting of George Washington's portrait on the headboard of his bed.

Educated at Miami University, where he showed an aptitude for drawing and music, Evans made teaching his profession for several years, first serving on the faculty of Smithson College and later as an instructor at Mount Union College, Ohio. After this, however, he turned to full-time painting, moving to Cleveland, where he opened a studio. In 1877 he went to Paris, studied under the eminent painter Bouguereau, and "received the attention of many distinguished artists and lovers of art in the great French capital." [13]

Returning from Paris to Cleveland, he re-opened his studio and became a professor at the Academy of Fine Arts there. From 1887 to 1898 he lived in New York, occupying a studio in the Carnegie Building. Although his fame swept back to his home state there is no record of his having visited Indiana again. In 1898 he left on his second trip to Paris on the *Burgoyne,* but the ill-fated ship sank on July 4, taking with it the artist and his two daughters.

Evans was christened David Scott, and his earliest canvases bear the signatures "D. S. Evans" or "D. Scott Evans." After his first trip to Paris he adopted "De Scott" as his first name, and he soon became known by it throughout the country.

Only four of his early Indiana canvases are now known: a portrait of Joshua Smithson (for whom Smithson College was named), painted at Logansport in 1872 and now in the possession of the Switzerland County Historical Society, Vevay; a portrait of Dr. George R. Chitwood, painted about 1870 (pl. 55), either at Liberty or Connersville, now owned by William H. Chitwood, of Indianapolis; and portraits of Francis Harwood and his wife Margaret, painted at Logansport between 1872 and 1875, owned for sometime by Louise Elliott. No landscapes or "ideal" pictures from his first period have come to light, which suggests that he did not attempt genre subjects, for which he later received high praise, until he removed to Cleveland and New York. There is little indication in those stern and rigid Indiana portraits of the fluent and colorful execution of his later work. [14]

Regarding the other Logansport artists of the 1870's whose names were mentioned above, we have scarcely any information.

Jerome McLean was here from 1873 to 1875. The only painting known to be by his hand is a portrait of Joseph Seiter, now owned by Victor E. Seiter of this city. It is flat and simple in style, suggesting that the painter had little, if any, formal training.

Jacob Ackerman was at Logansport during the same period, according to historian Powell,[15] with a studio in Dolan's Opera House where he both painted and taught art students. Portraits were his speciality but no work of his has survived, so far as we know. He may be the same Ackerman who painted in Lafayette the portraits of Stanis Barnhart and his wife, owned by Mary Barnhart, of Attica.

Robert Swaim (sometimes written Swain) is said to have come to Logansport from Chicago, but whether he was a native of the latter city or only a temporary resident has not been determined. He was a very competent painter, judging by his study in oil of Joseph Gammon Barron, son of Joseph Barron the Indian interpreter. It is a small oval canvas, signed and dated 1878, now in the possession of Mrs. H. H. Walker, Shelbyville. Swaim evidently left Logansport about 1880, returning to Chicago. The last appearance of his name in the city directories there (he was classified as a landscape painter) was in 1886. When and where he died is not known.

William J. Potter, one of the most obscure of the early Logansport artists, is known to us only through the publication of his name in the Indiana state directory of 1868. His classification as a landscape painter indicates that he was carrying on the tradition started in this region by George Winter and given additional stimulus by George Adams and John Forgy, adding his part to the movement that made Logansport an active center of landscape painting in the latter part of the century. Potter's ability as a landscapist will not be known until some of his work is found. He is not to be confused with a later American painter with the same name who was born at Bellport, Pennsylvania, in 1883.

According to historian W. Swift Wright, the painter Max Klepper (Wright misspelled it "Keppler") was a native of Logansport and his tutor in art was Robert Swaim.[16] Klepper's age is not known, but evidently he regarded himself as having reached technical maturity by 1877, because his name appeared that year in the local city directory as an artist. The following year he was among the half-dozen local painters who showed their work in the first important exhibition held in Logansport, under the auspices of the Presbyterian Church. He was apparently in Logansport for another two or three years, specializing in landscapes, a number of which are still in Logansport homes. Ambitious to become an illustrator and realizing the necessity of establishing himself in a large city, he went to New York. There he made illustrations and caricatures for various national publications, including *Puck* and *Harper's Weekly*.

Two women painters worked in Logansport in the seventies, swelling the little art colony on the Wabash and competing for patronage among the more affluent of the town's citizens. They were Lotta Guffin, a resident of Indianapolis, and Mary Carter Davis, a native of England. Mrs. Guffin, regarding whom more will be said in the section on Indianapolis, was a friend of Horace Biddle, Logansport's distinguished citizen and patron of the arts (Biddle was also a close friend of George Winter during the latter's residence at Logansport and was the owner of several of Winter's paintings, including a set of watercolor views of Biddle's Island).[17] Lotta Guffin painted a portrait of Horace Biddle that until recently was in the home of the late Eva Peters Reynolds. It is the only canvas of hers now known to have been made in Logansport.

Mary Carter Davis (christened Maria Ann Theresa Carter) was born at Preston, England, the daughter of an expert stained-glass artist. The Carter family, several members of which were glass glaziers or church decorators, came to America in 1848 and set up business in Cleveland, Ohio. The following year Mary was married to John Samuel Davis, of Philadelphia, and after making their home in Wisconsin for several years the Davises moved to Logansport. That was in 1865. Her husband's failing health forced her to turn more actively to portrait painting as a means of supporting the family, and later her income was increased by taking up commercial photography. She also had a few opportunities to carry out commissions in the field for which she was originally trained, namely, church decorating. She made the *Stations of the Cross* for the old St. Bridget's Church at Logansport and may have designed windows for other churches in this area. In the mid-1880's, after her husband's death, she went to Cleveland to paint and glaze figures for windows that the Carter-Davis Company was making for churches in various cities. Sometime later she moved to Kansas City, where she and her daughter, Mary Angela, had a portrait studio and where she continued painting until the close of her life.[18]

A number of paintings by Mary Carter Davis are still to be found in Cass County, among them the portrait of George Bevan, owned by Winifred Bevan, a carefully made likeness of Sophronia Murphy, formerly owned by Louise Elliott, and canvases owned by Mrs. Addie Eldridge and Mrs. Harry Baum, of Delphi. They were all painted in the seventies while she was living in Logansport. There is nothing that distinguishes her work when compared to that of her contemporaries. The portraits are faithful delineations of the subjects, without vitality or color, and appear to be based on photographs rather than living models.

In the 1880's an increasing number of artists contributed to Logansport's artistic enterprises, some as temporary visitors, others as residents. Among them were Joseph Mattes, Mary MacDonald and her sister Margaret MacDonald Pullman, Wils Berry, James H. Newport, and Charles E. Holbruner. But as their mature work was done toward the close of the decade and into the 1890's, they appear too late for more than a brief mention. However, Wils Berry (Wilson Read Berry) was so conspicuous a figure, and so long a resident here, that something more should be said about him. Born and reared at Logansport, he attended Smithson College, but evidently had no instruction in painting during that time. If he knew the artist De Scott Evans, or studied under him when the latter was at Logansport (1872–1875), no reference to their meeting has been found. His art career began by his painting of circus wagons. Then he turned to landscapes and toured different parts of this country and Canada, making drawings for firms that published county atlases. He also made a few portraits, figure compositions, and sketches of local subjects (pl. 56). His last years were spent in the old Horace Biddle house on Biddle's Island, and here he died in 1928, surrounded by his pictures and his small family.

III

Lafayette, seat of Tippecanoe County and a thriving river and canal town in its early days, was the home of several painters at different times, most of whom have already been introduced to the reader. Its founder, William Digby—who purchased the site for $1.25 an acre— became the subject of one of George Winter's most ambitious compositions (frontispiece), a work that now serves to commemorate two of Lafayette's famous early citizens: its founding father and its best-known artist.

Preceding Winter by about two years, Jacob Hegler (recently of Fort Wayne) reached Lafayette in the fall of 1849, becoming the town's first important painter. His arrival was made known to local residents by the customary announcement in the town's newspaper, in which he stated that he was prepared to paint, in addition to his usual studies from life, "portraits from good daguerreotypes and also from corpses if called upon immediately after death." [19] His room, according to the announcements, was in R. S. Ford's building above T. S. Cox's Stove Establishment. How long Hegler remained has not been determined, but on the evidence of the portraits he made of Dr. Turner Welch and his wife, which now hang in the Tippecanoe County Historical Museum, he was still here in 1853. He probably left soon afterward, going on down the river to Attica, where he spent the remaining two or three years of his life. The Welch portraits are the only known canvases by him in Lafayette, but he must have accomplished a good deal of work during those four years, and, in all probability, further research will bring more to light.

Arriving in 1851 from Logansport, George Winter soon became established in Lafayette, and quickly won the respect and affection of the citizens. Not only the quality of his work but his personality and pleasing disposition made him highly esteemed. At Lafayette he continued his output of landscapes and portraits, and conceived the idea of an annual raffle of his work in order to increase his income. He sold "chances" at one or two dollars each, placed a selection of his paintings on exhibition—totaling in value the amount realized from the sale of the chances—then held a drawing of numbers at a specified time. These raffles were held at various other places in the state and even as far away as Cincinnati and Toledo, and through them he distributed hundreds of his landscapes and romantic, idealized compositions. The landscapes were predominantly Wabash River views. Occasionally he had an opportunity to exhibit his paintings with other artists in Indianapolis and Cincinnati, which helped to make his name better known.

One of Winter's first projects to attract more than local interest was a series of oil paintings made in 1840 depicting different areas of the Tippecanoe battleground near Lafayette. The *State Journal* in 1851 gave one of the scenes its first public announcement when it reported:

"Mr. George Winter, an artist from Lafayette, was here [Indianapolis] a few days ago. His view of Tippecanoe Battle Ground, in the State Library is much admired, and proves him to be a skillful and talented artist." [20] This may be the canvas now owned by the Indiana Historical Society.

Although he was more successful, financially, with his landscapes, Winter painted a number of portraits in Lafayette. Perhaps the most notable of them is the large canvas of William Digby, mentioned above, representing the founder of the town in a landscape setting with the river in the distance; another is the more conventional study of John Purdue, for whom Purdue University was named. The former is owned by the Wells Memorial Library, the latter by Cable G. Ball, the artist's great-grandson. Some of his other Lafayette portraits are of Edward Reynolds and his wife Sarah, owned by Mrs. W. V. Stewart; Rebekah Tucker Squier, owned by Cable G. Ball; and Mary Canniff Wagstaff, owned by George B. Thompson. The largest single collection of the artist's work is still in the possession of Cable Ball, much of which has been lent by him to the Tippecanoe County Historical Society for the pleasure of visitors to the museum.

George Winter spent the remainder of his life in Lafayette surrounded by his family and friends. His death occurred here in 1876 when he had reached the age of sixty-six.

48. J. Ottis Adams: Portrait of
Sarah Heinsohn
Courtesy of Mrs. Robert H.
Hartley, Muncie (page 106)

49. Nelson Perry Adams: Landscape With Cows
Courtesy of Ball State Teachers College Art Gallery, Muncie (page 107)

50. Horace Rockwell: The Samuel Hanna Family
Courtesy of the Fort Wayne Art Museum (page 110)

51. R. B. Crafft: Portrait of
Robert Filson
    Courtesy of the Allen County-
    Fort Wayne Historical Museum,
    Fort Wayne (page 111)

52. Joseph H. Dille: Portrait of
Thomas W. Swinney
    Courtesy of the Allen County-
    Fort Wayne Historical Museum,
    Fort Wayne (page 114)

53. George Winter: Portrait of
Joseph Barron
Courtesy of Cable G. Ball,
Lafayette (page 116)

54. (below) George Winter:
Gathering of Indians
Courtesy of Eli Lilly,
Indianapolis (page 116)

Of the other artists known to have worked at Lafayette in the nineteenth century, two have already been discussed in previous sections of this history. Jacob Ackerman was reported as having been here in 1873 or 1874, the evidence of his sojourn being in the form of the portraits he painted of Stanis Barnhart and his wife, mentioned earlier. Henry Dousa is known to have lived in Lafayette before going to New Castle, and while a number of references to him have been uncovered nothing by his hand is known today. As stated earlier, his speciality was prize-winning cattle and horses, and it is reasonable to assume that his canvases adorn many walls of farmhouses in Tippecanoe County.

The remaining painters associated with Lafayette are even hazier personalities. The Lafayette city directory of 1873–1874 carried the name of Jacob Wakeman as an artist, but what type of work he did, or what he accomplished here, has not been discovered; Mrs. William Turner has a landscape bearing the signature H. A. Davis, and the date 1874, which might have been painted in Lafayette, but no information about the artist has been found; and in a number of homes there hang today portraits of ancestors, presumably painted here, whose authors are yet to be identified.

Attica, to which references have already been made in telling of Jacob Hegler's wanderings, was one of the early settlements that grew into a moderately prosperous town when the Wabash and Erie Canal reached this area in the late 1840's. Not only does its name suggest classical refinement, but many of its early houses, reflecting the Greek Revival style, indicate that the citizens tried to live up to the appellation in matters of architecture.

Two or three years before Hegler came and not long after the opening of the canal, there arrived in Attica a young man in his middle twenties named Barton S. Hays, who became recognized as a skillful painter not only here but also in Indianapolis. He was born in Greenville, Darke County, Ohio, in 1826, one of the six children of James Hays. Several members of the family moved west from Ohio, settling in Fountain and Montgomery counties, Indiana, around the year 1850 or 1851.

According to historian Jacob P. Dunn, Barton's early zeal for artistic expression brought him numerous rebukes from his parents for wasting his time sketching on fences, buildings, and other flat surfaces,[21] but that did not divert him from the goal he had set for himself. Although self-taught, so far as we know, his pertinacity and industry soon enabled him to compete with established painters in the region.

Records of his rudimentary stage as an artist exist in the form of two paintings owned by Mrs. Ira H. Englehart, of Brazil, Indiana: the Hays's homestead at Greenville, and a portrait of the artist's father, James Hays. The former was undoubtedly painted in Ohio and its timidity of workmanship suggests a youthful effort. Two landscapes, one apparently representing a farmer bartering for a horse and the other an expanse of fields with "farm hands" in the background, were also products of his early days, judging by the subject matter and style. They are owned now by Catherine Martin, of Crawfordsville.

Barton arrived at Pleasant Hill (now Wingate) in Montgomery County soon after 1850. It is believed that his first sitters were his relatives, and that after successfully painting them he obtained other orders in the region. His brother Samuel, who accompanied him to Montgomery County, was also an artist and may have made portraits in this area. However, Samuel's stay was short. He moved to Minneapolis at an early date and remained there the rest of his life.[22]

Barton's most ambitious undertaking at that time was a large panorama depicting scenes from *Uncle Tom's Cabin* which evidently met with considerable success. It led to a second equally monumental effort, but with the waning of popularity in panoramas the artist returned to easel pictures, turning out fruit pieces, cattle subjects, landscapes, and portraits.

A canvas portraying Dr. Lewis D. Lyons, of Attica (pl. 57), formerly owned by Minnie Parker but now in the John Herron Art Museum, and another of Daniel Kelsey Hays, owned by the late Mrs. William B. Reed, are typical of the work he did in and around Attica during his first years in Indiana. The simple direct manner in which they have been painted, combined with firm, if not fluent, brush work, gives them that forthright character that is evident in the best early American products.

Sometime after completing these, Hays was commissioned to paint members of the McClure and McKinney families southeast of Newtown, Fountain County. The oil portrait of James McClure, pioneer settler here, appears to have been made from a small water-color sketch owned by Mrs. J. H. Stahl. The oil is in the home of James McClure. Portraits of James McClure and his bride Phoebe Dagger McClure, formerly owned by Frank George, are now in the Chicago home of Arthur McClure. Mrs. J. H. Stahl has, in addition to the water-color sketch, an oil of Eleanor McClure McKinney, also by Hays.

The artist married Ellen Houser, presumably of Greenville, in 1846. About four years later she died, leaving two daughters, Julia and Martha, for the young husband to rear. During the next twenty years he remained a widower; then, on one of his sketching trips in southwestern Ohio, he met Amy Jane Woodmansee, of Hamilton, widow of Daniel Elliott, and married her in 1866.[23]

The family lived in Indianapolis from 1858 until 1882 when they removed to Minneapolis where the artist continued his work with success until his death in 1914. But Barton Hays returned to Fountain County many times to visit relatives and to paint portraits. Three canvases by him are in Covington today, two dated 1880, the third, 1881. The earlier ones, portraying Lewis Haines and Angelica Ransom Haines, are owned by Mrs. Gertrude Madigan; the other is a portrait of America Enseba Sewell, wife of William Sewell, and is in the home of Mrs. Julia Spinning.

The artist's parents lived at Covington a number of years. His father, James Hays, died here in 1857 and was buried in the old Covington cemetery. His portrait, a medallion relief, carved by his son Barton, is on the face of his gravestone.

In 1879 Barton Hays made a trip to Fairmont, Illinois, where he painted the portraits of James M. Dougherty, owner of the Centennial Hotel, and his wife; Mr. and Mrs. William Sandusky and their daughter; as well as James Sconce and his wife. The first two are owned by Maud Dougherty and the last are in the homes of descendants in or near Indianola, Illinois.

As the story of Barton Hays's activity at Indianapolis is told in the chapter dealing with the artists of the capital city, the work that constituted his late Indiana period is discussed there.

Jacob Hegler, who came to Attica around 1854, carried on a rather brisk business here and in the neighboring towns until his untimely death in 1856 at the age of forty-four. Several of his portraits of that period are known, and undoubtedly others will come to light as search for them continues. The most charming is that of Mary Alice Lyons (pl. 58), daughter of Dr. Lewis D. Lyons (whom Hays painted), accompanied by her dog, and pictured in an outdoor setting. For many years, following the death of Dr. Lyons and his daughter, the painting was affectionately cared for by Minnie Parker, and it has now passed into the collection of the John Herron Art Museum.

One of Hegler's best patrons, apparently, was William Kent, of the neighboring town of Williamsport. For him the artist painted four canvases: a large composition portraying William Kent with his children William and Mary, dated 1856; a second, of William; and companion portraits of Elisha Hitchens and Mary Kent Hitchens. They are still in the Kent home at Williamsport.

A charming study of Robert Milford as a boy, painted by Hegler, has been in Indianapolis a number of years in the home of Mrs. Samuel E. Perkins and is now in the Children's Museum there. The subject was a brother of Mrs. Benjamin Hegler, daughter-in-law of the painter. The portrait of the artist's wife, Julia Ann Richards, is owned by a grandson, Willoughby R. Hegler, of Fijole, Texas; the latter also has a painting of a raft on the Ohio River by his grandfather, the only known outdoor composition by Hegler.

Much of Hegler's time between 1854 and 1856 was spent on the farm of William Johnson in the southeastern part of Benton County, between Attica and Fowler, and for his patron the artist painted three canvases, each portraying two members of the Johnson family—William Johnson with his daughter Belle, and Margaret Finch Johnson with her son James, which are owned by W. J. Sheetz, of Benton County; and the charming composition of the sisters Nancy and Harriet Johnson, in pink dresses and holding flowers in their hands, which is owned by Mrs. W. E. Tubbs, of Fowler.

It appears that there were no artists in Attica for a decade or more after the death of Hegler and the departure of Hays for Indianapolis. Wandering painters may have stopped off, but if so, no one bothered to record or remember the occasions.

The third painter to be identified with the town was Virginia Wilson Todd, wife of Clayton Todd, a native of Pennsylvania. She was born at Beallsville in 1851, educated at the Pittsburgh Female Seminary and at the Springfield (Ohio) Female Academy, where she presumably got some instruction in drawing and painting. After making her home at Attica, she visited Indianapolis to study under Jacob Cox, the city's leading painter. Later, she and her family moved to Urbana, Illinois, where her death occurred in 1930.

While not a masterful technician, Virginia Todd produced some good portraits, mostly of members of her family. That of her grandmother, painted in Attica in the 1870's, is in the home of Will B. Schermerhorn here; likenesses of other relatives are owned by W. J. De Val, of Lebanon, Indiana, and Elizabeth Todd, of Athens, Georgia.

Covington, already mentioned in connection with Barton Hays's work, did not attract many painters in the early years of its growth, if we can judge by existing records. In fact, only one painter is known to have worked here besides Hays: a man named William S. Segar.

The city in which Segar was born has not been identified, but it was somewhere in the state of New York, and the year was 1823. He did not come to Covington until he was about fifty-five years old, so presumably he painted rather extensively in the eastern states before coming west. He moved to Covington in 1878 in order to be with a son who was a telegraph operator here, and remained until his death in 1887. He interrupted his residence at Covington in 1882 by a visit to Chicago, where he stayed about a year.

Only one painting by his hand is now known in Covington: a portrait of Michael Mayer, owned by the sitter's son. It is an academic and conscientious piece of work, literal in its delineation of features, and revealing a professional portrait painter's approach. As Segar was there for ten years it is reasonable to assume that many more of his canvases are in the town or surrounding region.

IV

Leaving the valley of the Wabash and turning east toward the center of the state, our attention is drawn to Crawfordsville, seat of Montgomery County and of Wabash College. The town's high regard for academic and cultural attainments won for it the name "Hoosier Athens," and it became the home of several distinguished scholars and statesmen. It has also had its share of itinerant and resident painters.

The most prominent of the latter was Lew Wallace, whose fame rested, of course, upon his achievements as a soldier and author rather than his skill as a painter. He was born at Brookville in 1827 and taken to Indianapolis in 1837 when his father was elected governor. There his burning desire to become an artist manifested itself and, against his father's wishes, he took every opportunity to grasp the technicalities of painting and to put his rudimentary skill into practice. In his autobiography he speaks of his earliest efforts and tells of his first paints and his first encouragement,[24] the essence of which is included in the chapter dealing with art activities in Indianapolis.

After his academic education Wallace studied law, but he was interrupted by the Mexican War. A period of legal practice followed the war only to be interrupted again by the Civil War. If, during those years, he made any attempts to draw or paint we have no record of them. After distinguishing himself in the army and attaining the rank of general, he returned to civilian life, made his home at Crawfordsville, practiced law, wrote, and occasionally painted pictures. He followed a diplomatic career for a few years after 1878, when he was appointed governor of New Mexico, and later U. S. minister to Turkey. He died at Crawfordsville in 1905.

Most of Lew Wallace's art work was done in the late sixties and seventies. Since no effort has been made to compile a chronological list of his drawings and paintings, dates of most of his pictures are matters of conjecture. His most important works in the field of portraiture are the likenesses of Isaac C. Elston, painted about 1866, and that of Henry Smith Lane, painted about 1875 (pl. 59). The former is owned by Isaac C. Elston, Jr., Crawfordsville, and the latter is in

Lane Place here. Wallace exhibited the Lane portrait at Indianapolis in the First Quarterly Exhibition held by the Indiana Art Association in 1878.

In the same exhibition there appeared one of his historical compositions based on a Civil War incident, entitled *Over the Dead Line*. A soldier, held prisoner in a stockade at Andersonville, is shot by the guard as he crawls, suffering from thirst, toward a stream that runs through the enclosure. The painting was presented to the G.A.R. Chapter of Terre Haute.

Another historical subject of large dimensions by the same hand is *The Conspiracy*, showing a group of men at a secret meeting place, plotting the murder of Lincoln. As John D. Forbes observed in his essay on Lew Wallace in the *Indiana Magazine of History*, "The romantic tendency can also be noted in Wallace's painting of the conspirators plotting the assassination of Lincoln. The conspirators are shown in a range of poses from furtive to poetic before a classical ruin, a favorite stage property of the age which revolted against the logic and reason of classicism." [25] As a member of the court that tried the Lincoln conspirators, Wallace obtained material firsthand for the composition, and made sketches of some of the characters in the courtroom; some of the drawings are now preserved in the library of the Indiana Historical Society, together with several portrait sketches and scenes in Constantinople. The Lew Wallace Study at Crawfordsville has, in addition to this painting, two landscapes in oil of scenes along the Kankakee River and some pencil drawings, which add considerably to our understanding of Wallace's artistic ability.

Most publicized of his paintings was one based on an allegorical theme and entitled *Reluctant Love*. It was shown in Lieber's Art Emporium at Indianapolis in 1875, where it caught the attention of the city's art critic, Alois Sinks. The picture depicted a young woman on her knees before a purple-winged Cupid, and several things about it touched the sensibilities of the critic, leading him to write a long and lively essay:

Gen. Lew Wallace, the author of the Fair God, is a candidate for the honors of the easel—but as long as his chances for success rest on such a specimen of work as that on exhibition at Lieber's there will be little to hope for. The idea of the picture—or let us say rather the idea that gave rise to the picture—is not without possibilities of much merit but the subject has been treated so often and buried beneath such an Olympian of paint that no one short of a second Rubens or Reynolds could hope to ever exhume and present it in attractive shape. We will not undertake to say that the General's conception of purple wings for his Cupid is out of place —for aught we know they are yellow—but we do undertake to say that the little imp appears at a great disadvantage with them when in juxtaposition to the colors surrounding him in the picture.[26]

Sinks then proceeded to call attention to the anatomy, contours, and facial expression of the girl, pronouncing them "palpably false and absurd," and closing his admonition with a suggestion that Lew Wallace would do better by going to nature for his models: "Painted Cupids are ridiculous at best. If the General would employ his time and talents in making a study of something in nature . . . we predict that the result would redound in his honor and be a source of real gratification to his friends."

A writer on the competing newspaper, *The Indianapolis Journal,* took occasion to interview Wallace to get the latter's story of how he happened to paint the picture. He then wrote an article of rebuttal in which he pointed out that Wallace had good authority for his treatment of the theme (particularly, the purple wings) since it was based on lines in Milton's *Paradise Lost:*

> Here Love his golden shafts employs, here lights
> His constant lamp, and waves his purple wings.
> Reigns here and revels.

"As Mr. Milton is generally considered an undisputed authority on mythology," continued the writer on the *Journal,* "the critic will have to step down."

But stepping down was the last thing the intrepid Sinks intended to do. In a later issue of his paper he published another long discourse. News of the battle of the critics reached other cities and at least two newspapers came to the defense of Lew Wallace's champion: the *St. Louis Republican* and the *New York Sun.* But still the *Saturday Her-*

ald's spokesman in art matters held his ground. A few weeks later he reiterated his charges, called attention to the fact that those who had stepped out in defense of the General had not seen the painting (referring to the out-of-town critics), and finished his article by saying: "In conclusion, had we known that General Wallace did not send his picture here for public exhibition, we should have said nothing about it. In the history of the late war, by the Count of Paris, he is mentioned honorably as a brave soldier; as a writer his 'Fair God' entitles him to Literary distinction; and we are certain that he has nowhere a friend who would more gladly record his success as a painter than the writer." That seems to have brought the controversy to a close.

The two canvases mentioned above as being in the First Quarterly Exhibition of 1878 were, so far as we know, the last of Wallace's artistic efforts shown to the public and probably the last serious paintings he made. While serving as U.S. ambassador to Turkey he made a number of drawings and sketches but none seems to have been carried to a finished state.

A second Crawfordsville painter, whose earlier work in Franklin has already been discussed, was John Nicholson. He arrived at Crawfordsville in April, 1879, with his family, and opened a photography and painting studio, concentrating on the former as clients for oil portraits were few. He spent the remaining years of his life here, dying in 1893 at the age of sixty-eight. Without doubt there are many of his oil-over-photograph portrayals of local citizens in and around Crawfordsville today, and some of the likenesses of former professors of Wabash College, of undetermined authorship, hanging in the library and other buildings, may be Nicholson's work.

A third painter temporarily living in Crawfordsville was Walter Sies, whose activity was touched upon in the chapter dealing with Terre Haute. He probably moved to Crawfordsville with his family in the mid-seventies (his name appears in *Beasley's Crawfordsville Directory* for 1878–1879), pursuing his specialty, carriage and landscape painting. To the historian he is an elusive figure; at present neither his birth nor death dates are known, nor have any of his Crawfordsville accomplishments been found.

A contemporary of Sies, also listed in the local directory, was W. D. Stillwell, sign painter. As he probably aspired to no higher form of painting, and as the products of his specialized skill have long since disappeared, he will receive only this passing notice.

Greencastle, about twenty-five miles south of Crawfordsville and the seat of De Pauw University, enjoyed some art activity in former years as attested by paintings (mostly portraits) in private houses and in the halls of the university. While some await the identification of authors, other canvases are by known painters.

One name associated with Greencastle is William S. Shackleford, whose work in the portrait field is demonstrated by two examples: the likeness of Isaac Reed, the artist's father-in-law, painted about 1845, and that of George Whitfield Reed, Isaac's son, which was painted in 1862. They are owned by Albert E. Williams here. Whether the portraits were made in Indiana or in Kentucky is uncertain. Shackleford was a Kentucky artist who lived for some years at Lexington, where he received instruction in painting from Matthew Jouett. Later he worked in Tennessee.[27] There is no record of his having visited Crawfordsville, and as the subjects of his canvases here were relatives of his he may have painted them in the South.

The artist most closely associated with Greencastle was Henry A. Mills, dean of the art department at De Pauw University from 1885 to 1894. His residence here was, in date, too late for this chronicle, but a summary of his career may be of interest. He was born at Bankers, Michigan, in 1848. Where he was educated and where he received his instruction in art have not been learned; in addition to teaching, he became proficient in both landscape and portrait painting. During his residence at De Pauw he painted the portraits of Reuben Andrus, Alexander Martin, and John P. D. John which are in the university's chapel. He also sent pictures to the exhibitions held by the Art Association of Indianapolis in 1891 and 1892. After leaving Greencastle, Mills became director of the school of art at Cornell College, Mount Vernon, Iowa, and died at Mount Vernon in 1921.

Mention was made earlier in this book of the portrait of Robert R. Roberts which hangs in the chapel at De Pauw University, believed to be the work of Augustus Von Smith of Vincennes. It was painted in 1841 or 1842 upon request of the Indiana Conference of the Methodist Church, meeting at Terre Haute in October, 1841, a collection having been taken at the conference to defray the expense of portraying the "venerable and beloved Superintendent."[28] Both the circumstance of the undertaking and the style of work points to Von Smith of Vincennes as the author, and it could have been painted either at Terre Haute or Vincennes. Its narrow escape from destruction by fire, as it hung in one of the university buildings, has already been mentioned; it was originally a full-length canvas but only the head and shoulders remain.

The only other artist who worked at Greencastle, to the best of our knowledge, was Theodore C. Steele, regarding whom we will have more to say in a later chapter. He visited here a number of times between 1878 and 1880 when he was an established painter in Indianapolis, and most of the portraits that he painted are still in the homes of descendants of the original sitters. Among them are the likenesses of Andrew and Elizabeth Lockridge, and of their three sons, Albert, Alexander, and Simpson (the artist showed the last three canvases at the 1878 exhibition of the Indiana Art Association); likenesses of Alexander Bryan and his wife Susan, and also of A. S. Farrow and his wife, the last based on photographs. The Bryan portraits, owned by Mrs. Elizabeth Hamrick, were painted on a farm south of Greencastle, and the artist received room and board for two weeks and some farm produce as payment for them.

The remaining painters who are known to have worked in the central part of the state (outside Indianapolis) were limited not only in their production but in their technical skill as well. Daniel Roberts painted portraits at Chesterfield, but whether or not he was a resident of the town has not been established. Three of his products are owned by Mrs. Flora Millspaugh here. They portray her parents and a group of three children, and the paint seems to have been applied over large photographic prints.

A self-taught painter associated with the towns of Cicero, Sheridan, and Noblesville, was Granville Bishop. Uncle Billy, as he was called, was a cripple. Incapable of doing any manual labor but finding that he had a natural aptitude for drawing, he turned to art and carried on a rather lively business with his landscapes, portraits in oil and crayon, store signs, and theatrical scenery. For several years one of his landscapes has attracted the attention of visitors to the State Museum in Indianapolis; a characteristic example of his composite scenes (arranged from other pictures and from his imagination) is owned by Mrs. R. R. Williamson, of Sheridan; and the artist's son L. O. Bishop, living at Westfield, has a number of his landscapes. By means of his varied talents, including the practice and teaching of penmanship, Bishop was able to support comfortably his family of five. Although his home was for many years at Noblesville he worked in different communities between here and Peru.

V

Due to geographical location and economic development, the most northern of Indiana's cities—Elkhart, South Bend, La Porte, and others —had, in the early years, little or no direct contact with those south of the Wabash River. Their history is linked with the Great Lakes. When the region was made available to American homesteaders it was settled by families from the East, traveling across northern Ohio and having little or no intercourse with the early settlers to the south. The towns mentioned became the principal stations on an important overland route that linked the East with the Northwest, and thus they rapidly became prosperous communities.

With the pioneer merchants and farmers came the painters. Their methods did not differ from those of artists previously discussed in these pages nor were their accomplishments more notable. They were equally migratory in their habits, but they apparently confined their activities to the territory immediately below the Great Lakes, remaining detached from, and probably ignorant of, similar enterprises in the central and southern sectors of the state.

The earliest known painting made in that northern belt is a scene in Elkhart County with a cabin in the foreground and two travelers negotiating for the purchase of sacksee (dried venison) from some

Potowatomi Indians. A long inscription below the picture, describing the incident, is followed by the artist's name, J. Heed, and the date, 1837. Unfortunately nothing more is known of Heed's activity either in Indiana or elsewhere. The painting, owned by the Chicago Historical Society, is not the work of an accomplished technician; it is probably the work of an amateur who made it as a pictorial record of an adventurous trip.

Goshen, seat of Elkhart County, preserves in its historical museum what is probably the first work of a resident painter. It is a self-portrait by James Mayfield. He appears as an attractive auburn-haired young man in a long black cloak. A window at the rear of the room in which he painted himself offers a view of a small town, perhaps Goshen. The style of work suggests that it was made about 1840, and that the artist was not overly adept in the technique of oil painting, although the simplicity of rendering and the choice of colors are pleasing. Painting, for Mayfield, was merely an avocation. He was a successful businessman, and his interest in civic affairs is commemorated by a park in Goshen bearing his name.

The next painter known to have worked in that region was Adolphus Van Sickle. He was a professional portraitist active in communities of northern Indiana from the late 1840's to the early 1870's. At Goshen he painted the portraits of Sarah Thomas, wife of William Thomas, and her sister Mrs. Joseph H. Defrees. They are signed and dated 1848 on the backs of the canvases. Mrs. George A. Riley, of South Bend, and Donald Defrees, of Winnetka, Illinois, now have the pictures. The work is competent, stolid, unadorned in style, and firm in drawing. Van Sickle was not a facile painter, but he possessed enough natural ability to produce work of strength and character.

Unfortunately we know nothing of his life. He probably came from the East, and after spending about twenty-five years in northern Indiana left for new fields of activity, or died in obscurity in this region. His work at South Bend and La Porte will be discussed later.

The third artist of Goshen, about whom we know the most, was Joseph H. Dille. A summary of his enterprising career has already been made in the section dealing with Fort Wayne, where he spent many years after leaving Goshen. He was in Goshen for about eight years, from 1857 to 1865, during which time he married Libby Crane, daughter of Oliver P. Crane, founder of the town. Dille supported himself and his growing family by the products of his brush, painting portraits, fruit and animal subjects, and scenery for the Thalia Theater. A large political banner, six by seven feet, bearing the likenesses of Abraham Lincoln, Hannibal Hamlin, and Henry S. Lane, was painted by him in 1860 upon order of the Wideawakes, the Republican Marching Club, which used it in the political rally that year.[29] It was largely a labor of love as Dille was an ardent member of the organization. The banner is preserved in the Elkhart County Courthouse.

A number of Dille's portraits are probably in homes of the older families here; among those known to the author is that of James Barnes, dated 1866, which hangs in the town's historical museum. It is well painted, and is a credit to the man who had neither formal training nor an opportunity to study the work of accomplished artists. He had hoped for some technical training abroad but it is reported that his health prevented his making a voyage to Europe.

In this connection it is of interest to learn that one of Dille's early associates was Alexander Wyant, who became one of America's leading landscape painters. In a letter written many years later to the editor of the *Goshen Daily News–Times,* recounting his early activities, Dille wrote in part: "But showing how little the doctors know of one's chances for long life, here is a case. I took with me to Goshen a large, stout young man as a pupil in painting in 1857. A Mr. Wyant by name. . . . He went to Europe, studied there but two years, returned to New York, became one of our best American landscape painters and, I am told got large prices for his paintings—his promise of long life ended 17 years ago." [30]

Wyant's original home was in Ohio. Presumably he did not remain long in Goshen, because his ambition to get ahead in the field of painting took him to Cincinnati and then to New York. Dille's letter is the only known reference to his sojourn in Indiana.

South Bend traces its history back to a meeting held by La Salle with certain chiefs of the Miami on this site in 1681, although the famous explorer is said to have set foot here two years before in making a portage from the St. Joseph River to the Kankakee on his journey into the Illinois country. If artists or cartographers accompanied him, or followed the *voyageurs* and *coureurs* into that area during the following century, no evidences of their visits have come down to us.

It is the period following the establishment of South Bend as an American community, and its cultural development in the nineteenth century, that concerns us here. The founder was Alexis Coquillard, an energetic promoter, who, with his father-in-law, Francis Comparet, purchased the agency of the American Fur Company for that region in 1823, thus becoming a leading figure in the new settlement.

Both names, Coquillard and Comparet, are conspicuous in the early annals of St. Joseph County, and, as was also true of the founders of several other Indiana communities, their names are linked with the first artistic enterprises here. It will be recalled that our survey of paintings at Fort Wayne mentioned portraits of Francis Comparet and his wife, believed to be the work of Rockwell and to date around 1847. Both families—Coquillard and Comparet—lived at Fort Wayne in the first years of the 1820's, moving to South Bend in 1823. The Comparet likenesses could have been painted either here or at Fort Wayne.

Alexis Coquillard sat for his portrait before the easel of J. H. Van Favoren in 1847 (pl. 60), according to the signature and date on the canvas. This is a new name in the annals of Indiana art, and up to this time no records have been found that throw any light on the career of Van Favoren. His only known work is this portrait of Coquillard. The painter has represented his patron as an astute, self-assured man, seated beside a table in a richly decorated room. The technique is not very adept but the drawing is clear and concise and the coloring is attractive. The manner of painting suggests that, while Van Favoren was an experienced portraitist, he had acquired his knowledge of the craft largely by self-training and observation rather than by apprenticeship or studio instruction. The portrait is now preserved in the art gallery of the University of Notre Dame.

Preceding Van Favoren's visit here was that of A. Merine, who is equally obscure as a person. His presence was made known to the small settlement through an announcement inserted in the *South Bend Free Press* on the last day of the year 1841. How long he remained is not known, nor is there any certainty that he got any orders. None of the portraits now in the city bears his name, and no record of his activity has appeared in any other part of Indiana. If he continued to practice as a professional portraitist he must have moved to a neighboring state.

The next artist known to have worked in the northern communities was Adolphus Van Sickle. As was noted above, on the evidence of two signed and dated portraits, he was at Goshen in 1848 and in South Bend at about the same time. Soon after he appeared in La Porte. For the next decade or more his movements are uncharted, but then he reappeared at South Bend equipped with the paraphernalia of the new art, photography, and prepared to take likenesses with either brushes and paint or the camera. According to the state and city directories he remained in South Bend from 1868 to 1874. Nothing made by him during those years has been identified, which is surprising in view of the fact that he was here six years and that he usually signed and dated his work.

Curran Swaim, best known of South Bend's resident painters in the years immediately following the Civil War, is a less nebulous figure. He was here between 1856 and 1869, painting portraits and landscapes and enjoying considerable success and popularity. He was born in Randolph County, Virginia, in 1826. While he was still a young man his family moved to Indiana, settling on a farm near Fountain City. There, in addition to farming, his father assisted slaves to escape to northern cities, an important depot of the "underground railway" being at Fountain City.

When about thirty years of age Curran Swaim came to South Bend, accompanying a brother who bought a farm in Green Township. Deciding to be a painter, he went to New York, studied intensively, married Mary Winter, and returned to South Bend to establish himself as a professional artist. Within a few years he was firmly settled in his profession and was earning enough to support his family. Some idea of his standing in the community ten years later can be derived from an article that appeared in the South Bend *Register*, of 1868:

55. D. Scott Evans: Portrait of
Dr. George R. Chitwood
Courtesy of William H.
Chitwood, Indianapolis
(page 119)

56. (below) Wilson Read Berry:
Logansport Street Scene
Courtesy of the Cass County
Historical Society, Logansport
(page 122)

57. Barton S. Hays: Portrait of
Dr. Lewis D. Lyons
John Herron Art Museum,
Indianapolis (page 126)

58. Jacob Hegler: Portrait of
Mary Alice Lyons
John Herron Art Museum,
Indianapolis (page 128)

59. Lew Wallace: Portrait
of Henry Smith Lane

Courtesy of the Montgomery
County Historical Society,
Crawfordsville, and heirs of
Henry Lane Wallace
(page 130)

60. J. H. Van Favoren:
Portrait of Alexis Coquillard
Courtesy of the University Art
Galleries, University of
Notre Dame (page 139)

61. Curran Swaim: Portrait of
Samuel C. Sample
Courtesy of the Northern Indiana
Historical Society, South Bend
(page 141)

62. Adolphus Van Sickle:
Portrait of
Frederick C. King
Courtesy of the LaPorte County
Historical Society, LaPorte
(page 144)

By invitation of Mr. Curran Swaim, we called at his room a few days since to see a portrait of Dr. Ham of this city, to which he had just put the finishing touches. It is an excellent likeness, every feature of the original being faithfully transcribed. The pose of the figure is easy and natural, and the accessories, such as furniture and books, are quite in keeping with the leading object of the composition. With the exception of a faulty foreshortening of the right hand, the whole work cannot be regarded otherwise than a superior production.

The best specimen from Mr. Swaim's easel, for color, is a kit-cat portrait of the late Sol Miller. It is also an admirable likeness, the artist having succeeded in infusing into it all the force and individuality that characterized the original . . . Besides these portraits there are several landscapes which will well pay one to see. A large one, "A Dream of Arcadia," is commendable for study of tree forms and leafage, while the tints are managed with a due regard for harmony of color.[31]

Although the portraits mentioned by the reporter-critic cannot at this time be found, others by Swaim are preserved in homes and public buildings at South Bend. The historical museum has on its walls companion portraits of Reynolds Dunn and his wife Phoebe Tatman, painted about 1856, which are Swaim's earliest known works. A likeness by him of Judge Samuel Sample, also in the museum (pl. 61), and that of Judge Thomas S. Stanfield, owned by Anna H. Stanfield, appear to be at least five years later.

After the middle of the 1860's Swaim apparently became interested in the processes of photography and began to use the photographic print as the foundation of some of his portraits. The likenesses of Thelus Bissell and his wife Ellen, owned by Mrs. Esse Bissell Dakin, are examples of the combined techniques, dating from about 1868.

In 1869 Curran Swaim and his family left South Bend and moved to McHenry County, Illinois, where he continued painting for almost ten years. In 1878 he moved again, that time to Jasper County, Missouri. There he bought a farm and spent the remaining years of his life. He died in 1897.

The *Indiana State Gazetteer and Business Directory* for 1860 and 1861 carried the names Swaim and Clark as partners in a portrait-painting enterprise at South Bend. What Clark's first name was has not been determined, nor have any canvases been found to show his ability or manner of working.

Three other names are associated with South Bend's artistic activities in the last half of the nineteenth century, all of whom were native sons: Heaton, Kotz, and Comparet.

Charles M. Heaton, Jr., was born at South Bend in 1840. What training he had in drawing and painting has not been learned, but a portrait of his mother, painted in 1870, reveals the hand of a capable draughtsman.[32] Later he went to Washington, D. C., maintaining a studio there for many years and specializing in oil portraits and miniatures. About 1895 he gave up professional painting and entered the real estate business at Tacoma Park. It was there that he died in 1921.

Daniel Kotz was born in 1848, received his elementary education at South Bend, and then studied art under Henry F. Spread at Chicago. He returned to South Bend, where he opened a studio and in the latter part of the nineteenth century was the best-known painter in the city. He specialized in landscape painting and much of his work is still in local homes. Later he went to New York and then to New Jersey, continuing his output until his death in 1933.

In the University Art Galleries, University of Notre Dame, there hangs a portrait of Mrs. Alexis Coquillard by Alexis Comparet (or Compera). It is a very competent piece of work and reflects the painter's training in France. He was probably a descendant of Francis Comparet, who was referred to above as a pioneer of Fort Wayne and South Bend. At about the age of eighteen (he was born at South Bend in 1856) Comparet went to Paris and studied under Benjamin Constant. When he returned to South Bend he remained only a short time before finding it necessary to move to Colorado for the sake of his health. Living in Colorado City and Denver, he was inspired by the mountains, which he came to depict in soft, misty tones. His last years were spent at San Diego, California, where his death occurred in 1906.

Comparet never referred to his South Bend origin, preferring to be regarded as a Frenchman. Later he changed the spelling of his name to Compera, presumably to retain the French pronunciation even at the expense of losing the original French spelling.

VI

The first wayfaring painter recorded at La Porte, the next point on our survey, was J. R. Richards. His name appeared among the first artists of Logansport (mentioned by Powell in his *History of Cass County,* as a "painter of some reputation"),[33] but whether he was there before or after his visit to La Porte has not been determined. On the evidence of several advertisements of a John R. Richards in the *La Porte County Whig* in 1838, offering for sale all kinds of dry goods, liquor, soap, and glassware, with the intention of selling out and moving west, we are led to believe (if this was the same man) that he turned from merchandising to painting prior to 1840.

Our first definite information about him as a wielder of paint brushes is derived from the same newspaper in 1844:

PAINTING

I have a room over the store of Newell and Woodson, where I am ready to receive orders for Painting Portraits, Miniatures, Landscapes, Window Shades, Fire Screens, Scenery, Transparencies on Cambric, Glass, &c., Landscapes on the walls of Rooms, Halls, &c., Hall, Stairs and Fire proof Hearth Carpets on heavy Canvas; Landscape, Perspective, Ornamental, Gilt, Shaded and Plain Signs; Doors and inside work, plain or imitation of Oak, Maple, Mahogany, Rosewood and Marble; Perspective drawings of buildings, &c., for Advertisements.

My charge shall be low for all good jobs, and nothing for bad ones. Please give me a call and judge for yourselves.

J. R. Richards.[34]

An artisan with more diverse skills would, in all probability, have been hard to find, and yet Richards was typical of most of the men who worked in the frontier towns. However limited their technical abilities, judged by the usual standards, they were the only people with even a rudimentary knowledge of paints and the manipulation of brushes. And being able to turn from imitative graining of wood to the delineation of human features enabled them to survive in places where economic conditions demanded diversity rather than highly specialized skills. It is unfortunate that nothing by the hand of J. R.

Richards has come to light to reveal his talent as a portrait and landscape painter.

Sometime in the 1840's another itinerant limner, named Joseph Mason, is believed to have stopped in La Porte. This supposition is based on the existence of a portrait of Maria Jane Andrew, age seven, said to have been painted by him here. The age of the child would place the work in the year 1841, according to Charles F. Cochran, owner of the portrait. Joseph Mason's name first appeared in the *Annals* of Cincinnati, written by Charles Cist, with the statement that he was painting in that city in 1822.[35] In the early forties he was practicing in Michigan, and it is probable that his visit to La Porte coincided with his removal from Ohio to Michigan. Unfortunately nothing more is known of his movements, nor has an account of his life come to our attention.

Adolphus Van Sickle had come to La Porte after working in Goshen and probably in South Bend. Upon the evidence of a portrait of F. C. King (pl. 62) in the historical museum here, which is signed and dated on the back, he had reached La Porte by 1849, and had found at least one client. Doubtless King was pleased with the result because the painting has been carefully preserved by him and his descendants. Although it lacks brilliant brush work it is well executed, and King's personality has been pleasantly expressed.

On the basis of stylistic similarities to the King portrait, canvases bearing the likenesses of members of the Webber family at La Porte, owned by Mrs. Emmet Scott, can also be assigned to Van Sickle. Those of Thomas Webber and his wife Emaline Pope appear to have been executed by him the same year (Emaline Webber's dour expression is in sharp contrast, however, to that of the amiable King), but those of Le Roy and Sarah Deniston Webber were probably made a decade or more later. Technically, the latter are much better—drawing, coloring, and interpretation of personalities reveal a more experienced eye and hand.

Another visitor to La Porte in the early days was the fiddler-painter of Springfield, Vermont, Aaron Deane Fletcher. While his peripatetic activity, combining strong musical and pictorial talents, was well known in New England,[36] historians were unaware of his migration into the Midwest until his name was discovered on the back of canvases bearing the likenesses of Jacob Replogle and his wife Sinia—staunch members of the Dunkard faith—in the home of L. W. Replogle here. The date 1855 accompanies the signatures.

From the standpoint of quality, these canvases are competent productions; compositions are simple (the severe, unadorned style seems appropriate to what one imagines the character of the sitters to have been), colors are gray and muted, and the drawing is firm.

Fletcher was born at Springfield, Vermont, in 1817. Being a migratory type, he traveled around Vermont, Massachusetts, and neighboring states. His tour west into Indiana was probably of short duration, and there is no evidence that he visited any town in the state other than La Porte. He died at Kuseyville, New York, at an undetermined age.

During the period of the Civil War there was, apparently, a lull in art activities at and around La Porte, but in the 1870's two more painters had arrived. One, the unidentified author of the portraits of James Ridgway and his wife; the other, W. Whitlock, who is known only through the appearance of his name in the La Porte city directory of 1876–1877, where he was listed as a portrait painter. None of his work has been found, nor are any facts available regarding his life. If the date of the Ridgway portraits (1871) had coincided with the directory listing, one would be tempted to conclude that Whitlock painted them. Unfortunately, the present owner of the canvases, John A. Ridgway, does not recollect having heard the name of the painter mentioned by elder members of his family.

Indianapolis

Chapter 7

INDIANAPOLIS 1820–1860

"THE UNDERSIGNED have endeavored to connect with an eligible site the advantages of a navigable stream and fertility of soil, while they have not been unmindful of the geographical situation of the various portions of the state. . . ." So went the report of the committee appointed to select a site for the new capital of Indiana in 1820.[1] By act of January 6, 1821, the legislature ratified the selection—a dense forest at the junction of Fall Creek and White River—and appointed three new commissioners to lay out the town. Christopher Harrison, a summary of whose life was given in an earlier chapter, was the only one to appear at the appointed time so he carried out the assignment alone. Later the town was to receive the name Indianapolis.

This is not the place to discuss the actual advantages and disadvantages of the site, nor to tell in detail the problems that beset the first settlers, but it was soon apparent that the navigability of White River was a delusion, and that the fertility of the soil was offset by the difficulty of clearing away the timber and draining the swamps. For years the lack of roads connecting Indianapolis with other communities kept it in a state of isolation.

And yet the town grew. A number of lots were sold in the autumn of its first year (1821) and settlers began to filter in. Among the first to arrive were two artisans (one hesitates to call them artists), Caleb Scudder, cabinet maker and the community's first Sunday-school teacher, and Samuel Rooker, sign painter and limner.

Rooker was not a wayfaring painter. He had come to Indianapolis with the intention of making it his home, and he became affectionately identified with its cultural and political life. In addition to his specialty [2]—house and sign painting—he tried his hand at portraits, and represented his ward on the town council for a number of years; he was president of the town's board of trustees from 1845 to 1847. His first artistic efforts afforded the townspeople some amusement due to his inability to draw and spell correctly. His biographer, John H. B. Nowland, is the source of a number of anecdotes relating to the designer of the community's first signs:

In addition to the joy felt at having gained a new citizen and neighbor, all were glad to have one qualified to announce their names and businesses in glowing letters. The first to order a sign from the painter was Caleb Scudder, cabinet maker. This, Mr. Rooker painted on white ground with firey red letters and when finished it read, "Kalop Skodder, Kabbinet Maker."

Mr. S. R. soon received an order from Mr. Carter for a sign for the "Rosebush," and one from Mr. Henderson for the Eagle tavern. It was said that Mr. Hawkins' sign was that of a turkey with a surname attached.

He afterwards painted one for Major Belles. The design was "General Lafayette in full uniform." This was a fine opportunity for the painter to show his skill in portrait painting. When he commenced, it was his intention to paint it in full size, but after finishing the head and body he found there was not room for the legs full length; so he left out the section between the knee and ankle, and attached the feet to the knee joint, which gave the General the appearance of a very short legged man . . . .

In justice to Mr. R., I must say he improved very much in his profession in after years. He painted the portrait of the writer, which was very complimentary to the subject and a great credit to the artist . . . .[3]

Unfortunately, no one knows what became of the Nowland portrait, and nothing by Rooker—not even a signboard—can now be found. There is a portrait of A. A. Louden that on circumstantial evidence might be assigned to him. Both men were town trustees for a number of years, and for two terms Louden represented the same ward as Rooker, suggesting that they were neighbors and knew each other intimately. It would have been natural for Rooker to paint Louden's portrait under those circumstances. This assumption is strengthened by the fact that the style of painting does not resemble that of any other known painter working in Indianapolis in the 1820's or 1830's. It is not technically proficient, being executed in a flat, simple manner —what one would expect in a Rooker painting after reading Nowland's analysis of his work. The Louden portrait is now owned by Mrs. Floyd E. White, of Indianapolis, who is not in possession of any facts regarding its history.

Nowland informs us that Samuel Rooker came from Tennessee, but evidently he knew nothing more of his origin or early history. Subsequent research has revealed that he was the son of William Rooker, an English silversmith, who was seized with some of his companions in a London tavern, forced into military service, and sent to America during the Revolutionary War. He remained in this country, married, and raised a large family near Knoxville, Tennessee.[4] There Samuel Saffel was born about 1800. In 1821 he came to Indianapolis, accompanied by some of his brothers who settled in neighboring towns: Jesse in Mooresville, and William in Noblesville.

Samuel Rooker may have originally aspired to the field of portraiture, but limited talent and too few patrons kept him at sign and house painting. He is listed in the directories as a "painter," meaning a house painter, and not as an "artist" or "portrait painter" as others were. After 1865 he left Indianapolis and is believed to have taken up residence first in Mooresville and then in Martinsville. His death occurred there about 1875. This is all we know about Indianapolis' first dauber of paint.

In 1828, seven years after Rooker's appearance in Indianapolis, the first professional portrait painter came to the capital. He was Richard Terrell, a native of Kentucky, who had been painting in southern Indiana. Upon his arrival in Indianapolis, he bought space in the *Indiana Journal* and inserted his announcement:

PORTRAIT PAINTING.   R. TERRELL

Respectfully informs the citizens of Indianapolis that he is prepared to take the portraits of those who are willing to encourage the Fine Arts. Ladies and Gentlemen are invited to call and examine a specimen of his work at the Senate Chamber.

He will also execute the following kinds of paintings in a superior style: Signs for Public Houses, Stores, Shops &c., Regiment and Company Colors, together with all kinds of oil guilding and fancy painting.[5]

Until the portrait of Rebecca Cook Coe was found (pl. 63) in the home of Evelyn Sickels, bearing Terrell's signature on the back of the canvas, no work by him, produced in Indianapolis, was known. In addition to Mrs. Coe's likeness (that of her husband, Isaac Coe, was destroyed a few years ago because the family did not like it) Terrell painted James Mitchell Ray and his wife Marie Coe. These, owned by Mrs. Louis McHenry Howe, of Fall River, Massachusetts, are known to date from 1828, the year Terrell printed his announcement, and they might have been the "specimen" of work awaiting the community's examination and admiration at the senate chamber.

To what extent his work pleased the early citizens we do not know, but to modern eyes his canvases appear very inadequate from a technical standpoint. The visages of his sitters are hard and bony, proportions are awkward (small, deformed hands and large heads) and figures lack roundness and grace. The portrait of Ruth Parker Hobbs, wife of Samuel Hobbs, now in the home of Carrie Hobbs, of Plainfield, possesses the same stringent style and it may be another example of Terrell's work.

After his last advertisement on June 12, 1828, no more is heard of Terrell. We can only assume that he returned to Kentucky where life was more settled and artistic efforts more highly appreciated.

Another three years went by before the next artist wandered into Indianapolis. The newcomer was Michael G. Rogers, an Ohioan, twenty-six years of age, and probably without formal training. After setting up his equipment in a room in Henderson's tavern he had the local newspapers, the *Democrat* and the *Journal,* announce his presence, inviting the townspeople to come and see "specimens of his painting." [6] There is no record as to the amount of work he obtained from these advertisements, but he got one order, at least: the portraits of Isaac Dunn (pl. 64) and his wife Frances. They are oils on oval canvases, signed with the name "Rogers" on the back, now in the possession of Caroline Dunn, of Indianapolis.

Rogers' style of painting is more gracious and mellower than that of his predecessors in Indianapolis. The tones are softer, expressions are less grim, and some attempt has been made to model the forms of the head. His study of Isaac Dunn would have been better had he not tried to show a hand in the lower edge of the composition.

After his final announcements in the July papers no more is heard of Rogers for several months. The next time his name appeared it was on the list of those who had unclaimed mail at the post office—on January 27, 1832. Evidently the postmaster had not been informed that the artist had died on the eighth of January that year.[7]

Three and a half years later a fourth young painter arrived in Indianapolis and hopefully inserted his professional card in the *Indiana Journal*: "John I. Williams, Portrait Painter, Respectfully informs the Ladies and Gentlemen of Indianapolis that he will remain here for a few weeks . . ." The notice appeared first on August 14, 1835, and continued more than a month.

J. Insco Williams, as he later wrote his name, was the most promising of the young painters to reach Indianapolis. As related in an earlier chapter, he came to Indiana from western Ohio and, even though a novice, revealed unusual artistic sensitivity and good draughtsmanship. It is gratifying to learn that he found one client at least: Lewis Crowell Freeman had two portraits made—one of his wife Susan Harris (pl. 36) and one of himself, the former bearing the date 1835. The pictures are small profile studies in pencil and water color, showing heads and shoulders only; Williams' precise drawing, pleasing interpretation of character, and soft coloring give them a great deal of charm. They are now in the home of Mrs. William E. Gavin, of Indianapolis.

Another painter who appeared in the capital during the 1830's and attracted some attention to himself and his work was a portraitist named Ephraim Brown. The *Indiana Journal* in 1837 introduced him to the community as a person having a "particular claim upon the favor of the people of this place and this state. In Indianapolis he first commenced, and here he has lived, and by the force of his own industry and genius, advanced until we have high reason to be proud of him." In conclusion the editor implored: "Let not the people of Indiana fail to encourage the genius of her own soil." [8]

Neither the artist's "genius" nor the editor's entreaty brought immortality to Ephraim Brown. Nothing more is heard about him except a brief statement by a later chronicler, Louis Gibson, who, in his "Indiana Monographs," wrote, "Mr. Ephraim Brown became acquainted with Mr. Cox in 1838. He determined to become an artist, studied with Mr. Cox for a time, and afterwards went to Cincinnati, returning to open a studio. He painted portraits of Robert Dale Owen, Thomas Dowling, Hon. A. L. Chamberlain, and other prominent persons of this state." [9] We might add that William R. Holloway, in his sketch of Indianapolis, mentions a Brown who was here in 1867, and refers to portraits he painted of Governor Whitcomb and Bazil Brown; and Berry R. Sulgrove, in his local history, states that "a portrait painter named Brown had a studio in the Sanders Block a year or two." [10] If these writers refer to Ephraim we have two more portraits to add to the list of his recorded work, but no additional facts about his life. Unfortunately, none of the canvases listed above can now be found.

Probably when Ephraim Brown was studying with Jacob Cox another painter was a frequent visitor to the same studio. James Cameron, like those who preceded him, announced his presence in the town by inserting a notice that ran from November 1839 through January 1840, in the *Indiana Journal*. He professed to be a portrait painter, but if he got any business in line with his specialty nothing has come to light in recent years to prove it. He formed an art organization of some kind with Charles and Jacob Cox, which terminated in February, 1840; the *Indiana Journal* carried a notice that the partnership "hitherto existing between James Cameron & Co., is dissolved by mutual consent;" it was signed by the two Cox brothers and Cameron.

II

As our story thus far suggests, Indianapolis was not large enough in the 1830's to attract many painters, nor could it support more than one at a time. In 1835 its population was slightly over 1,600 persons, with probably not more than a score of them interested in artistic activities or wishing to have their portraits painted—even if they could afford it. The town was still difficult to reach, and such travelers as made the arduous journey were not always impressed by the place when they arrived. One such visitor, Hugh McCulloch, wrote that "nothing had been done to the streets except to remove the stumps from two or three . . . There were no sidewalks, and the streets most in use, after every rain, and for a good part of the year, were knee-deep with mud . . . I have seen many of the incipient towns of the West, but none so utterly forlorn as Indianapolis appeared in the spring of 1833." [11] Only the fertility of its soil redeemed it.

If Jacob Cox, tinsmith and artist, found the community so depressing when he arrived in January of that year he said nothing about it; nor did it dissuade him from his plan to make Indianapolis his home.

The story of the rise of this young man from an obscure tradesman to the most beloved and honored of the city's artists is an engaging one. He came to Indianapolis from Pittsburgh where he had started his career as a tinner, and where, in 1832, he married Nancy Baird. His original home was Burlington, New Jersey, where he was born November 9, 1810, the eldest of ten children of David Cox and Abigail Town. His parents died when he was young, so he grew up in the home of his grandfather and aunt at Washington, Pennsylvania.

From the beginning the boy had an insatiable desire to draw and paint, but realizing the necessity of learning a trade that would enable him to earn a livelihood, he became apprenticed to a tinner. His brother Charles went into business with him in Pittsburgh and they were joined later, in Indianapolis, by a third brother, David.

In Indianapolis the brothers opened a shop on the south side of Washington Street, a door east of Washington Hall, and advertised in the local newspaper that they had established a copper and tinware business and were prepared to make and sell, wholesale or retail, copper wash tubs, pans and teakettles, as well as whiskey stills.[12] Evidently during the early years of the company's development Jacob Cox never gave up hope of being a painter, and when the business got well under way, and his economic station was secure, he began to draw and paint in his spare time. He became more and more absorbed in the technical problems of painting, with the result that less time was spent in the shop than in his improvised studio. Finally he was bold enough to undertake the painting of portraits as a profession.

His earliest attempt in this direction, now known, is a small oil on cardboard of William Sullivan, painted about 1835, owned by William George Sullivan, of Indianapolis. It reveals the hand of an amateur, but indicates that the author has enough natural ability to go far as a painter.

Encouraged by his progress during the next five years and, perhaps, by the attention his work was receiving, Cox opened a studio of his own in the business district. Although evidence is lacking, circumstances suggest that he did so in 1840, and that he intended making portrait painting his speciality. A few canvases are in the city today that originated in that year, showing that he enjoyed some degree of success. In 1840 he was also engaged to design and paint a large political banner that was carried at the head of the Indianapolis delegation (known as the "Wild Oats of Indianapolis") to the Tippecanoe Battleground in their campaign for William Henry Harrison.

Cox's first formal announcement as a portrait painter appeared in a local newspaper, the *Indiana State Sentinel,* on December 30, 1841:

J. COX, PORTRAIT PAINTER

Has removed to the room over the store of Morris & Brother, adjoining the Post Office, where he may be found at all times by his friends and public. Specimens of Portraiture by himself are to be seen at the State House, in the committee room at the North-west end, in which collection are portraits of several distinguished individuals.

The following winter, 1842–1843, he closed his studio, took a leave of absence from the copper and tinware shop, and went to Cincinnati. There he opened a studio, which he shared with John Gibson Dunn, and sought portrait commissions and orders for "fruit and fancy pieces." He was surprisingly successful, considering his limited technical knowledge and the competition of established painters.[13] In less than six months, however, he was back in Indianapolis and again at his easel—a wiser and more confident artist.

"Still he did not find painting sufficiently remunerative to justify his retiring from the prosaic business of tinning," wrote historian Nowland, "and he continued an active partner with his brother in that business until about twelve years ago [1858]." [14] A sale of his paintings, together with canvases by Whittredge, was held at Wiley's Auction Room soon after his return from Cincinnati, but the proceeds were modest. Then he obtained a number of important orders for portraits, including those of Oliver H. Smith, Governor James Bigger, and former Governor David Wallace (pl. 65). His advertisements began to appear again in the newspapers, which, together with laudatory articles from the pens of editors, stimulated business.

One of the first critical appraisals of Cox's work came from the pen of Peter F. Reed, a poet and painter of Cincinnati who visited Cox's studio in 1851. It was reprinted in the *Weekly Indiana State Journal,* October 23, 1852, from the *Cincinnati Nonpareil:*

I was really astonished to see such worthy artistic pictures from a pencil that works in obscurity. I have never seen an article of praise or criticism to Mr. Cox, and I wondered, when I gazed upon the fine paintings that graced his studio, that he did not go to Cincinnati and be *puffed!* His last original production, called "The Mountain Lake," is a fine painting, and shows the artist to be a genius, and one of the first of our Western artists. His subject is always pleasing and agreeable, and handled with great care and taste.

Incidentally, Reed stated that Cox had at that time given up his interest in the tinning business (six years earlier than Nowland reported) and that he was devoting his powers entirely to art, adding: "This will afford him more comfort but less *tin!*"

During the next decades his progress was steady and sales were adequate to maintain his home and support a growing family. With the help of the American Art Union, an agency that exhibited and sold paintings—or more correctly, raffled them off—he experienced a period of prosperity and promptly set off for New York, where, during 1860, he had an opportunity to see excellent paintings and meet some of the eastern artists. According to family tradition he was successful in securing commissions there and painted New York's most prominent citizens. It is also believed that he enrolled in the school of the National Academy of Design for his first formal instruction in painting—a belated undertaking, as he was by that time fifty years old.

Upon his return from New York he maintained his studio in Indianapolis, changing its location from time to time, until his death in 1892. It was the hub around which the majority of the city's art activities revolved, and the point to which most of the artists gravitated. Many younger men and women, eager to learn the rudiments of drawing and painting, worked there under the kindly supervision of the town's most revered artist—most of whom we will have occasion to speak about later.

The list of Cox's paintings is long. Portraits of six Indiana governors are in the Statehouse; the John Herron Art Museum has his canvases of Dr. Charles G. McLean and Achsa McCollough, as well as several landscapes (pl. 66); his portrait of William Conner is in the Conner Homestead; and likenesses of many prominent early citizens—among them, Alexander W. Russell, George M. Lockerbie, Jesse Fletcher, Samuel Merrill, and John L. Spann—are in the homes of descendants. The most attractive of his group portraits is the large canvas bearing the likenesses of the three Spann children: Thomas, John, and Eliza in an outdoor setting (pl. 67).[15]

Cox was not an adroit technician. Although he steadily progressed toward a more skillful manipulation of brushes and a broader concept of his subject, he did not achieve a rich and fluent handling of paint. His portraits are direct, straightforward statements about the people who sat before his easel, with no suggestion of flattery nor emphasis on decorative backgrounds. Lacking sound technical instruction in his formative years, he never got over a certain timidity in applying paint to canvas; and being, himself, a plain and unpretentious man, he did not try to give his models an air of suavity and artificial grace as did many of the fashionable painters of his time.

While he achieved considerable success as a portraitist, Cox was also recognized as a leading landscape, still-life, and figure painter. His figure paintings, often inspired by other pictures, were usually referred to as "fancy pieces," since they were romantic and rather fanciful compositions of children and pretty girls, often in gypsy or peasant costumes. Their distribution among local homes exceeded that of other subjects because they were lower in price and more widely appreciated. He also succumbed to the panorama craze.

The decade of the 1850's witnessed the making of a number of panoramas in Indianapolis, according to the *Journal* of March 15, 1854: "This is a great town for panoramas, not only showing but making them. We have already sent out two or three and there are still a couple behind." One of the principal figures in these enterprises was Jacob Cox, who, in the winter of 1853–54 painted one dealing with the temperance theme. It was ordered by four local businessmen who paid the artist $1,500 for the work, based on thirty scenes at fifty dollars each. Cox was assisted in its execution by a younger man, Henry Waugh, who had arrived in Indianapolis not long before in the theatrical troupe of Yankee Robinson. The panorama met with considerable success as long as the temperance fever was high, and it was shown before large audiences in several Indiana towns as well as in Cincinnati, Dayton, and Louisville.

Henry Waugh, who helped Cox, had arrived here in 1853, as scenery painter as well as actor in Robinson's company. His ability as an artist attracted the attention of a reporter on the *Journal*, who called attention to his landscapes on exhibition at Jones Music Store, as well as to the "excellent scenery used at the Athenaeum." The article went on to say that Henry W. Waugh was "of a race of artists. It was his uncle who painted Waugh's Panorama of Italy . . . a perfect mirror of the lovely scenes and important views of that classic land." [16]

Little is known of Waugh's life. He was eighteen or twenty years old when he came to Indianapolis, but neither the date of his birth nor the name of his original home is known. He evidently had a good deal of artistic talent and, eager to become more proficient as a painter, he joined a circus after leaving Indianapolis for the purpose of earning enough money to go abroad to study art. He became very popular throughout the country as Dilly Fay, "the parlor clown," and was able to save $3,000. With that he went to Rome where he made rapid progress in painting. Unfortunately he had little opportunity to use

63. Richard Terrell: Portrait of
Rebecca Cook Coe
Courtesy of Evelyn R. Sickels,
Indianapolis (page 149)

64. Michael G. Rogers:
Portrait of Isaac Dunn
Courtesy of Caroline Dunn and
Eleanor Dunn Moore,
Indianapolis (page 149)

65. Jacob Cox: Portrait of
David Wallace
Courtesy of the Indiana
Historical Bureau,
Indianapolis (page 154)

66. (below) Jacob Cox:
The Morris Morris Farm
John Herron Art Museum,
Indianapolis (page 155)

67. Jacob Cox: Thomas, John, and Eliza Spann
Courtesy of Anna H. Spann, Indianapolis (page 155)

68. Joseph O. Eaton: Portrait of Peninnah Mills Pope
Courtesy of Mrs. Robert B. Moynahan, Indianapolis (page 162)

his new skill, for he died suddenly of consumption in England on his way back to America.

The only known painting by Waugh in the city is a small landscape, probably a scene near Indianapolis, owned by Eleanor Whitcomb. It was formerly in Jacob Cox's possession.

Another panorama to which the Indianapolis *Journal* referred was the *Mirror of Intemperance,* painted in 1853 by James F. Harris, formerly of Madison, and at the time a student of Jacob Cox. According to the editor of *The Locomotive,* it was intended to illustrate in a series of episodes the course of a man who, from virtue and happiness, sinks to drunkenness and death: "The plan is something after that of the 'Rake's Progress' by Hogarth; but, though the course of dissipation must necessarily be somewhat the same in both cases, the scenes and characters in that great masterpiece are entirely different from those used by Mr. Harris; originality of conception is the merit of his panorama . . . How far Mr. Harris has succeeded will be for the public to say when his work is brought before it . . . There is a kind of silent eloquence therein, which sinks deeply into the soul." [17]

Four months later the panorama was finished and was being visited by large numbers at the Masonic Hall. From the editor's comment we learn that it covered more canvas than any other shown at Indianapolis, and that while it was not without its technical shortcomings, particularly in the proportion and position of figures, he considered its moral subject matter of enough value to shield it from criticism.

Instead of warding off criticism, the editor's kindly appraisal brought forth a long denunciatory reply (signed, T.T.), stating that however noble the theme, the execution was poor, and that the moral tone of the work "should afford its blunders no immunity from candid criticism . . . Such a rule would stuff the world full of paintings as poor as this panorama, and books as dull as Dr. Thompson's explanation of it." [18]

Young Harris then undertook a second and more dramatic panorama called *Evils of Intemperance,* possibly to demonstrate to his critics that he was capable of better technical performance. How well he succeeded we have not been informed. In the same year he received a commission to paint the Indiana banner for the World's Fair in New York, which was hung with those of other states: Indiana's coat of arms was in the center surrounded by a wreath, with agricultural scenes in three corners and a railway train in the other. It was designed and executed in his studio in the north end of the Statehouse, where he had painted his panoramas.

No more is heard of James Harris after this. He left Indianapolis for other fields, and his subsequent movements are as obscure as are his pre-Indiana activities.

The rage for making panoramas was not confined to the painters of Indianapolis. As we have seen, the movement in the state began with John Banvard's undertaking at New Harmony in 1836. In 1849 and 1850 J. Insco Williams painted two, and although the work was done in Ohio, the fact that he had been practicing in Indiana and that his panoramas were exhibited in this state, justifies the inclusion of his name here. The products of Marcus Mote in this line have also been discussed.

A painter who has not thus far been mentioned, Clark Gordon, of Spiceland, was moved to paint a panorama depicting events he had experienced during his service in the Civil War. He did not get around to making it until almost two decades later; reports indicate that he enjoyed considerable success exhibiting it in nearby communities and explaining the episodes as they came into view. The large roll of canvas, titled *Battle Scenes of the Rebellion,* has been preserved by the painter's daughter, Mrs. Frank Davis, of Spiceland;[19] so far as we can determine, it is the only early Indiana panorama still in existence.

III

To continue the story of art activities in the 1840's (interrupted by our discussion of panoramas), Indianapolis was at that time the temporary home of several aspiring young painters who deserve some attention here. Fortunately for them Indianapolis had become a town of respectable size; adequate roads linked it with other large communities; the railroads began to come; commerce and industry expanded; and artistic enterprises increased.

Nearly all early accounts of local art affairs mention six budding painters of the decade who achieved distinction in after years, either in Indiana or in eastern cities. Thomas Worthington Whittredge and Joseph O. Eaton attained professional status during that period; William Miller, Lew Wallace, John Gibson Dunn, and a man named Elliott were in the embryonic stage.

Whittredge, or Whitridge,[20] who became one of the nation's leading landscape painters, came to Indianapolis in the summer of 1842 from Cincinnati, where he had made a start as an artist. He was about twenty-two years old, had already tried his hand at portrait painting, and believed that Indianapolis would recognize and appreciate his ability. The duration of his residence here was short—only about a year—and although a few of his paintings of that period are mentioned by early chroniclers, nothing remains. In a letter written many years later to William Henry Fox, Whittredge had the following to say about his sojourn here:

I went to Indianapolis in the very first days of the Daguerrotype with a camera and plates to take Daguerrotypes. I had been a portrait painter. I took sick in Indianapolis, and this, together with the shinplaster state of our currency, soon brought me and my business to grief. I had known old Dr. Lyman Beecher of Cincinnati all my life, and all his family, and his son Henry Ward came to Indianapolis when I was there and began his preaching, and soon converted everybody in the town, myself among the number. I lay sick at Parker's Hotel for some time, when Henry Ward came for me in a carriage and took me home with him, and I lived in his family just one year, and as I had no money, and wanted to offer some reward for Henry's kindness, I painted his portrait as well as the portraits of the whole Beecher family except Edward, who was away off in Chillicothe.[21]

It is unfortunate that the Beecher canvases have not been located, and that another of Whittredge's early efforts, a drawing of Harriet Beecher Stowe, later belonging to one of her relatives in Simsbury, Connecticut, has not yet been traced. His only other recorded portrait made in Indianapolis, that of General Tilghman Howard, is also missing. The latter was mentioned in the *Indiana Daily State Sentinel*, December 31, 1842 (the first published report on Whittredge): "We yesterday stepped into Mr. Whitridge's rooms. We saw there some of the best likenesses we have ever seen. An unfinished one of Gen. Howard promises to be excellent."

If Whittredge worked seriously at photography there is no contemporaneous reference to it. In fact, his own announcement inserted in the local newspaper in January, 1843, gives no hint of any such intention:

PORTRAIT PAINTING

Mr. Whitridge's room is on Washington Street nearly opposite the Post Office, where he will paint portraits at the following very reasonable prices. For a Head, the usual size, $20.00. For a Head, half size, $10.00. Small Panels or Miniatures, $5.00. His Paintings are in Oil, and Warranted good likenesses.[22]

A month later he was enjoying the fruits of this advertisement and, no doubt, of his industry, because he had canvases under way for several members of the legislature. The last mention of him was in May when he and Cox had a sale of paintings at Wiley's Auction Room.[23] Not long afterward he returned to Cincinnati, where he worked five or six years; then he went abroad for ten years, studying in London, Paris, Antwerp, and Düsseldorf; he returned to America in 1858, and spent the rest of his life in the East. He died at Summit, New Jersey, in 1910. While in Cincinnati he painted both portraits and landscapes, but gradually gave up portraiture. In fact, few historians today know about his early products in that field.

In an interview with a reporter on the *Indianapolis News*, Jacob Cox gave his recollection of Joseph O. Eaton, when the young, aspiring painter first came to Indianapolis:

One morning, in 1848, I think it was, he sauntered into town. He had run away from home. He lived somewhere in Ohio, where his father wanted him to stick to the soil and be a farmer. He had on an old coat of his father's, which was much too large for him, and the furtive look from his eyes showed he was on the lookout for pursuers. He was then maybe 18 years old and had two pictures with him, portraits, one of some itinerant Methodist preacher, the other of George Washington. The latter looked like the sign board of an ancient tavern, while both of them were frightful daubs. Upon the strength of these samples he intended to get some work to do here. He had nerve and cheek and the boy actually did get work. He opened a studio here and painted whole families at $5 a head. He painted Governor Whitcomb's portrait, which recently came into Judge Biddle's possession. I took an interest in Jo and encouraged him. Henry Ward Beecher, who was here then, said to me the boy had no talent and would never do me any credit, but I knew better. Jo had a will that no obstacles could prevent from going onward to a goal. He got a little money together, $30 I believe, and went to Cincinnati where he worked until he had made by his own brush $50,000 and was the most popular and best portrait painter there.[24]

Cox was correct in most points regarding Eaton's stay at Indianapolis, but his memory failed him (the interview was more than thirty years later) with respect to the date of his arrival. An editorial in the *Indiana State Sentinel* of December 6, 1845, reported that Eaton was already established here, and that he was painting "admirable likenesses of a few who have taste enough to appreciate genius, and faces of which they are not ashamed." Contrary to Cox's estimate of the young man's cheek and aggressiveness, the editor pointed out that there was but one fault with the artist: he was "too modest ever to get along in this world, which is a hard one for men of his profession especially."

It is hard to believe that Eaton was only about seventeen years old when that encomium appeared in the paper. He must have made incredible strides, technically, if the samples he brought with him were as bad as Cox reported. His paintings of 1845 and 1846 were not astounding, but the ones that are still around confirm the editor's appraisal. They are "admirable" in view of the man's stage of development, particularly when compared to the usual portraits limned in the frontier settlements.

Most of the canvases painted in Indianapolis by Eaton bear the likeness of some member of Abner J. Pope's family. This is significant because an advertisement inserted by the artist in the newspaper about the time the editorial appeared, stated that he had his studio (or "room," as he called it) over Pope's store, south side of Washington Street, a few doors east of the Palmer House.[25] He also lived in the home of Dr. Abner Pope during his stay in Indianapolis, according to Mary Q. Burnet,[26] and he painted his landlord's likeness, possibly in lieu of rent. While the present whereabouts of the Abner Pope portrait is unknown, those of the son and the son's wife, Peninnah Mills, are in the possession of descendants in Los Angeles. A second canvas of Peninnah by Eaton (pl. 68) is owned by Mrs. Robert B. Moynahan, Indianapolis, and one of Joseph E. Pope is in the home of W. K. Stewart, of Louisville. A pair of portraits depicting Charles Good and his wife Margaret Schofield, owned by Mrs. Alice Good Holloway, Indianapolis, can also be attributed to Eaton.

As might be expected, these paintings show a simple, direct approach to the problem of depicting likenesses. They are not technically suave or brilliant; and yet the drawing is firm. The characterization of each sitter is good, although marked individual traits are not brought out as they are in Eaton's later and more developed work.

In stating that Eaton lived somewhere in Ohio in his youth, Cox was not mistaken: he was born at, or near, Newark, in 1829. Why he chose Indianapolis as his destination after surreptitiously leaving his home no one knows. He was in Indianapolis about a year, moving to Cincinnati probably late in 1846.[27] He remained in Cincinnati sixteen or seventeen years, rising to the front rank of the portraitists there, and earning, according to Cox, $50,000 during that time. Then he went to New York, where his reputation and popularity did not diminish. He died at Yonkers in 1875, soon after completing his self-portrait for the National Academy of Design.

The third artist associated with Cox's early studio days was William Miller. In the *Indianapolis News* interview referred to above, Cox said Miller was in Indianapolis three or four years (about 1846–1848), and that "he did not amount to much here, being in the embryonic state." If our information that he was born in Lexington, Kentucky, in 1835 is reliable, it is not surprising that he did not paint very well when he was at Indianapolis—he was only eleven or twelve years old. However, he did develop into a first-rate miniature painter in Cincinnati, and when he went to New York some years later, he was at the "top of the heap," as Cox expressed it. He died there in 1907.[28]

One of Jacob Cox's most ardent admirers in the early forties was young Lewis (Lew) Wallace. He was about ten years old when, in 1837, his father, David Wallace, became governor and moved to Indianapolis from Crawfordsville. His most passionate interest during the years in Indianapolis was drawing pictures, but it was not until 1843, or thereabouts, that he became acquainted with Cox and got his first encouragement in what heretofore had been a furtive venture. In his *Autobiography* Wallace gives us an intimate report on the meeting that meant so much to him at the time:

"When I heard that Mr. Cox painted pictures in oil, I nerved myself and boldly invaded his studio. He was painting my father's portrait when I went in. The coincidence excused me. We became good friends, and not a few of my truancies were passed watching him at work." He went on to tell how Cox gave him some dabs of paint on a sheet of tin, how he improvised brushes by cutting hairs off his dog's tail, and painted a portrait of Black Hawk from a picture in a book on American Indians.

Lew Wallace was hindered in his progress by a stern and practical father. One day David Wallace called the boy into his study and said, "You must give up drawing. I will not have it. If you are thinking of being an artist, listen to me. In our country art is to have its day, and the day may not come in your time. There is no demand for pictures. Rich men are too few and the poor cannot afford to indulge a taste of that kind. To give yourself up to the pursuit means starvation." Whereupon the boy made an attempt at argument, bringing up the name of Cox. "Oh, yes," the father replied; "Mr. Cox is a good man, but he has a trade to fall back upon, a shop to help him make the ends meet." [29]

The admonition continued, and the son listened, but he could not easily push aside so absorbing an interest. Throughout his youthful days he went on drawing and sketching. But when he became a man other interests dominated his thoughts and actions. In the 1860's and 1870's he began painting again, and although he was living in Crawfordsville during that period—perhaps working on *Ben Hur* much of the time—he sent some of his paintings to Indianapolis exhibitions.

Wallace's artistic activities have been dealt with in the section dealing with Crawfordsville painters.

Returning to the period of the 1840's, the last two artists mentioned above—Dunn and Elliott—contributed little to the story of Indiana art. What little is known of the career of John G. Dunn has been told in Chapter 3. Elliott, who is referred to as one of Cox's pupils in early accounts, cannot be identified now. His first name was never given, nor was reference made to his age or place of origin. The first printed notice about him appeared in the *Indiana Journal* on February 19, 1853, more than ten years after he had left Indianapolis: "Elliott, the best portrait-painter of Cincinnati, when a ragged boy in our streets was taken in and received instruction from Cox." Unfortunately an investigation of portrait painters in Cincinnati in the 1850's has failed to throw any more light on this puzzling figure.[30]

Another artist in Indianapolis during the 1840's of whom we have some definite knowledge was William S. Unthank, a mature portrait painter. He was born at Richmond, of Quaker parents, in 1813. His early life remains quite obscure, but, like most lads brought up in communities of Friends, he had little or no opportunity to exercise his artistic talents and doubtless met opposition rather than encouragement. His work suggests that he had had no formal training; as he reached maturity he probably got such technical information as he could by studying paintings already in that region and by gathering crumbs of advice from visiting painters.

By 1840 Unthank had arrived in Indianapolis where he married Nancy Moreland and where he and his bride made their home. His first datable portraits are those of Dr. Henry Wishard and his wife Harriet Moreland (pl. 69), painted about 1840 or 1841, now hanging in the Greenwood Presbyterian Church, south of Indianapolis. About the same time he painted the likenesses of Edward McGuire and his wife, owned by William M. McGuire, Lima, Ohio, and those of Samuel Moore and his wife Eliza. Samuel Moore was the founder of Mooresville, and the portraits were painted there by Unthank about 1840. They were inherited by Ida Fogleman.[31]

Unthank's manner of painting is blunt in its directness of statement and simplicity of drawing. Relatively flat forms, strongly emphasized folds of garments and wrinkles, and stiff poses indicate that he had no opportunity to get beyond the elementary stage of the painter's craft. And yet, as with many similar products, there is a decided homely charm about his work.

After residing in Indianapolis a number of years, he took his family to Centerville and then back to his native town, Richmond. That was in 1857. From there he ventured into Ohio, living for a time in Cincinnati where he experimented with a perpetual motion machine. The outcome was failure, both scientific and financial. In 1860 he was back in Indianapolis, having turned photographer, and announced himself an expert ambrotypist. About that time his domestic affairs went awry; his wife left him and he became a lonely vagabond painter, traveling farther and farther west. In 1891 he wandered into the Christian Home Orphanage at Council Bluffs, Iowa, destitute and almost blind. He was received kindly and arrangements were made for him to remain. His death occurred there the following year.

There are a number of portraits besides those listed above that appear to be Unthank's work. A black crayon drawing of Sophia Sloan Watt, owned by Mrs. Henry W. Buttolph, of Indianapolis, might be a preliminary study by him for an oil portrait; it is also reasonable to assign a pair of portraits in the historical museum at Richmond to him on the basis of stylistic affinities with his known work: they portray in a simple, forthright manner William Allen Reddish and his wife Sarah Smith, and appear to have been painted about 1840.

IV

Cultural affairs in Indianapolis differed but little in the 1850's from the preceding decade, even though the personnel comprising the Bohemian group changed considerably. According to the *State Journal* there were three artists in town in May of 1851: "Messrs. John G. Dunn, James B. Dunlap, and Jacob Cox. The latter has long been a resident of this place, and has deservedly won for himself a high position among the painters of the land. Mr. Dunlap is also a resident of this city, and though young, has the name of a good painter. Mr. Dunn resided in our city several years ago, and took his first lessons here. He is also a versatile genius, having become quite celebrated as a painter, poet, and physician—he too, is a young man."

James Bolivar Dunlap was the son of a distinguished Indianapolis physician, Dr. Livingston Dunlap. He was born here in 1825, received a good education, and was allowed to follow his artistic bent. His interest in draughtsmanship and caricature led to the career of cartoonist and engraver, although he painted portraits and landscapes as well. Only a few portraits in oil that can be assigned to him are known. One represents Woodville Browning, a small study on copper (pl. 70), and another is the likeness of Mrs. James Dignan. The former is owned by Netta B. Pittman, the latter by Elizabeth Browning. A painting that is said to be the likeness of Dr. Livingston Dunlap, now at the library of the Medical Center, was thought to be his work, but neither the identity of the sitter nor that of the artist has been proved. A barnyard scene, owned by Merrill Berkley, of Indianapolis, appears to be his only known landscape.

He was first mentioned in the Indianapolis *Locomotive*, August 31, 1851, for engravings he had done for advertisements appearing in the paper: "We can recommend any person wanting any wood engraving, or designing, to James Dunlap, of our city. For a specimen of his work see the coffin and bier in the advertisement of Fitler & Co." The following year, the young artist began to insert his own advertisements in the same newspaper, hoping to get more orders for commercial drawings and engravings: "J. B. Dunlap, designer and engraver on wood. Also drafting of patents and machinery. Office over Wm. Smith's clothing store, one door east of Wright's House." [32] He also did some cartooning, a few characterizations of local citizens being reproduced in Jacob Dunn's *Greater Indianapolis*.[33] His versatility led him to try his hand at sculpture, a field in which he might have attained distinction, judging by the quality of the bust of Captain John A. Sutter in the Statehouse, had he not died prematurely. The Sutter bust was made in California where Dunlap had gone in the hope of finding relief from tuberculosis.

A number of early chroniclers spoke of Dunlap's artistic abilities, but his most ardent admirer was Laura N. Ream, who proclaimed him as one "whose talent was so versatile that he could have become renowned in half a dozen different fields. . . . 'The Voyage of Life' is his most beautiful painting. It is a scene viewed in pure air and sunshine, when every leaf and sprig stand out clear and distinct, and one feels as if the vision extended beyond the hills and the sky into the furthermost realms of space. Blessed be genius that lifts us, even for a moment, above the cares of life."[34] This was written in 1867, nearly three years after the artist's own "voyage" had ended.

As the decade of the fifties advanced, other artists arrived in Indianapolis. Two of them—Waugh and Harris—have already been mentioned. Barton Hays, who had become a recognized painter in Attica, moved to the capital in 1858, and established with William Runnion the principal daguerrean parlor. As he did not give up his creative work, his part in the enterprise must have been the tinting of photographs and painting over enlarged prints. His early plain and unembellished style gradually gave way to a professional and photographic manner, becoming more proficient and polished as time went on.

Among the first portraits Hays painted after coming to Indianapolis were those of George F. Adams and his wife Rebecca Raymond (pl. 71). As his work was seldom signed and never dated, exact periods are difficult to determine. On the basis of the ages of the sitters (either obtained from records or deduced from their appearances) approximate dates can be reckoned, and in the case of the Adams portraits 1859 or 1860 seems about right. Formerly owned by Mrs. Frank Lewis, they are now in the home of Bertha Ellis. About ten years later he painted the oval portrait of Mary A. Alford, now in the John Herron Art Museum; and at about the same time he made the portrait of his second wife Amy Jane Woodmansee, owned by Jean Black, of Indianapolis. Many of his canvases are in local homes; and descendants of the artist—here in the state and elsewhere—are affectionately preserving his work. The largest collection is in the home of his daughter Naomi Hays Hinshaw, of Elmhurst, Illinois.

Much of Hays's renown in later years came from his having tutored William M. Chase (coming, of course, after Chase had attained international recognition as a painter); but during his residence in Indianapolis his reputation rested solely upon the quality of his own work. He remained in the capital about twenty-five years, producing many portraits and fruit pieces (pl. 72), as well as a few landscapes; for a period of time he taught drawing and painting at the McLean Female Seminary. In the summer of 1866 he spent several weeks sketching in southern Ohio, where he met his second wife. In 1869 he was asked to paint the portrait of William Henry Harrison for the collection of pictures of Indiana's former governors which was being made for the Statehouse, the model for which must have been a photograph or an engraving. He moved to Cincinnati in 1870 to try his fortune there, but he did not stay more than a few months. In 1882 he and his family moved from Indianapolis to Minneapolis, where he spent the remaining thirty-two years of his life.

No critical appraisal of Hays's work appeared in the local press, so far as we can determine, until Alois Sinks, a local critic, visited his studio in 1875. In his characteristic blunt and self-confident manner, Sinks remarked that the pictures he saw "did not impress us as being meritorious," and that "it may not be fair to judge of his [Hays's] ability by what we saw in his room, otherwise we should simply say that his forte lies in painting very elaborately sandpapered fences and exquisitely regular houses." Then he concluded, "Mr. Hays is a fine man, socially, but he is not in the strict sense of the word, an artist, and we are prepared to prove our assertion." [35]

In deference to both Hays and Sinks, it should be stated that the critic realized that Hays had little on hand at the time, most of his pictures having been sold recently at auction. Also, Sinks was adhering to a thesis or philosophy stated in his "Art Notes," namely, that imitation of outward appearances of people and things does not necessarily produce a work of art. His argument is of interest:

In portraiture, and in landscape painting as well, the function of art is not to copy, speaking paradoxically, but to represent; and therefore the effect, and not the imitation, must be the aim. But in ordinary works, the very reverse of this is true . . . nature is painted literally, and how badly may be seen in the score of lifeless, spiritless pictures which daily come under observation—pictures which neither give pleasure to the eye nor refinement to the mind . . . pictures painfully smooth, horribly precise, softened, sweetened, polished, until the remotest possibility of soul has been consigned to the tomb of the Capulets.[36]

Photographic precision in art irked him, and Hays's work was too close to the borderline.

Another artist who was to be seen in Indianapolis in the 1850's was John H. Niemeyer, whose long and distinguished career in the East as painter and teacher is well known. He was born in Germany in 1839 and was brought to America as a child; he turned up in Indianapolis in 1858 at the age of nineteen, having previously been in Cincinnati. His beginning was humble enough; he found work in the shop of John B. Osgood, sign and house painter, where Jacob Cox met him and offered to give him gratuitous instruction. The offer was accepted and young Niemeyer took the first serious steps toward portrait and landscape painting that eventually led to further study in New York and Europe, and finally to important teaching positions in New Jersey and at the School of Fine Arts, Yale University. No work done by him in those early years here in Indianapolis is now known; it is doubtful if he was far enough along in his studies, anyway, to produce anything of importance.

Before leaving our survey of the 1850's, reference should be made to enterprises that gave considerable stimulus to art among the residents of Indianapolis. In 1850 a chapter of the American Art Union was started, with Charles B. Davis as secretary. The procedure was to sell tickets at $5.00 each that gave the purchasers chances on paintings, sculptures, and prints which were placed on exhibition, and drawings were held at specified times. As the Art Union was a national affair, the items raffled off were usually by eastern painters and sculptors. In 1856 the Indianapolis Art Society was organized, following the plan of the Art Union, primarily to promote the sale of work by resident painters, but it was of short duration. In the meantime the Indiana State Fair was started (1852) and art exhibits there soon became annual affairs, affording artists an opportunity to show their pictures to a large number of people and to win premiums. Another exhibition center was created with the founding of the Lieber's Art Emporium in 1854, where many local artists found an outlet for their products as years went by.

Though many of these undertakings were evanescent, they indicated a general movement toward a wider acceptance of art and a general feeling of the need for broader community participation in cultural programs. As the editor of the *Indiana Journal* put it in 1853: "We are bound in some sort as a metropolis of the State to make competent provision for their [the public's] entertainment at concerts, operas, galleries of paintings, lectures, and in short whatever can minister to a refined and intellectual taste." [37]

Indianapolis

Chapter 8

INDIANAPOLIS 1860–1885

THE DECADE OF THE 1860's, according to historian Holloway, was, for Indianapolis, the "most important, not only as regards events affecting the whole country, in which it bore a conspicuous part, but in those affecting its immediate development and prosperity. It saw us rise from a mere flourishing inland town and prominent railroad station to the condition of a manufacturing and commercial centre, increasing our population 130 percent." [1] After the close of the Civil War economic and social life changed greatly, the quiet, neighborly village suddenly becoming a noisy, bustling city, with expanding cultural and artistic activities.

According to the *Business Mirror*, the classified section of the Indianapolis city directory, for 1860–1861, ten artists and professional portrait painters were in business, seven more than in the previous year. A *Business Mirror* is not necessarily a complete roster of local artists, but it serves as a good barometer. The ten were Mrs. J. G. Adams, E. & J. Bruening, Jacob Cox, James B. Dunlap, Samuel Gulich, Barton S. Hays, Henry N. McEvoy, John H. Niemeyer, Peter Fishe Reed, and William Smallwood. Of these we have already been introduced to Cox, Dunlap, Hays, Niemeyer, and Reed; the others are no more than names to us today. Gulich, listed as a scenic and fresco artist, is said to have painted a war panorama with the help of Thomas B. Glessing, which was exhibited in 1863.

Peter Fishe Reed, the most eminent of the ten, had visited Indianapolis ten years before, and had written a laudatory article about Cox's work. He was a native of Boston, where he was born in 1817. He de-

171

veloped into a nationally recognized poet, critic, and painter;[2] and while his reputation was made to a large extent on work he did after leaving Indiana, he was, nevertheless, prominent in art circles here for several years.

The first time his name appeared in midwestern annals was in the *Cincinnati Business Directory for the Year 1844* (R. P. Brooks) where he was listed as a house and sign painter. A special card inserted in the "Supplement" is of interest not only as his first formal professional announcement, but also as an enumeration of the services offered by a sign and ornamental painter in those days:

P. F. REED

SIGN PAINTER

N.E. corner of Vine and Pearl streets

CINCINNATI

Is prepared at all times to execute every description of Plain and Fancy Signs, Transparancies, Enameled Signs, Door Plates, Banners, Pictures, Imitations of Wood and Marble, & c., in the neatest style, and in the most reasonable terms.

To the best of our knowledge he remained in Cincinnati only a few years and then moved to Vernon, Indiana, in 1850. There he painted and wrote, sending articles to Cincinnati journals. He lived in Indianapolis from 1860 to 1863, but interrupted his stay by accepting a position on the faculty of the Whitewater College, Centerville, Indiana, for a year. From 1865 to about 1874 he lived in Chicago, during which time he went on sketching trips to Vermont, the Adirondacks, Vernon—his earlier home—and Brown County, Indiana. His activity at Chicago was so varied and persistent that he came to be known as "the father of art" there.[3] He visited San Francisco in the late seventies and then presumably remained in the West. His death occurred at Burlington, Iowa, in 1887.

Unfortunately none of the work done by Peter F. Reed in Indiana has come to our attention. He was evidently a painter of romantic sentiments, and his landscapes doubtless emphasized the lyrical moods of nature. An address he made on the subject of art at the opening of

69. William Unthank: Portrait of
Harriet Moreland Wishard
Courtesy of the Greenwood Presby-
terian Church, Greenwood (page 164)

70. James B. Dunlap: Portrait of
Woodville Browning
Courtesy of Netta Browning Pittman,
Indianapolis (page 166)

71. Barton S. Hays: Portrait of Rebecca Raymond Adams
Courtesy of Bertha R. Ellis, Indianapolis (page 167)

72. Barton S. Hays: Melon and Peaches
Courtesy of Carl B. Shafer, Indianapolis (page 168)

73. Thomas B. Glessing: Cold Springs, Riverside Park
Courtesy of the Arthur Jordan Foundation, Indianapolis (page 174)

74. William Merritt Chase: Portrait of William Gurley Munson
Courtesy of Mrs. Felix Wurzburg, Berkeley, California (page 179)

the fall session of Whitewater College substantiates this supposition, and reveals his skillful use of words in creating mental images. In speaking about how the eye of the artist is "greeted by a thousand beauties" when looking at nature, he said in part:

The sparkling tide of sunshine, the deep transparent shadow, the cool and inviting halftints that separate the two, and the gentle gradations of perspective, till the enchantment of the distance has melted the very mountains into the soft blue sky, are all studies and conspire to entrance him with their beauties. He dwells in a new world of feeling . . . in which his soul revels, and where, amid groves and vineyards and fountains of water, where the sun never goes down on its loveliness, he may gather fruits upon the confines of this realm of glory and bask enchanted in the beamy sunshine of beauty.[4]

Probably the paintings Reed sent to the Indiana Art Association exhibition in 1878 (*On the Susquehanna* and *In the Adirondacks*) reflected this point of view.

The *Business Mirror* for 1860–1861 should have included the name of Thomas Glessing among the resident painters. Although his name does not appear in the Indianapolis city directories until 1862, he was here in 1859 decorating the Metropolitan Theater,[5] which later became the Park. Glessing was a native of England, born in London in 1817 or 1820, and was trained by his father as a maker of violin strings. When and where he began painting is not known. He first visited America when he was about twenty years old to see his sister and brother-in-law, and he came again about a year later to stay. Presumably he became interested in scenic painting in one of the eastern cities, and had become proficient in the art before coming to Indiana.[6] In Indianapolis he continued to work for the Metropolitan Theater until 1873 when he left for Boston to accept a position as scenic artist at the Boston Museum (theater). He was also in New York for a time where he painted scenery for the Booth Theater. His death occurred in Boston in 1882.

If Thomas Glessing had done only scenic work for theaters the probability is that nothing would have survived as an example of his artistic capabilities. However, he painted landscapes too, and painted them very well. He was a close observer of nature and her moods, adding a poetic touch to the subjects he depicted and organizing his pictures with balance and symmetry as might be expected of a skilled decorator.

His best-known canvas, and probably his most creditable, is *Cold Springs, Riverside Park* (pl. 73), formerly owned by Rose Holmes and now in the Benjamin Harrison Memorial Home, Indianapolis. Several of his landscapes are in the possession of Mr. and Mrs. Herman L. Peck, while others are scattered among local homes. He also enjoyed painting still lifes; Mrs. Hayden Webster owns one that is signed and dated 1862.

An important assignment that came to Glessing in his last year at Indianapolis was the painting of four large canvases illustrating the history of the city, to be hung in the "exposition" here in 1873. They represented the selection of the site, the new settlement in 1821, the city in the Civil War period (with the capital building as the central feature), and the state seal. According to Jacob Dunn, they were not very accurate historically but they were reproduced several times, and came to be regarded by many people as reliable records of local events.[7] As late as 1910 they were still preserved by the Indiana Historical Society, but no trace of them can be found today.

Perhaps the most able of the artists here in the mid-sixties was James M. Dennis. He was originally from Dublin, Indiana, where he was born in 1840. When about eighteen years of age he studied painting in Cincinnati under Joseph O. Eaton, and while there came to know Alexander Wyant, a rising landscape painter from whom he received additional instruction. In 1865 he was in Indianapolis, and here he remained until 1873. In that year he went to New York for a year to get additional technical training.

Although Dennis had embarked upon his professional career as a painter during his first eight years in Indianapolis, none of his work of that period is known. But from his second Indianapolis sojourn (1874–1883), during which time he painted many portraits and landscapes, a sufficient number of his pictures has survived to give a clear idea of the quality and character of his work. His most important commissions were for portraits of John C. New, for the Treasury Building, Washington; of James A. Mount, for the Statehouse, Indianapolis; and of Jefferson Davis (the present location of which is unknown). The Governor Mount portrait is a pastel, a medium that Dennis employed almost exclusively during his mature years; being in a poor condition today (its surface has been damaged by careless cleaning), it does not convey the merits of his work. Crayon portraits of a Mrs. Daggett and Major J. W. Gordon, shown in the 1878 exhibition of the Art Association, have, unfortunately, dropped out of sight. Two of his landscapes, one formerly owned by Mrs. Frank Lewis (now in the home of Bertha Ellis), and another depicting a scene in Christian Park, owned by Mrs. Edna Christian, reveal him as a sensitive artist. His manner of drawing is free, light in touch, and yet sure. His colors are soft and atmospheric.

In 1883 Dennis moved to Detroit with his wife (Marion Webster, of Indianapolis) and their son George, where he continued painting until his death in 1918.

About the time Dennis came to Indianapolis there arrived in the city an itinerant painter named Thomas J. Davies, whose birthplace and place of final settlement are not known. According to the city directories, he was here from 1865 to 1866, but no notice was taken of him by the local press. The penciled name "Davies" on the back of the frames of canvases depicting John and Margaret Boyd Carlisle, owned by Arthur Moore, of Indianapolis, have led to the assignment of the portraits to him.

Davies' technique as seen in these portraits is competent but not distinguished. The likenesses appear to be good, and may have been derived to a large extent from photographs. Several other portraits might be assigned to him on the basis of the Carlisle pictures, such as that of Mary Johnston Tutewiler owned by Isabelle Johnston, and those of Fabius M. Finch and his wife in the Conner Prairie Homestead on the Noblesville road.

Reference has already been made to the commission from the city council of Cincinnati to T. Buchanan Read, of that city, to paint Oliver P. Morton, Indiana's Civil War governor, which brought the celebrated poet-painter to Indianapolis in February, 1865. Read stayed at the Bates House, the city's finest hotel, and his presence must have caused not a little stir in local art circles—his standing as a writer, architect, and painter was such as to make him a notable figure; and one of the town's principal literary events that year was the reading he gave of his poems before a large and appreciative audience on the evening of February 24.

As Oliver P. Morton was at the time occupying the office of governor, sittings for the portrait may have taken place in the Statehouse. Contemporary rating of the finished work was so complimentary that it must have attracted many admirers when it was exhibited at Lieber's Art Emporium:

The portrait of Governor Morton, which Mr. Buchanan Read has been painting for a week past, for the City Council of Cincinnati, is finished, and has been placed in the room of Lieber and Co., the picture and frame dealers on Pennsylvania street, near the Post Office, where it will remain a few days for the gratification of the many citizens who are desirous of seeing how the Governor looks on canvas, as depicted by the hand of genius. The painting, we think, is a most admirable one. The coloring is perfect, the flesh tints natural, and wholly free from the 'painty' suggestion of many portraits. The drawing is excellent, and the likeness close and striking. We have seen no photograph that presents the Governor so accurately, or his expression so naturally. It may be objected that it is a little smooth and unwrinkled, but those who are most familiar with the Governor will be least likely to notice this defect, if it really exists. As a work of art, it has no superior of its kind in the country. And as a likeness, it is not probable that it will be equalled for a long time, if ever.[8]

To the best of our knowledge this was Read's only commission carried out in Indianapolis; and as the finished canvas was soon dispatched to Cincinnati nothing "depicted by the hand of genius" remained for the gratification of the local citizens.

Not long after Read's visit there arrived in the city a woman from Connecticut who was soon to occupy a prominent place among the professional painters of Indianapolis: Ellen M. Ingraham. She was born in New Haven in 1832, had studied art there and in New York, married Charles B. Ingraham, and then came west. She was well known as both a teacher and painter; her work in the latter field included miniatures (she had studied with William Miller in New York) and portraits in oil, executed in a labored academic manner. Several of her miniatures painted in the East are listed by Mary Burnet,[9] who also states that her portrait of Thomas A. Hendricks, Indiana's governor from 1873 to 1877, was shown at the Columbian Exposition of 1893, and that she won first honorable mention at the New Orleans Exposition in 1885. The Hendricks canvas is now lost, but one of her best-known portraits in oil is that of Bishop Joseph Talbott, owned by Harriet Talbott, Indianapolis. He is represented in his ecclesiastical vestments, and looks toward the observer with a kindly, yet strong face. Water-color portraits of Florence and Minnie Coffin, as children, are in the California homes of the subjects. They were made in the early seventies, and appear to have been painted from photographs.

Nothing is said in local chronicles to indicate that Charles Ingraham, Ellen's husband, was also a painter, except that his occupation is listed intermittently in city directories between 1882 and 1890 as "artist." So far, no work by him has been identified. A daughter Lena was born in Indianapolis, received her first instruction in art from her mother, continued her studies in New York, and then taught art in California. She is believed to have died there in 1924.

The number of professional women painters in Indianapolis began to increase at that time, becoming very impressive by the close of the century. The year Ellen Ingraham arrived, the city directory carried the name of Mrs. N. M. Suffrins as a portrait painter with a room at 8 West Washington Street; she stayed only a year or two and was last heard of as being in Muncie in 1868. Mrs. S. S. Starling appeared in 1870; then, a few years later, came Lotta Guffin, Sallie Archer, Julia Ludington, Mary Hill Culbertson, Eliza Bates, Margaret Rudisill, Julia Cox, and Elizabeth Nicholson.

II

During most of the decade of the sixties there lived in Indianapolis an eager and talented art student by the name of William Merritt

Chase, who was destined to become one of America's most distinguished painters. As the story of his life has been told many times,[10] it will not be necessary to give here more than the briefest summary of his early activities.

He was born in Williamsburg (now Nineveh) in 1849. His family moved to Indianapolis late in 1861 when the aspiring artist was twelve years old. His father, David H. Chase, entered the retail shoe business, and the boy went to local schools, helping in the shoestore in his spare time. His incessant drawing on wrapping paper led his father to conclude that he would accomplish more in an art class than in the store, so he was taken to the studio of Barton S. Hays. There he received his first serious instruction in painting and also became acquainted with other students and established painters. That was in 1866. About a year later he went east, spent three months on the naval training ship *Portsmouth* and a couple of seasons at the National Academy of Design. Early in 1869 he was back in Indianapolis and had resumed his work in Hays's studio, although it was evident that he was already outstripping his master, technically.

A fellow student, Frank J. Howell, has left some reminiscences of that phase of Chase's development that are of more than passing interest. He said in part:

Mr. Hayes [*sic*] had with him David Munsey, a still life enthusiast, who was testing the merits of a red apple, in study work of its various tints of color, light and shades.

Mr. Hayes's charges of $20 for lessons for a calendar month was the price for every aspirant in color work.

Near Mr. Munsey's easel was William M. Chase using his well arranged palette and brushes with masterly strokes, that bespoke the artist whose father was then a prosperous shoe merchant.

Artist Hayes, quite capable of teaching art, had urged his youthful pupil to study at America's fountain head, New York city. Now back again to Indiana's metropolis, he was temporarily using his first teacher's studio in a three-story building adjoining the government postoffice on "Meridian Circle." He was indulging his striking technique even then admired by Mr. Hayes.

One subject was that of a half length figure on an 8 x 10 canvas of an old German barber, clipping the frowsy locks of a weeping youngster. His subjects were various and always interesting, whether of still life or story telling figure works.[11]

Frank Howell went on to say that the next year (in October, 1870) he met Chase again in St. Louis where he was sharing a studio with James W. Pattison. Not long afterward, Chase, through his extraordinary performances, attracted the attention of several businessmen in St. Louis who decided to advance him a sum of money for study in Europe; in the late summer of 1872 he sailed for Munich; six years later he was back in New York, and within a short time was regarded as one of the leading painters and teachers of America. He never again returned to his native state except for brief visits.

Only half a dozen pictures by Chase dating from his Indiana period (1866–1869) are known, and they are all portraits. The canvas of a German barber and a weeping youngster, mentioned by Howell, has not come to light, nor have any of the still-life compositions that played a very important part in the first stage of his technical development. Probably his earliest work now known is the crayon portrait of Wallace Foster, owned by the John Herron Art Museum, dating from 1866.[12] Another is a study, in the same medium and of the same date, of Mary Elizabeth Browning, owned by Mrs. R. H. Browning, Indianapolis. An oil portrait of William Gurley Munson (pl. 74), a close friend of the artist, painted about 1868, is owned by Mrs. Felix Wurzburg, now residing in California. Remaining oil portraits of the period represent William Orbison, owned by Robert Orbison, Indianapolis; Benjamin F. Love, owned by Mrs. Prudence Douglas, Shelbyville; and Emma S. Carpenter as a child, a small oval canvas owned by Mrs. A. G. Brumenshenkel, of Gates Mills, Ohio.

There is no suggestion in these of the virtuosity, the brilliant brush work, and sparkling color so characteristic of Chase's mature work; nor of that "striking technique" displayed during his last year at Indianapolis, to which Howell referred. The conclusion is reached, therefore, that they were painted before he went to New York, and at a time when his concepts were based on local commercial portraits and on the precepts of Hays: firm, precise drawing and a paucity of color. He was only about nineteen years old when he painted them.

As the 1860's drew to a close a project of considerable importance, artistic and historic, was undertaken by the state. Governor Conrad Baker conceived the idea of assembling portraits of the former chief executives of Indiana, and won the support of the legislature in carrying out the program. Seventeen men had preceded him but as yet no likenesses of them were owned by the state, and there was no assurance that any existed. The Governor's first step was to have the legislature appropriate money to purchase such portraits as could be found and to commission artists to paint others, at $200 per canvas. Then the search began for existing portraits of the seven governors who had died, while plans were made to have those who were still living sit before the easels of local painters.

Since the story of the acquisition of each is told in the author's report, *Portraits and Painters of the Governors of Indiana*,[13] only a summary will be given here. As no existing portrait could be procured of William Henry Harrison, first territorial governor, Barton Hays was commissioned to paint one; the model used by Hays was probably the portrait of Harrison at Bowdoin College. No likeness of John Gibson, acting territorial governor, could be found, and repeated attempts to discover one were fruitless.[14] The portrait of Thomas Posey was painted by John B. Hill, probably from a miniature. John Bayless Hill was a young painter of twenty, a student of Jacob Cox, just starting out on his career—a career that was cut short by his premature death five years later. In addition to the Posey portrait, Hill received the commission to paint former Governor Abram A. Hammond, from life.

The canvases portraying Jonathan Jennings, Ratliff Boon, James Whitcomb, Paris C. Dunning, Oliver P. Morton, and Conrad Baker (pl. 75) are by James G. Forbes, to whom reference has already been made in the section dealing with Evansville. As was pointed out there, Forbes had come to Evansville from Chicago to paint the portrait of Mayor John Baker, brother of Conrad Baker, which, in all probability, led to his introduction to the Governor.

Jacob Cox, the most popular of the city's painters, was not overlooked in the project: he was privileged to have six of his canvases in the collection (more than any other resident artist), all made from life, and all but one, apparently, painted before the collection was assembled. The one that was commissioned by the state is that of Henry S. Lane, who was living in Crawfordsville at the time but came to Indianapolis to pose for the portrait. Those of Samuel Bigger, Noah Noble, James B. Ray, David Wallace, and Joseph A. Wright had all been painted by Cox in the forties and fifties, and in all probability were still in the artist's possession when the official collection was being formed. The canvas of David Wallace was probably the one upon which Cox was working when the Governor's son Lew surreptitiously entered the studio to watch the painter at work—an incident referred to previously.

The portrait of Ashbel P. Willard was the work of George W. Morrison, whose activity in New Albany has already been reported. It was painted in 1857 when Willard was residing in New Albany, and was purchased from the artist in 1870.

Securing a likeness of William Hendricks, the only predecessor whose portrait had not been found or commissioned by 1870, gave Conrad Baker and his associates considerable trouble. In desperation, the commission was finally given to a man in New Castle, Kentucky, by the name of R. H. Buckley, who claimed to have known Hendricks well enough to recapture his features—even though Hendricks had been dead thirty-five years. It turned out that Buckley was not a professional painter, although he had done a little daubing many years before. Nevertheless he boldly attempted the impossible. The picture was accepted and paid for, but it was so unsatisfactory that when Thomas A. Hendricks, the subject's nephew, assumed office as governor in 1873 he had the canvas destroyed. Many years later (1926) the gap was filled by S. Burtis Baker, a painter of Washington, D. C., who used as his model the likeness of Hendricks in the famous composition, *The House of Representatives*, by Samuel F. B. Morse.[15]

Since Conrad Baker's tenure of office the collection of governors' portraits has grown steadily as each incumbent has sat before an artist of his choice. Thomas A. Hendricks was painted by William R. Freeman in 1873 or 1874, during the artist's brief residence in Indianapolis. James D. Williams was painted by an itinerant named Harry M. Colcord, who was here for only a year between 1878 and 1880.

With Albert G. Porter begins a series of portraits by Theodore C. Steele, whose long and active career will be summarized in the section dealing with the artists of the 1870's. His canvas of Governor Porter was probably painted in 1885, the date we have chosen for the termination of this chronicle.

III

In spite of the panic that came in the middle of the decade, the years between 1870 and 1880 were significant ones for the arts. First, there was the post-war boom. Not everyone was rich, but many people had money far beyond their ordinary necessities, enabling them to acquire luxury items, build and furnish large pretentious houses, buy pictures by foreign and native painters, and contribute to the support of art associations and schools. Second, the artists themselves were beginning to have a different attitude toward their work and their place in society. In contrast to their predecessors —many of whom were rather inept itinerants, particularly in the frontier areas—the younger men and women of the seventies thought of themselves as a professional group whose calling was noble and whose work was a part of that great stream into which Raphael, Michelangelo, and Rembrandt had poured their best efforts. This attitude was largely the consequence of unprecedented travel and study abroad, which not only increased the artists' technical capacities but broadened their cultural horizons and sharpened their sensibilities. Both of these factors had some bearing on the third, namely, the establishment of art societies and schools, and the organization of large public exhibitions. The latter served as valuable agencies in introducing a painter's work to the public, as well as enabling the artist to judge the success of his labors in relation to that of his colleagues.

It was late in the decade—January, 1877 to be exact—when the first organization was formed designed to bring together the artists and art patrons of the city. Incorporated under the name Indianapolis Art Association (not to be confused with the Art Association of Indianapolis, of 1883), with an active membership of seven painters and a list of patrons that included many prominent citizens, it opened an art gallery in the Bates block. Here was held the city's first major exhibition; about fifty paintings by the seven members of the association were arranged on walls hung in seal-brown cambric.

A peculiarity of this first art association was its rule that membership was open only to men. According to an account in the *Saturday Herald*, John Love, who, with T. C. Steele, drew up the regulations, was responsible for that stipulation. The editor, not being in sympathy with the idea, wrote a long, caustic article about the organization, predicting its early extinction. He pointed out that "Mr. Love's experience abroad had taught him art could not be elevated by but one sex, and that his own. Art and femininity were incompatible in his opinion, hence femininity was to be excluded from the Association." Toward the end of the article the writer showed his utter disgust by remarking: "Here was displayed a petty and contemptible jealousy of the workmanship of women which would better have fitted a trades union of low degree than an association of artists, supposed to be cultivated and traveled gentlemen." [16]

The president and secretary of the Indianapolis Art Association were Dewey Bates, a new arrival in the city, and Theodore C. Steele. The other members were John Love, Jacob Cox, Theobald Lietz, Carl Fetsch, and Barton Hays. In their exhibition of January, 1877, only one painter outside the membership was invited to submit a picture. She was Lotta Guffin, the leading woman artist in the city; the inclusion of her work was probably designed to ease the sting of the male-only clause in the association's by-laws.

The editor's prediction of an early death for the organization was fulfilled. A year later no more was heard of it. Then some of the artists and their friends turned to a new project, a school, and in the fall of 1877 the Indiana School of Art was established, opening its doors to students on the fifteenth of October. As an adjunct, a new organization called the Indiana Art Association was formed, designed to enlist interest and financial aid from the citizenry.

The school was located on the upper floor of the Sacks Building, known at that time as the Fletcher-Sharpe block, where several rooms were equipped with easels, tables, and plaster casts of classic sculpture.

The announced courses were free-hand drawing, machine and architectural draughting, perspective, artistic anatomy, sculpture, figure
composition, landscape, decorative painting in oil and water colors,
engraving, lithography, ceramic art, wood carving, and industrial art.
The two men most active in its organization and management were
James F. Gookins, who was made director, and John W. Love, assistant
director. The other instructors were Ferdinand Mersmann, John H.
Warder, and Henry C. Chandler.

According to historian Dunn, the school was successful while it
continued, and enjoyed excellent prospects, but "Gookins and Love
did not agree in their art ideals. Gookins belonged to the old school,
and most of Indianapolis people who cared for art had its ideals."[17]
After a year Gookins dropped out, but Love kept it going for another
season. By that time patronage had all but evaporated, for Indianapolis was feeling the full pressure of the panic of 1873. Its work, however, was not in vain. The serious younger men and women of the
state had had their first taste of professional instruction in art and were
well launched upon their future careers before the doors were closed.
And, more than anything else, asserted William Forsyth, "this school
and these men brought to Indiana art seriousness of purpose, that con-
tinuity of effort, and that joy in work and craftsmanship that has never
ceased and is its most pronounced characteristic today."[18]

The first major project of the art association, adjunct to the art
school, was the organization of a large exhibition of paintings and
ceramics, held in May of 1878. It was made up of work by resident
painters, with a number of invited canvases by eastern artists. A section was devoted to a bric-a-brac display, and another to students'
work. Called the "First Quarterly Exhibition," it was optimistically
thought of as the first in a series of major shows, a projected plan that
did not materialize because of the organization's brief existence. However, with the formation of a third art association five years later, the
torch was again taken up by artists and laymen, and the city was treated
to even larger and more splendid displays of artistic talent.

Most of the painters who participated in the exhibition of 1878
will be discussed in the following pages, if they have not already been

mentioned. Gookins, the favored exhibitor, with twenty paintings on the walls, left for Terre Haute soon after, and then went to Chicago; Assistant Director Love showed nine pictures, most of which, judging by their titles, were made in Europe. His portrait of Louis A. Kiefer, number 34 in the catalogue, is now in the John Herron Art Museum —the only one of the nine known to be in the city.

John Washington Love was a native of the state, having been born in Ripley County, near Napoleon, in 1850. His family moved to Indianapolis when he was a boy, and here he attended local schools and Northwestern Christian University. When nineteen he studied for about a year with Barton S. Hays (William M. Chase had left not long before for New York) and then went to Cincinnati to continue his art training under Henry Mosler. In 1872 he went to Europe, but attended the National Academy of Design in New York for a few months en route; he enrolled at the Ecole des Beaux-Arts in Paris, and also received instruction from Gérôme, probably the most eminent painter in Paris at the time. The fact that Love exhibited his paintings twice at the Paris Salon while still a student gives an indication of his ability. His vacations were spent at Barbizon and in Brittany, where many of the paintings he exhibited later in Indianapolis were made.

Love returned to Indiana in 1876, full of enthusiasm and with a desire to expand the art activities of Indianapolis. He began to lay the foundation of a professional art school and found a sympathetic helper in Gookins. The city had little of that atmosphere so congenial to artists living abroad, and we may reasonably assume that Love did everything possible to recreate something of the Bohemian tone by encouraging friendly gatherings of painters, writers, and musicians, and by promoting exhibitions.

The establishment of the art school that autumn was unquestionably a difficult and responsible project, and one that he was well suited to carry through. His ideals were high, his experience had been extensive, and his ability as a painter and teacher could not be questioned. One of his first pupils, William Forsyth, wrote that he had "vigorous ideas as to drawing which made him almost merciless as a teacher to those of his pupils who showed talent and staying powers. In painting he was liberal and showed equal liking for the academic and its opposite and was influenced strongly by widely different masters . . . He died too young [1880] to have formed any settled manner, or to have organized his knowledge into a distinct style . . . In person he was tall, broad shouldered and distinguished, a handsome blond giant whose appearance would have attracted attention anywhere." [19]

The few extant canvases by Love attest to his power as a painter, and reflect both his foreign training and the germ of an individual style. He worked in a strong, direct manner, based on sound draughtsmanship and a good understanding of form and color. Both portraits and landscapes interested him, although outdoor subjects apparently appealed to him most. Several of his canvases are owned by the John Herron Art Museum: in addition to the portrait of Louis Kiefer, it has two of his landscapes, *Fontainebleau Forest* and *The Sycamores* (pl. 76), and a sketch of the head of a boy. A portrait of Henry L. Sielken, in hunting attire (pl. 77), is in the home of the grandson of the subject, who bears the same name.

IV

Some idea of the position occupied by the arts in Indianapolis in the 1870's may be gained by studying the roster of painters active during that decade, compiled from such sources as newspaper reviews, city directories, and the catalogue of the 1878 exhibition. There were more than forty. Many, like Cox, Hays, Dennis, and Glessing had been active in the previous decade, as we have seen, and they continued to hold their own in spite of growing competition. The list of new arrivals included men who had worked in other communities in Indiana—several of whom, such as Fetsch, Lietz, Freeman, and Davenport, have already been introduced to the reader—and a score of new transients whose sojourns varied from a few weeks to several months. Some, like Steele and Sinks, made Indianapolis their permanent home.

The first, with professional ratings, to arrive in 1870 were Carl P. Fetsch and Theobald Lietz. They were both trained as photographer-artists, using photographs to a large extent as models for their portraits, or actually painting over enlarged photographic prints. As previously stated, Fetsch, or Pfetsch, was born at Blankenburg, Germany, about 1817. He came to New York when he was twenty-six years of age, opened a studio where he taught and painted, and joined the German-American Art Club. When his work was destroyed by fire, he moved to Cincinnati. That was about 1853. Fire again destroyed his studio and possessions three years later, prompting him to move again—this time to New Albany, Indiana, where he lived until his removal to Indianapolis in 1870. It is reported that during the Civil War he served as a photographer with Grant's army. He died here in 1898.

Fetsch's output in Indianapolis must have been extensive, but his use of photographs reduced the possibility of his showing a marked individual style, with the result that little of his work can now be identified on the basis of personal technique. A portrait of John Heitkam, formerly owned by the late Walter Heitkam of Indianapolis, and a composition depicting an elderly woman preparing to bathe her grandchild, owned by Carlton Weiss, of Indianapolis, are characteristic of his best efforts. The latter, combining sentimentality and lifelike delineation, won for the painter, according to family tradition, a prize at the Philadelphia Centennial Exhibition. Another honor came to him in the form of a silver cup which he won on a painting shown at the Indiana State Fair in 1859.

Theobald Lietz, also a German by birth, was presumably about Fetsch's age. His training in art was probably obtained in his native land, where he also received his academic education. It is not known when he came to America or when he arrived in Indianapolis. He may have had friends in the city's large German colony, which could have influenced his selection of Indianapolis for his home.

Lietz seems to have enjoyed the reputation of being a good teacher, as well as a painter and photographer, because several of the younger aspiring artists received their technical training under him. (The best-known of his pupils was Samuel Richards). The difficulty of identifying his work today rests, as in Fetsch's case, upon his practice of employing photographs as the foundation of his oil portraits. The closing years of his history are not known. He was living in Indianapolis in 1884, the last year his name appeared in the city directory.

By 1873 the panic had hit Indianapolis with grim force, having been brought on to a large extent by the collapse of the real-estate boom that followed the Civil War. Perhaps the most hopeless victims of the depression were the artists, most of whom had no other trade to fall back upon, and were forced to weather the period as best they could. Their fortitude was reflected in an article about Cox that appeared in the *Saturday Herald:*

> During the dull times since the panic, Jacob Cox, the patriarch of Indianapolis art, has been amusing himself and keeping off the blues by painting little landscapes and figure pieces, and now and then a work of greater magnitude. Among the latter is an original composition entitled "The Tired Sewing Girl," which is full of sentiment and has been admirably executed.[20]

While Cox and other resident painters were building up their stock of small and large compositions, awaiting better times, several more artists arrived, hoping to find some business in the metropolis. Perhaps the situation was worse in the communities from which they had come, and they probably hoped that Indianapolis could offer them a few commissions, however modest, to tide them over. We know little about their success, but the fact that their visits were of short duration indicates that they did not enjoy the patronage they hoped to find. Among them were William Fredericksen, Joseph Sternback, David O. Adams, J. B. Mendenhall and Mrs. M. E. Lewis, who left nothing behind but their names in the city directories; more is known about Royal H. Millison, Dewey Bates, Lotta Guffin, Mary Culbertson, John Antrobus, James Dennis, Alois Sinks, and William Freeman.

William Freeman, whose proclivity for wandering around the southwestern part of the state has already been pointed out, arrived as the economic situation was less severe—in 1874—and remained about a year. His most important commission at the time was the portrait of Governor Thomas A. Hendricks for the Statehouse collection. During the same sojourn here he made the posthumous portrait of Almus E. Vinton, which is owned by Mrs. Frederic Krull, and probably that of David F. Vinton, owned by Douglas Pierce. One of his finest performances is his portrait of Jacob Cox (pl. 78).

Freeman was brought abruptly into the spotlight of local art affairs when, early in 1875, he became the target of some scathing jabs from the pen of the local newspaper critic, Alois E. Sinks, a recent arrival in Indianapolis. Reference has already been made to Sinks's censure of Lew Wallace's composition. The painting by Freeman that disturbed his sensibilities not a little was one labeled *Rainy Day*. Sinks denounced it as "a violation of nearly every principle of art," and the verbal battle that ensued is of interest in the story of local affairs because it is the first recorded controversy in the state between critic and painter.

Sinks's attack upon the Freeman canvas is too long to print here in its entirety. He began by reporting that the artist had thrown "a third part of heaven, or Indianapolis, rather, into a spasm of admiration over a picture entitled—facetiously, we suppose—Longfellow's Rainy Day," and went on to say that he had heard wild rumors of fabulous prices, ranging from five hundred to two thousand dollars, having been paid for the picture, adding, "we have only to say most truthfully and solemnly that if any man did pay $500 for this picture he paid just about $450 too much." [21]

His criticism was based primarily on the photographic appearance of the picture and its false sentiment or expression: "One can almost see the photographic prop behind the head [the painting represented a girl seated in a room], to say nothing of that effect of stiffness in other parts of the body. Add to this the vulgar green bedroom carpet, the commonplace and precise appearance of things in the room, the fuzzy church spire and trees out of the window, the shivering, unwholesome suggestions of ague and liver complaint in the hue of everything—well, enough of it."

After pointing out the incongruous lighting and the "love-sick, dreaming look that almost any young woman can assume when she desires to attract attention or admiration," Sinks added that if anyone doubted the justification of his "very moderate criticism" of the picture one could take it to any recognized and competent critic or artist and get an opinion.

Freeman's reply was restrained and concise, but reflected the sting he had felt. It appeared as a letter to the editor of the *Sentinel* and was reprinted in the *Saturday Herald* on the twentieth of February. He made no defense of technical shortcomings or maudlin expression of sentiment, but revealed that the painting was to have been reproduced by a chromolithograph company in Boston, who placed on it a value of $2,400. While the picture was in Boston several critics and art dealers were asked to examine it, and "it received their emphatic approval." Freeman ended his letter with the statement that "justice demands that the public should judge between the opinions of some of the best Boston critics and this wandering egotist."

The counterthrust came from Sinks the following week, asking for the identity of the Boston critics and adding that he felt obliged "to correct an erroneous but very general impression that a painting reproduced by the chromo process is a work of art," reminding the reader that most of the leading artists of that day objected to having their pictures "chromoed," and that "daubs, the most monstrous, have often been found sufficiently meritorious by chromo artists to be duplicated." Finally, after pointing to some specific examples of this "vile anamorphosis" type of art, he condescended to admit that "Mr. Freeman's Rainy Day, with its sweet face, compared with these abominations, is a master-piece," and with that the controversy was brought to a close.

When Sinks's articles first appeared in the *Saturday Herald*, in January, 1875, an unknown citizen, signing himself "An Admirer of Genius" (who may have been Sinks himself), sent a long letter to the editor extolling the critic's ability. After dwelling upon the city's growth, its industrial and cultural status, he pointed out that the sad state of the art of painting was not due to a lack of artists but rather to the want of a competent art critic—and now Indianapolis was no longer to suffer on that account. "It may be death to many of the poor miserable artists," he continued in his zeal, "who are struggling on in their mean way to make the two ends meet, but it will be better for the future greatness and glory of the greatest inland city." [22]

The city's first professional art critic, Alois E. Sinks, was a native of Dayton, Ohio. He came to Indianapolis from New York, where he had received some training as a painter and where he acquired a certain amount of experience as a writer, both critical and creative. According to historian Dunn, he "was as genuine a bohemian as ever reached this place, and was a source of perpetual entertainment to John W. Love, who maintained that Sinks was out of his proper setting anywhere but in the Latin Quarter in Paris."[23] Dunn went on to say that Sinks had run away from home, joined the Union army as a drummer boy, was wounded and discharged, and then went to New York. He reached Indianapolis late in 1874 or in the very first part of 1875. From William Forsyth we get a description of him as "a rather small man, smooth shaven, his face framed in a shock of long, brown hair, with a large soft hat over it and always, weather permitting, wearing a cloak . . . Sinks painted in the interval of his newspaper work, mainly imaginative pictures—moonlit castles, Grecian temples, etc. He had had probably little or no training and was not master of his dreams. Nevertheless, he was a picturesque and interesting figure, and when in the mood quite entertaining."[24]

As an artist, Sinks was neither as lucid nor as sparkling as he was as a writer. As Forsyth remarked, he was a dreamy sort of painter, preferring romantic scenes drawn more from imagination than from actuality. However, the titles of paintings exhibited in local shows indicate that he also aimed to depict certain scenes with objective fidelity: *View of Indianapolis from Union Stock Yards, Battle Field of Stone River, Study of Beech Trees.*[25] But whatever his intention, the few pictures that one can see today reveal him as a mediocre technician. A small canvas depicting a country school, owned by Mamie L. Bass, and two landscapes owned by Mrs. F. E. Wickard, are characteristic examples of his output.

Sinks made Indianapolis his home from the time of his arrival until his death in 1881. He married Elizabeth Wickard soon after settling here; their one child, a son, died in infancy. Sinks became a heavy drinker and died from injuries suffered from a fall. He was buried in Crown Hill Cemetery among his comrades who had served in the Civil War.

As we look back now to the years when Sinks was in Indianapolis, we fail to see any marked improvement in the arts as a result of his preachments or critical appraisals. He was bold, if not ruthless, in his attacks upon mediocrity, but a certain arrogance coupled with impatience reduced the effectiveness of his crusade.

Of interest to the historian, nevertheless, are his estimates of work produced by such men as Cox, Steele, and Dennis, in addition to those already mentioned. He was understanding and tolerant in regard to "the fine looking, elderly gentleman, Jacob Cox . . . a man of unquestionable talent, if not genius." He felt that Cox's best pictures emanated from his soul and that his works would be admired long after he had "gone beyond them."

Of Steele's portraits he remarked that they gave promise of unusual artistic talent, but that they were deficient in color (which was true) and that under favorable auspices he would develop rapidly into a real artist. Sinks compared one of his portraits to the work of Healy, but added that the background was "dead and unaccessory," and that his drapery was stiff and flat.

Sinks found some newly painted landscapes in the studio of James M. Dennis and remarked that there was not one of them but could be made much better if Dennis were to "try right hard." "Of course," he continued, "a warm-hearted impulsive young man like Mr. Dennis must live, but then he would live just as long if he took pains to always do his best." Then the critic proceeded to analyze two portraits and a study of a nude, remarking that the "Venus is a failure, but the same is justly said of Page's Venus. We would suggest to Mr. Dennis that in painting a nude figure great care should be observed if drapery is introduced at all, not to have just enough to suggest immodesty." The reader will recall that Dennis was one of the established painters in the city, having opened his studio about ten years before this review appeared in the local press, and presumably had enjoyed as much success as any of his fellow-painters in town.

Another visiting painter whose work did not come up to the critic's specifications, was John Antrobus. He had not been in Indianapolis long when he was favored by a visit from Sinks, and soon after the citizens read the following in the *Saturday Herald,* under the caption "Art Matters," that weekly column of vitriolic art criticism:

75. James G. Forbes: Portrait of Conrad Baker
Courtesy of the Indiana Historical Bureau, Indianapolis (page 180)

76. John W. Love: The Sycamores
John Herron Art Museum, Indianapolis (page 186)

77. John W. Love: Portrait of Henry L. Sielken
Courtesy of Harry L. Sielken, Indianapolis (page 186)

78. William R. Freeman: Portrait of Jacob Cox
Courtesy of Cyril C. Spades, Saint Augustine, Florida (page 188)

As regards John Antrobus, but little can be said. So far as his pretentions to be a painter—if by that term an artist is meant—are concerned, he is a peripatetic humbug . . . Mr. Antrobus once perpetrated the clever joke of caricaturing some of the prominent citizens of the city, and in order to make the matter more funny still, he took surreptitious leave of the Capital at an hour considerably in advance of that in which his ex-Honor, Mr. Jim Mitchell, discovered that his portrait appeared to most flattering advantage with the face turned prone to the wall.[26]

Which of the prominent citizens Antrobus "caricatured" we are not informed, but a pair of portraits has recently been identified as his work. They represent George J. Stilz and his wife, and are now in the home of Walter Bozell. While they cannot be classified as great technical performances they are not as bad as Sinks would have us believe, either from the standpoint of technique or characterization.

Antrobus is today a very nebulous historical figure. The scattered references to him inform us that he was painting in Savannah, Georgia, and Montgomery, Alabama, in the 1850's, and in Chicago during the 1860's. Where he went after taking "surreptitious leave" of Indianapolis we do not know. The next report announced his death at Detroit in 1907.[27]

V

Of the several painters mentioned by Sinks in his various articles or reviews there were three women: Lotta Guffin, Mrs. De la Matyr, and Margaret Rudisill. "No Indianapolis artist has shown more rapid progress than Mrs. Harry Guffin," he wrote on January 30, 1875. "She has on exhibition at Lieber's a copy of one of Mr. Eaton's pictures— a Greek-faced woman—which shows great strength. Mrs. Guffin shows great promise for animal painting, and has scores of little pieces in various stages of development. It is one of her peculiarities to have a great many pieces under way at the same time." In another article he referred to her "handsome portrait, life size, of Annie, daughter of Hon. Ben F. Davis."

Lotta Guffin's output was more considerable than that of many of her contemporaries, judging by existing examples, which may have accounted for the fact that her reputation beyond the state was greater than most. On the other hand, she was not an exceptional painter from a technical standpoint. Her drawing was accurate but her brush work was labored and the tones of her pictures now appear dark and sooty. Colors may have been brighter when first applied: her aim to create moody, dreamy pictures led her to use deep colors that probably have darkened considerably during the intervening years.

Her portraits may be classed as her finest work, particularly that of Addison C. Harris (pl. 79), in the Allisonville home of the late Mrs. Addison Harris, and of Dr. Thomas C. Harvey, in the Indiana Medical School Library, Indianapolis. Among her other known portraits are: Horace P. Biddle, noted Logansport citizen; Conrad Baker, former governor, owned by Thaddeus R. Baker; Elizabeth Burgess Harvey, owned by Linton Cox; and John Froelking and his wife Charlotte Wehlermann, owned by Emma Bushman.

Charlotte Elmire Hollis Guffin, familiarly and professionally known as Lotta Guffin, was born in Decatur County, near Greensburg, Indiana, in 1844, one of the seven children of William Hollis and Harriet Davidson. The father, who had been a schoolteacher in Kentucky prior to coming to Indiana, was engaged chiefly in raising horses. Lotta had considerable training in music under teachers in Cincinnati; she also studied at Northwestern Christian University (later Butler University), Indianapolis, and later became a teacher of music on its faculty. There she met Henry Clay Guffin, a law student, whom she married in 1864.

About ten years later she decided to paint and became a student of Jacob Cox. During her husband's prolonged illness she supported her family (they had two daughters) by her pictures. Afterward she went to New York, and then to Chicago. She died in the home of her son-in-law, in Chicago, in 1896.

The second woman painter mentioned by Sinks was Mrs. Gilbert De la Matyr, and about all we know of her work is the critic's brief and complimentary report in the *Saturday Herald*: "Mrs. De la Matyr, wife of the pastor of Roberts Park church, is not only a charming lady but an artist of great ability. The walls of her residence on East Ohio street are enriched with many fine oil paintings from her easel." If any of the pictures painted during her five years of residence in Indianapolis are still in the city their whereabouts is not known. She was a native of Mount Morris, New York (her maiden name was Marietta Osborn), and she accompanied her husband to Indianapolis in 1874, when he became pastor of Roberts Park Church. About three years later he became pastor of Grace Chapel, and from 1879 to 1891 he was in Congress. Presumably they made their home in Washington after leaving Indianapolis.

While Sinks mentions Margaret Rudisill in the same article, he says nothing enlightening about her or her work. But from Jacob Dunn we learn that she was a native of Montgomery County, Indiana, studied for seven years in Paris under Thompson, Bouguereau, Fleury, and Stevens, and then came to Indianapolis to take her rightful place among its leading painters.[28] However, the care of an invalid mother prevented her from giving as much time to art as she wished and her output was curtailed. She was born in 1857, and died in Indianapolis in June, 1933.

In speaking of Margaret Rudisill as a pupil of Jacob Cox, Dunn states that the Indianapolis master had two other promising female pupils—India Underhill Kirkland and Mary Hill Culbertson—in addition to his own daughter Julia. India Underhill, daughter of Robert Underhill, prosperous foundryman, was born and educated in Indianapolis. While studying with Cox she displayed such talent in modeling that he advised her to turn from painting to sculpture. Her bust of Oliver P. Morton, made in 1880 for the Morton monument competition and shown in the 1903 exhibition held under the auspices of the Flower Mission, is frequently referred to in early reports.[29]

Mary Hill Culbertson, daughter of John F. Hill, a nurseryman and florist, and sister of John B. Hill, the young painter mentioned earlier, was born in Richmond, Indiana, in 1848, and died in Indianapolis in 1913. Her first instruction in drawing was received from Mrs. M. A. Talbott, wife of the Episcopalian rector; for about two years she studied under Jacob Cox; then she went abroad in 1890 to pursue her studies in painting and music. Much of her life was devoted to teaching art, and scarcely anything of significance remains today that was painted by her in those first years of her professional career.

In his "Art Notes" of February 27 and March 20, 1875, Sinks introduces his readers to another painter who had arrived in the city: Henry F. Spread. The critic was attracted to the portrait of a lady by Spread in Styles's show window, and feeling inclined to say something about it, analyzed the color and drawing (which he did not regard as superior) and pronounced it "decidedly good, for the kind." He then went on to say: "We understand that Mr. Spread is an affable and highly cultivated gentleman and hope to have the pleasure of meeting him at his studio and seeing something more of his work." In the second article Sinks mentions a portrait of Judge Martindale that had taken the place of the lady's portrait in Styles's window, the merits of which were "pretty effectually" obscured by the garish light. We presume he had met Spread by that time and found him as affable and cultivated as reported.

The portrait of Judge Elijah B. Martindale that Sinks examined on that March day in 1875 is still in Indianapolis in the possession of the subject's grandson, and seems to be the only identifiable painting by Spread in the city. It is far from being an arresting performance, artistically; the likeness impresses one as good, but the technique is prosaic and unrelieved by either adroit brush work or attractive color.

Henry Fenton Spread had probably reached Indianapolis from the East late in 1874 or early in 1875. He had come to America about five years earlier from his home at Kinsale, Ireland, where he was born in 1844. Having studied art in England and Germany, he was equipped to undertake portrait painting on a professional basis when he arrived in the United States.

It appears that he left Indianapolis in the fall of 1875, lingering for a brief period in Terre Haute, and then proceeding to Chicago. It was there that he made his permanent home. His reputation grew and he became a popular painter, teacher, and leader in art circles. He founded Spread's Art Academy, which eventually became the Chicago Academy of Fine Arts, forerunner of the Art Institute of Chicago, and he exerted a good deal of influence through his instruction and advice to students; he was best known as a painter of anecdotal compositions like *Sad News* and *Chicago Arising from Her Ashes*. His death occurred there in 1890.

Sometime during 1875 a sixteen-year-old aspirant to an artistic career by the name of Otto Stark left Indianapolis (where he was born in 1859) for Cincinnati, to apprentice himself to a lithographer. There he attended the night classes at the art academy; becoming absorbed in problems of painting, he later went to New York, where he entered the Art Students League; from there he went to Europe and studied at the Julien Academy in Paris for a period of three years. Returning to America in 1887, he settled in New York; but the death of his wife three or four years later, and the responsibility of caring for four motherless children, brought him back to his native city. The story of his career after 1890, while occupying a conspicuous place in the city's cultural history, is beyond the domain of this book.

An announcement in the Indianapolis *Saturday Herald* of January 27, 1877, to the effect that five paintings in the First Quarterly Exhibition were by Dewey Bates, probably attracted little attention, and yet Bates was one of the best-trained and most competent artists in the city at the time. Although a recent arrival, his abilities were not unappreciated by the local artists, for he was elected president of the newly formed Indiana Art Association.

Bates was born in Philadelphia in 1851. He had studied art at the Antwerp Royal Academy, Belgium, at the Académie Gérôme and Ecole des Beaux-Arts, Paris, and in London. His coming to Indianapolis doubtless hinged upon his friendship with John Love, whom he had met in Gérôme's studio; also, he was related to the Bates family, so prominent in Indianapolis at the time. Both young men arrived in the city the same year, 1876.

Bates took an active part in the city's cultural life during his year's residence, managing the affairs of the art association and painting portraits and other subjects that were well above the average in quality. His superiority was recognized by the editor of the *Indianapolis Saturday Herald*, who wrote on May 26, 1877: "It is but simple justice to state that the recent revival of interest in art matters in this city, and the more correct standard of judgment and appreciation, has been mainly due to the efforts of a gentleman whose sojourn here has been limited to a few months." He went on to describe Bates as a young man of medium height, rather fastidious in dress, with moustache and chin whiskers *a la cavalier,* clear, keen grayish-blue eyes, and a strong cranial development in the region of the perceptive faculties. He also referred to one of the portraits in Bates's studio, a full-length painting of Ella Bates, as "his best work and certainly one of the most attractive pictures, whether in subject or execution, ever exhibited in the city."

The editor's closing remarks indicated that the painter intended leaving the city as soon as he had finished the portraits on hand.

Two characteristic examples of his work still remain in the city: a portrait of John Love, seated informally in a room, wearing a stocking cap and an overcoat, and a very pleasing portrait of Josephine Landis, done with great simplicity and technical knowledge (pl. 80). The former is in the collection of the John Herron Art Museum, the latter in the home of Mrs. William M. Rockwood. It is recorded that his paintings *Dutch Comfort* and *Little Jannetje* were shown at the Society of British Artists, London, in 1875, and that the latter was acquired by Mrs. M. M. Landis, of Indianapolis.[30]

Where Bates went after his short sojourn in Indianapolis is not known, but eventually he reached England, and his death occurred at Rye in 1899.

Speaking of the arrival of Bates in 1876 calls to mind the spectacular Centennial Exposition held at Philadelphia that year, with an art exhibition that surpassed anything previously held in this country. Comprehensive as was the display, the influence it had on the progress of art in the Midwest is a debatable point. In architectural circles excitement ran high as a result of experiments in certain constructional features, particularly the use of the steel frame, but there was little that was new or novel among the pictures to stimulate discussion or creative thinking among painters. This does not mean that the displays in the art building were insignificant. They were extensive and impressive. A dozen foreign countries were represented by their most eminent painters, and each painter by his most striking canvas. Crowds poured through the galleries; men and women from every state of the Union and from every walk of life were seeing for the first time a comprehensive survey of the art of their day.

So far as the Indiana painters of 1876 were concerned, no records exist to prove that any of them saw the exhibition or had much to say about it. Local newspapers carried accounts of the exposition, written by correspondents in Philadelphia to stimulate attendance, and their occasional remarks about the art section were too general to give the artists much of an idea of the actual paintings. It is possible that John Love, on his way home from Europe, and Dewey Bates, striking out for Indianapolis that year, went by way of Philadelphia; if so, they would have brought a firsthand report to their comrades who could not afford to take the trip.

It now appears that the Centennial's greatest value was its effect on the average citizen. Thousands of men and women upon seeing it must have thought, consciously or unconsciously, about bringing large impressive art exhibits to their own communities; such an idea, born in those extensive exhibition galleries in Fairmont Park, bore fruit sooner or later in many an American town, Indianapolis being no exception. The local exhibitions of 1877 and 1878, already discussed, may have had a remote connection with the Philadelphia project, but the first enterprise here approaching it in plan and scope was the 1883 loan exhibit assembled and shown by the Art Association of Indianapolis, composed of 453 paintings by 137 artists. The fact that more than thirty local painters were represented in the exhibition is significant.

According to the catalogue, the exhibit was to be the initiatory movement in what was "hoped will be a continuous effort by the Association to elevate, instruct and gratify a taste for genuine works of Art," a hope that was realized as the organization tenaciously struggled through difficult formative years into full maturity after the turn of the century, and after the erection of its permanent home, the John Herron Art Museum. Nothing approaching in size the 1883 Loan Exhibit was undertaken, however, for the next two years; then in 1886 the ambitious projects were resumed, continuing for another decade.

VI

Of the remaining ten or twelve painters who were active in Indianapolis in the 1870's, we have information, though scanty, about the work of two, Colcord and Fowler; and much more about a third, Theodore C. Steele.

Harry M. Colcord, to whom we alluded in discussing the portraits of the governors, painted, in addition to the James D. Williams canvas, a portrait listed in the 1878 exhibition as that of W. McRea. It has not been tracked down, nor have any facts been brought to light about the painter's earlier or subsequent activities. He was already in the city in May, 1877, when two of his portraits, representing Mr. and Mrs. Reed (which Reeds, we are not sure), were shown in Lieber's Art Emporium, together with products of other painters' brushes "for the public eye to pick to pieces, or damn with faint praise," according to the newspaper reporter.[31]

Harry Fowler, another peripatetic portraitist, was in the capital city in 1877 according to the city directory, but what he accomplished is not known. His visit to Gosport about that time resulted in his painting the likeness of Curtis G. H. Goss and his wife Angelica, owned by Anna L. Gray, of that town; perhaps he was also responsible for those of Joseph E. Goss and his wife Elizabeth, now in the Indianapolis residence of George C. Goss.

In contrast to these temporary and rather ephemeral personages, such a man as Theodore C. Steele, to whom references have already been made, stands out conspicuously. As mentioned above, he was recognized as one giving promise of unusual artistic talent by the critic Alois Sinks when the latter visited his studio in 1875. By that time Steele was well established as a portrait painter, having been in the city nearly two years. Although largely self-taught he had behind him about ten years of painting experience.

Steele's original home was near Gosport on the eastern edge of Owen County. He was born in 1847, the son of Samuel Hamilton Steele, a sadler, and his wife Harriet Newell. When he was five years of age his family moved to Waveland, where he later attended the

Waveland Academy. Something of his innate talent is revealed by the fact that he was made a teacher of drawing there while still a student. It is reported that in his formative period he studied art in Chicago and in Cincinnati, but names of his teachers are not known. Early in 1870 he married Mary Elizabeth Larkin, whom he knew at Waveland Academy, and not long afterward they went to Rushville, her original home, to live. There he painted, among others, some members of the Alger and Kinney families. A few months later the Steeles moved to Battle Creek, Michigan, where the artist soon became established, and where, judging by the list of paintings that accompanies his journal,[32] he was very successful. Three years later he was back in his native state and had opened a studio in Indianapolis.

During the last five or six years of his residence in Waveland—from about 1865 to 1870—Steele's journal reveals that he painted not less than fifty portraits, many in communities some distance away: Peru, Rensselaer, Delphi, Greencastle, Lafayette, and Attica. Some of those early contacts must have helped him when he returned to the state in 1873, because he found additional clients in some of the same towns, judging by existing canvases.

While primarily a portrait painter—and as successful as any, judging by the list of his known canvases—Steele had begun to sketch outdoor subjects with great earnestness, even as early as his Waveland days. An illuminating report of this facet of his work, as well as a description of the man himself, has come down to us in the form of an article that appeared in the local press in 1877. A reporter on the *Saturday Herald* (not Alois Sinks), hoping to stimulate public interest in the work of the local artists, wrote an account of his visits to several studios. After describing that of John Love in the Bradshaw block, he penned the following eulogy:

In friendly contiguity to the door of Mr. Love's studio is another, which, being of glass, is pretty certain to afford a view of a tall romantic-looking fellow, hard at work at the easel. Mr. Steele is almost an ideal artist in personal appearance, wearing his hair and whiskers long, after the manner of Bohemians generally, and moving always in a genial atmosphere of good fellowship that renders him a general favorite with his brother artists and acquaintances. His studio is a pretty large room, and the walls only contain a fixed number of square feet, and in despair the pictures have given up the effort to find places, and lie in heaps on tables and under them, in corners and on chairs—everywhere—delicate, ethereal little sketches, in cool gray and neutral tints, with a carefulness and fidelity in detail which bears out the artist's assertion that his work has been more and more toward a strict and accurate following of nature. Mr. Steele never fails to improve any little vacation he may get from portrait painting by a stroll into the suburbs or country, and as he is a rapid worker his collection increases almost daily. The trunk of a beech tree, a little stretch of corn stubble with the shocks still standing, a winter foreground of snow and dry grass and weeds, with a thousand other like things, all executed with a lightness and airy sparkle much resembling water-color effect. Here is a little study still unfinished looking up Wabash alley from the canal, with a distant view of Christ Church and other buildings about the Circle. It is an early morning effect, entirely executed before most of us have begun to suspect the presence of another day. His portraits are characterized by ease, finish, and the same fidelity seen in his higher work. Among those now in his studio are the well known features of Major Gordon and Doctor Fletcher both characteristic pictures.[33]

In addition to creating a vivid word picture of Steele and his studio, the report includes two statements of particular interest to the historian of art. The observation about Steele's portraits being characterized by the same fidelity seen in his "higher" work, shows that compositions other than portraits were looked upon as products of greater significance. Landscapes were beginning to be more highly regarded in some circles than accurate portrayals of visages. This was probably due to the stigma that was attached to the commercial aspect of the latter, and the greater opportunity for individual perception and self-expression in the former.

The other observation that is of interest relates to the way Steele painted his small outdoor sketches: "executed with a lightness and airy sparkle. . . ." There has long been a tendency among writers on art matters to credit the rendering of airiness and atmospheric effects to the French painters of the last quarter of the nineteenth century. It is doubtless true that the broken brush stroke and spotty-paint method, known as impressionism, was primarily a French development (if we disregard its use by the baroque painters of seventeenth-century Italy), but the awareness of the luminosity and vibrant quality of sunlight and shadow, of fog and haze, of frost and snow, must have been as prevalent among painters in America as among those in Europe. So far as Steele was concerned, he never quite lost that first intense curiosity about out-of-door light (although he was obliged to neglect it almost to the point of losing it during his five years in Munich), as the canvases that mark the successive stages of his development show. This delight in subtle effects is revealed in his writing as well. In his journal of 1870–1871 there occur a number of passages reflecting it; for example:

The sky is full of purplish haze and the dim clouds are almost motionless. While there is not much haze in the air the light and shade has the peculiar indecision or indistinctness that with the golden sunshine is the charm of autumn. The full foliage and tasselless corn are leaning from their summer beauty toward the riper beauty of the fall. The change is small, but to eyes that love to watch the delicate changes of the seasons, it is distinctly marked . . .

Day by day the year is drawing to its close. Already the atmosphere is that of autumn. Not yet has the Indian haze wrapped the landscape in its illusive vapor, in the blue distance and gold and purply near-at-hand . . . A sentiment of harmony, a feeling of calm delight is upon the earth. It floats upon the warm-tinted clouds and upon the vapor slowly rising from its rivulet bed. Like a dream it is upon the variegated leaves of the forest.

Nothing exceptional occurred in connection with Steele's professional operations in the last years of the 1870's. He continued to paint portraits (pl. 81) and to sketch diligently the features of the country surrounding Indianapolis, advancing steadily in his technical skill. But in 1880 the opportunity came for him to go abroad to perfect himself in his chosen profession, so he embarked with his wife and children for Munich, Germany.

In those first years of the 1880's there was a marked exodus of artists from the city and state, resulting in a noticeable scarcity of "Bohemians" in Indianapolis. According to Forsyth, Cox was about the only professional left, "while a few of the students who had been in the Art School, not long since disbanded, continued as best they could to practice what they had been taught." [34] This was not actually so. Hays and Dennis were around until 1883; Lietz was here until his death in 1884; Fetsch, until 1898; the three professional women painters, Lotta Guffin, Ellen Ingraham, and Margaret Rudisill, continued actively for a number of years; and half-a-dozen lesser known commercial portraitists were in town, residing for varying lengths of time. The veteran Cox was certainly not alone.

Among those who moved away was Charles Fiscus, who apparently went soon after James Gookins left, because he entered the latter's studio in Terre Haute. Later, Fiscus went to Chicago, as did Gookins, but he soon returned to Indianapolis, where he died in 1884, at the age of twenty-two. One of the few remaining pictures by Fiscus is a still-life composition in oil, owned by the John Herron Art Museum; there is also a self portrait in charcoal in the possession of Elmer Taflinger, of Indianapolis; a recorded portrait of John Stern by him has not been traced.

Speaking of Fiscus, we are reminded of a listing in the 1881 city directory: "Fiscus and Scott." In that year Charles Fiscus was but twenty years old and his partner in the enterprise, Frank Edwin Scott, was eighteen. Although quite young and inexperienced, they felt they had enough technical ability and business acumen to compete with the professional artists then in the city. Fiscus died too soon to produce very much work or to attain the heights predicted by his colleagues; Scott lived to enjoy the acclamation of collectors and critics in both America and Europe. After that brief partnership with Fiscus, Scott left for New York, studied for a time at the Art Students League, then went on to Paris. Most of his life was spent in Europe, his death occurring at Paris in 1929.

VII

Those joining the artistic evacuation of Indiana in the fall of 1880 to attend academies abroad were (in addition to Steele) J. Ottis Adams, whose early career has already been reported; Samuel Richards, who had a studio at Anderson; August Metzner, a local lithographer; and Carrie Wolff, a student in the Indiana School of Art.

Two and a half years later (January, 1883) they were joined by William Forsyth.

Forsyth had been living in Indianapolis for a number of years, his family having moved to the city when he was a child from their original home in Hamilton County, Ohio, where he was born in 1854. It is doubtful if the city had anyone among its youthful citizens with so much zeal for things artistic as he, and with such determination to reach the top in the practice of painting. His earliest introduction to an artist's studio was about 1869 when his father took him to the painting rooms of Barton S. Hays with the intention of enrolling him as a student; but Forsyth's immaturity and the charges for instruction made the scheme impractical. Both Chase and Love were probably studying under Hays at the time, and Forsyth must have met them. It is said that Chase's work, which Forsyth saw in local exhibitions and in Hays's studio, aroused still more his determination to become a painter.

Less than ten years later the Indiana School of Art was established and William Forsyth was one of the first to enroll. He remained until it closed its doors, then opened a studio of his own in the Ingalls block; this he maintained for about two years, at which time the opportunity came for him to go abroad to study. His only known paintings made in this pre-Munich period are a self portrait, dated 1878, and a watercolor rendering of his mother (pl. 82), owned by Mrs. William Forsyth, Indianapolis.

During the first two years of the 1880's there was in the city a fraternity of artists, organized largely upon Forsyth's instigation, which was not only Bohemian in its conduct—or supposedly so—but also in its name: Bohe Club. Its informal membership included about a dozen young men whose personalities and aims made them unusually compatible. The leading spirits, in addition to William Forsyth, were Frank Scott, Charles L. McDonald, Fred A. Hetherington, Thomas E. Hibben, Charles Nicolai, and William O. Bates. Associate members included Hartsel Stem, Clarence Forsyth, George Cottman, and others. Although most of the active members painted, etched, and went on sketching trips, none of them, except Forsyth, Scott, and

McDonald, made a career of art. Most of the others became successful businessmen, but took keen interest in the cultural programs of the growing city. One of the club's unified efforts was the making of transcriptions in pencil and ink of paintings by Forsyth and Steele, which served as illustrations in the catalogue, *Ye Hoosier Colony in München,* an exhibition held at Lieber's Art Emporium in 1885.

William Forsyth's stay of almost seven years in Munich was of great profit to him as a maturing painter. He studied principally at the Royal Academy, and as he advanced in his work he received awards and medals of merit. When he returned to Indiana he was well equipped to take his place as one of the leading painters and teachers in the state.

Members of the Indiana colony in Munich returned to America at different times. Steele came back in 1885; Adams, in 1887; Forsyth, in 1888; and Richards, in 1891. Metzner returned later in the 1890's, and died soon after.

Theodore C. Steele opened a new studio in Indianapolis in the Vance block, and took up his work where he had dropped it five years before, carrying out portrait commissions and increasing his output of landscapes (pl. 83). J. Ottis Adams selected Muncie as his home, where he painted and taught classes in art. William Forsyth came back to Indianapolis, joined Adams in setting up art classes in Muncie and Fort Wayne, and assisted Steele in establishing a school in the Circle Hall, Indianapolis. Samuel Richards returned to Anderson, but his serious illness forced him to leave within a short time for Denver, Colorado.

Upon their return to Indiana, these men learned that a new and active art association had been founded, that superior exhibitions were being brought to the community, that several new artists had become residents, including Richard Gruelle and Sue Ketcham, and that a new spirit of artistic activity seemed to be permeating the city.

Of the younger set, Gruelle and Susan Ketcham moved most rapidly to the fore. Richard Gruelle was a Kentuckian, born at Cynthiana in 1851. As a young man he had taken up professional portrait painting in Decatur, Illinois, and had been moderately successful before coming to Indianapolis in 1882. He stayed here twenty years, turning from portraits, dull in color and execution, to landscapes that are colorful, airy, and vibrant. The most ambitious example of his portrait work is the likeness of Captain Henry M. Socwell, owned by the Indiana Historical Society Library. Several of his landscapes are in the city (pl. 84), most of which were painted in the latter years of his Indianapolis sojourn, or after he went east. He spent a good deal of time in Washington and Baltimore, and passed his last years in Connecticut. One of Gruelle's most important undertakings was the descriptive catalogue of paintings in the collection of William T. Walters, Baltimore, Maryland, published in 1895 under the title *Notes: Critical and Biographical.* His death, following a stroke of paralysis, occurred at Indianapolis in 1914.

Few people exerted more influence in local art circles, and commanded higher respect among her colleagues, than did Susan M. Ketcham. She was a native of Indianapolis and a member of one of the city's oldest families. Her preliminary training was in the Indiana School of Art under Gookins and Love, after which she remained in the city for several years, painting and assisting in promoting a more general interest in cultural events. With the organization of the Art Association of Indianapolis in 1883, she was given the responsible assignment of selecting the paintings for the organization's first major art exhibition, a project that took her to Chicago, Detroit, and New York. With the establishment of the art association's school that fall, she was given the responsibility of finding an instructor, and after consulting some of the leading painters of Chicago, she engaged Charles L. McDonald. This school opened on January 10 ,1884, first conducting classes in the parlors of the Denison Hotel and then moving to the old Plymouth Church. Sue Ketcham taught in the school until it was forced to close its doors for lack of support in 1886.[35]

Soon after the school closed Miss Ketcham sailed for Europe, where she spent two and a half years studying music and art. Upon her return to America she decided to live in New York, entered the Art Students League, and also studied with William M. Chase. Later she maintained a studio in Carnegie Hall, and spent most of her summers at Ogunquit, Maine. Practically nothing remains of her early Indianapolis productions, but many of her later pictures, particularly those made at Ogunquit, are in local homes.

*   *   *

In designating the mid-1880's as the termination of this survey, the author realizes the impossibility of drawing a fine line between periods in the evolution of the arts, or of establishing a fixed point where one movement ends and another begins. From our place of observation, more than half a century after the events took place, the decade of the 1880's appears to mark the end of the old order and the start of the new. The older established artists like Cox and Fetsch fade out of sight; the old method of painting—smooth, precise, labored—gives way to a more dashing, colorful style; what we have chosen to call the pioneer phase of Indiana art is over.

As we look back across the years covered by this book, and attempt to form an impression of the total output of pictures, we conclude that the dominant characteristic of our early painting was sobriety and sturdiness, with an emphasis on factual subject matter. Thrift and industry were as much a part of the artist's character as of the businessman's, and these traits are reflected in the former's concise and unadorned—even blunt—manner of painting. In comparison to more polished and sophisticated pictures of other times and places, the canvases discussed here may appear crude, but their positive, forthright quality makes a strong appeal once we recognize it.

This interlocking of basic character traits and native artistic styles gives American art its greatest significance; and on the plane of frontier or provincial painting, farther removed from foreign or artificial influences, the merging of the two is most clearly seen and, therefore, is of more consequence in the understanding of our native American culture.

79. Lotta Guffin: Portrait of Addison C. Harris
Courtesy of John W. Becker, Allisonville (page 194)

80. Dewey Bates: Portrait of
Josephine Landis
Courtesy of Mrs. William
M. Rockwood, Indianapolis
(page 198)

81. Theodore C. Steele:
Portrait of
James Whitcomb Riley
Courtesy of Lesley Payne,
Indianapolis (page 203)

82. William Forsyth: The Artist's Mother
Courtesy of Mrs. William Forsyth, Indianapolis (page 205)

83. Theodore C. Steele: Pleasant Run
Courtesy of Carl B. Shafer, Indianapolis (page 206)

84. Richard B. Gruelle: The Canal, Morning
John Herron Art Museum, Indianapolis (page 207)

NOTES

BIBLIOGRAPHICAL GUIDE

ROSTER OF PAINTERS

INDEX

Notes

CHAPTER I

[1] John D. Barnhart (editor), *Henry Hamilton and George Rogers Clark in the American Revolution* (R. E. Banta, Crawfordsville, 1951), p. 126. Journal and drawings are owned by the Houghton Library, Harvard University.

[2] Will Ball and Robert B. Whitsett, historians at Logansport, are also of the opinion that the sketch shows the east end of what is now known as Cedar Island, property of the Logansport Country Club.

[3] The drawings are in the National Archives, Cartographic Records Branch, Washington, D.C. That of Fort Dearborn is dated January 25, 1808; that of Fort Wayne was made about 1815. An earlier map of old Fort Wayne, drawn by P. McNiff in 1797, is in the manuscript collection of the Library of Congress; see, *Indiana, The Sesquicentennial of the Establishment of the Territorial Government* (Washington, 1950), cat. no. 29, p. 8.

[4] Elizabeth R. and Joseph Pennell, *The Life of James McNeill Whistler* (J. B. Lippincott Co., Philadelphia, 1909), I, 5.

[5] Reproduced in Dorothy Riker, "Fort Finney," *Year Book of the Society of Indiana Pioneers*, 1944, pp. 14–20.

[6] Benson J. Lossing, *Pictorial Field-Book of the War of 1812* (New York, 1868), pp. 189 and 283.

[7] Edwin James, *An Account of an Expedition from Pittsburgh to the Rocky Mountains in the Year 1819 and '20 . . . under the Command of Major Stephen H. Long* (Philadelphia, 1823) I, 3.

[8] William H. Keating, *Narrative of an Expedition to the Source of the St. Peter's River . . . in the Year 1823 . . . under the Command of Stephen H. Long, Major* (Philadelphia, 1824), I, pl. 3.

[9] J. O. Lewis, *The Aboriginal Port Folio* (Philadelphia, 1836); *The North American Aboriginal Portfolio* (New York, 1839); other editions followed.

[10] The camera lucida was constructed in various ways; in its simplest form it consisted of a prism of glass through which the artist viewed his subject and which at the same time caused the image to fall on a sheet of paper, thus allowing the pencil to trace it accurately. The exact nature of Hall's device is not known.

[11] In the published account of his trip, *Travels in North America in the years 1827–1828* (Edinburgh, 1829), Basil Hall speaks of passing through southwestern Indiana in May, 1827, but no sketches of this region are known to exist.

[12] *Reise in das Innere Nord-Amerika in den Yahren 1832 bis 1834* (Coblenz, 1839–1841); the prints were published without text in *Illustrations to Maximilian Prince of Wied's Travels in the Interior of North America* (London, 1844).

[13] *National Gallery of American Landscape* (New York, 1869). Three western subjects drawn by him serve as illustrations in Robert Carlton, *The New Purchase, or, Early Years in the Far West* (New Albany, Ind., 1855).

CHAPTER 2

[1] Gilbert Stuart's name was occasionally spelled Stewart, even by the artist himself.

[2] Lewis Peckham to Thomas Peckham, October 28, 1810, letter owned by Mrs. Clara P. Davis, Providence, R. I.

[3] Vincennes *Western Sun,* June 18–29, 1816.

[4] Records of Marriage Licenses in Knox County, Indiana, 1807–1820, I, 141, photostats in Indiana State Library, Genealogy Division.

[5] Sept. 27, 1819; Records of the Parish of St. Francis Xavier, Vincennes, Indiana, 1801–1823, V., photostats in Indiana State Library, Genealogy Division. Mary Dagenet had been married to Thomas C. Shields.

[6] Charles J. Kappler (editor), *Indian Affairs, Laws and Treaties* (Washington, 1904), II, 169–170.

[7] Peckham Letters, Indiana Historical Society Library.

[8] Mary Q. Burnet, *Art and Artists of Indiana* (The Century Co., New York, 1921), p. 387.

[9] The attribution is based on a memorandum written by Charles B. Lasselle, the subject's son.

[10] Burnet, *op. cit.,* p. 10.

[11] Chester Harding, *My Egotistigraphy* (Cambridge, 1866); reprinted and edited by Margaret E. White, *A Sketch of Chester Harding, Artist, Drawn by His Own Hand* (Boston, 1890), and by W. P. G. Harding, (New York, 1929).

[12] Abner Morse, *A Genealogical Register of the Descendants of Several Ancient Puritans* (Boston, 1855–1864), IV, 49–50.

[13] Vincennes *Indiana Centinel & Public Advertiser,* February 2–May 27, 1820.

[14] Owned by Oscar Everhart, Indianapolis.

[15] Little Rock *Arkansas Democrat,* April 22, 1951.

[16] Painting owned by Capt. Chester Harding, Fayetteville, Arkansas.

[17] Owned by the Filson Club, Louisville, Kentucky, and by Mrs. V. C. Turner, St. Louis, Missouri.

[18] Draper Manuscripts, State Historical Society of Wisconsin, Madison, 10J 108, pp. 2–3.

[19] Donald C. Peattie (editor), *Audubon's America* (Houghton Mifflin Co., Boston, 1940), pp. 152–153.

[20] Minutes of Board of Directors of Vincennes Library, Feb. 4, 1839. The painting has been in the custody of Vincennes University since 1879.

[21] Vincennes *Saturday Gazette,* December 25, 1842; repeated through January 28, 1843.

[22] Charles E. Slocum and Robert S. Robertson, *History of the Maumee River Basin, Allen County, Indiana* (Indianapolis, 1905), II, 78.

[23] Burnet, *op. cit.,* p. 12. Freeman's visit to southern Indiana was probably after 1845. He was in New York in 1844 (*New York Business Directory, 1844*) and he is believed to have been in Cincinnati about 1845.

[24] Ralph Clifton Smith, *A Biographical Index of American Artists* (Baltimore, 1930), p. 37.

[25] Records of the Bethel Church, Freelandville, give Tester's birth date as September 11, 181_, the last number having been torn away.

[26] Burnet, *op. cit.,* p. 14.

[27] The drop curtain for the theater was also painted by Lesueur. It bore a scene of the cut-off of the Wabash River at New Harmony, probably the first large-scale landscape made in the state.

[28] Robert W. G. Vail, *American Sketchbooks of Charles Alexandre Lesueur, 1816–1837* (American Antiquarian Society, Worcester, 1938).

[29] David Starr Jordan, "Sketch of Charles A. Le Sueur," *Popular Science Monthly*, February, 1895, pp. 549–550. Jordan states that a most spirited portrait of old Governor Vigo by Lesueur was still extant in 1895, but it is now known only through an engraving.

[30] Walter B. Hendrickson, *David Dale Owen* (Indiana Historical Bureau, Indianapolis, 1943), facing p. 126.

[31] Experiences of the Duclos brothers at New Harmony are given in Victor Duclos, Diary and Recollections, manuscript, Indiana State Library.

[32] The building was converted into a garage in 1913.

[33] Miner K. Kellogg, Private Journal, Remembrances and Sketches of incidents in the life of the author . . . . pp. 3–4, manuscript, Indiana Historical Society Library. In his Notes for Autobiography, another manuscript in the Indiana Historical Society Library, Kellogg states: "Mr. Parsons assisted me in my [art] labors. He had learned drawing at West Point." No other reference to this artist has been found.

[34] *Description of Banvard's Panorama* . . . . (Boston, 1847), p. 10. The earliest recorded panorama made by an American artist was John Vanderlyn's "Versailles," exhibited in New York 1815–1816.

[35] London *Morning Chronicle*, December 27, 1850, as quoted in the above pamphlet, *Description of Banvard's Panorama*.

CHAPTER 3

[1] A lithograph, titled *Fort Harrison on the Wabash*, was published by Modesitt & Hager in 1848, made from a drawing by an unnamed artist; reproduced in, *Indiana, the Sesquicentennial of the Establishment of the Territorial Government* (Library of Congress, Washington, D.C., 1950), facing p. 11.

[2] Mary Borromeo Brown, *History of the Sisters of Providence of Saint Mary-of-the-Woods* (New York, 1949), I, 166.

[3] Mantle Fielding, *Dictionary of American Painters, Sculptors, and Engravers* (Philadelphia, 1926), p. 217.

[4] Mary Q. Burnet, *Art and Artists of Indiana*, (New York, 1921), p. 12.

[5] *Terre Haute Sunday Tribune and Terre Haute Sunday Star*, May 9, 1943.

[6] *Harper's Weekly*, June 22, 1861, p. 388, and July 6, 1861, p. 423.

[7] A. T. Andreas, *History of Chicago* (Chicago, 1884–85), II, 561.

[8] Fielding, *op. cit.*, p. 244.

[9] Newburgh *Warrick Democrat*, November 27, 1855.

[10] Peat Papers, John Herron Art Institute Library.

[11] Reynolds was the first president of the Royal Academy and no one named Wilson ever held that position. Forbes doubtless referred to Charles Heath Wilson (1810–1882) who, for a short time, was head of the schools of the Royal Academy.

[12] Tradition assigns it to a "celebrated artist, Coot, at Washington City" and to the year 1835, when Boon was a member of Congress: *Boonville Standard,* July 21, 1939.

[13] *New Albany Tribune,* November 27, 1939.

[14] These portraits by Morrison are owned respectively by E. A. Reily, New Albany, Lloyd Collins, French Lick, Harry Austin, New Albany, Blanche Stillson, Indianapolis, and Katharine Woodward, Middleburg, Virginia.

[15] William Wesley Woollen, *Biographical and Historical Sketches of Early Indiana* (Indianapolis, 1883), pp. 160–167.

[16] The first known reference to Terrell was an advertisement in a Lexington, Kentucky, newspaper of 1795: "Richard Terrell announces he will move from Lexington to Bear Grass and will continue in business at that point." Transcribed in Charles R. Staples, *History of Pioneer Lexington,* 1779–1806 (Lexington, 1939), p. 107.

[17] Exhibition catalogue, National Academy of Design, New York, 1858.

[18] *Indianapolis Journal,* March 29, 1885. The term, *Salle d' Heur,* is not used in the catalogue of the Paris Salon and may be an error.

[19] *Indianapolis Sunday Star,* Hoosier Tabloid Section, November 15, 1925.

[20] Owned by Caroline Dunn, Indianapolis.

[21] William T. Coggeshall, *Poets and Poetry of the West* (Columbus, 1860), p. 537.

[22] *The Indianapolis News,* February 14, 1879.

[23] *Cincinnati Commercial,* March 21, 1882.

CHAPTER 4

[1] George Pence, "General Joseph Bartholomew," *Indiana Magazine of History,* December, 1918, pp. 287–303; Columbus *Daily Evening Republican,* April 9, 1881.

[2] Marguerite Hall Albjerg, "A Nineteenth Century Hoosier Artist, Samuel Richards, 1853–1893," *Indiana Magazine of History,* June, 1948, p. 147.

[3] Indiana Seminary, founded 1824, became Indiana College in 1828, and Indiana University in 1838.

[4] Madison *Republican Courier,* September 2, 1846.

[5] *Louisville Herald,* November 9, 1923.

[6] Indiana University owns a portrait of Andrew Wylie, the painter of which is not known.

[7] The portrait of Lincoln is owned by Dr. Rodney D. Smith, Bloomington, who also provided biographical material on Blair. Articles about the portrait appeared in the *Indianapolis News,* February 10, 1925 and the *Indianapolis Star,* June 17, 1936.

[8] *History of Montgomery County, Indiana* (A. W. Bowen & Co., Indianapolis, 1913), III, 1231–1232.

[9] *Indianapolis Sunday Star,* Hoosier Tabloid Section, November 15, 1925.

CHAPTER 5

[1] Reproduced in T. A. Goodwin (editor), *Autobiography of Rev. Joseph Tarkington* (Cincinnati, 1899), p. 64.

[2] Mary Q. Burnet, *Art and Artists of Indiana* (New York, 1921), p. 50. The name Sullivan is given instead of Sully.

[3] From Samuel Swan Walker, Richmond, June 5, 1841, to Harriet S. Walker, Hamilton, Ohio. Letter owned by Claude F. Walker, Darien, Conn.

[4] *Richmond Palladium,* June 5, 1841. The editor was mistaken about Williams being a native of Indiana. William A. Cammack was the artist's brother-in-law.

[5] March 13, 1842. Letter owned by Claude F. Walker, Darien, Conn.

[6] Edna Maria Clark, *Ohio Art and Artists* (Richmond, 1932), p. 111.

[7] William Forsyth, *Art in Indiana* (Indianapolis, 1916), p. 28.

[8] *History of Wayne County, Indiana* (Inter-state Publishing Co., Chicago, 1884), I, 643–644.

[9] Burnet, *op. cit.,* p. 385. This number is so large that it may be a typographical error. The article in the *History of Wayne County,* cited above, referred to it as a school for women.

[10] Opal Thornburg, "The Panoramas of Marcus Mote, 1853–1854," *Art in America,* Winter, 1953, pp. 22–35.

[11] A number of his drawings, owned by Emily Kersey, Pasadena, California, were reproduced in the *Richmond Palladium,* November 1–18, 1950.

[12] The resolution was passed December 5, 1849.

[13] *Indianapolis Sunday Star,* July 7, 1929.

[14] Indianapolis *Indiana Saturday Herald,* February 20, 1875.

[15] The portraits still hang in the old Conklin house, the property of Pauline and Robert Montgomery.

[16] *New Castle Courier-Times,* May 16, 1923.

[17] Owned by Josiah K. Lilly, Indianapolis.

[18] Burnet, *op. cit.,* pp. 148–155; Marguerite Hall Albjerg, "A Nineteenth Century Hoosier Artist, Samuel Richards, 1853–1893," *Indiana Magazine of History,* June, 1948, pp. 143–160.

[19] Albjerg, *op. cit.,* p. 156. *Day Before the Wedding,* painted at Davos, Switzerland, and regarded by Richards as a technically more meritorious work than *Evangeline,* is now in the Public Library, Spencer.

CHAPTER 6

[1] Bert J. Griswold, *Pictorial History of Fort Wayne, Indiana* (Chicago, 1917), I, 307.

[2] Indianapolis *Indiana Daily Journal,* January 12, 1852.

[3] Frank Sumner Bash, *History of Huntington County, Indiana* (Chicago, 1914), I, 166.

[4] Edmund M. Wasmuth, *The Saga of a Hoosier Village* (Huntington, [1946]), p. 65.

[5] On the back of his canvas portraying Robert Filson, the artist inscribed: "Painted by Crafft, Clinton, Parke County, June 10, 1839."

[6] Owned by Mrs. Richard E. Edwards and May Bloomfield, Peru.

[7] Charles E. Slocum and Robert S. Robertson, *History of the Maumee River Basin, Allen County, Indiana* (Indianapolis, 1905), II, 78.

[8] *Ibid.*

[9] Harvey W. Crew, *History of Dayton, Ohio* (Dayton, 1889), p. 563. The artist's first name is given as Edmond, apparently a mistake.

[10] Letter owned by Mrs. Arrilla F. Fortney, Fort Wayne, dated January 9, 1917.

[11] The most definitive work is *The Journals and Indian Paintings of George Winter, 1837–1839* (Indiana Historical Society, 1948). A selection of his paintings was listed and illustrated in the catalogue, *Exhibition of the Work of George Winter*, November 5–26, 1939, John Herron Art Museum, Indianapolis.

[12] Jehu Z. Powell, *History of Cass County, Indiana* (Chicago, 1913), I, 252.

[13] Mary Q. Burnet, *Art and Artists of Indiana* (New York, 1921), p. 52.

[14] The Richmond (Indiana) Art Association owns one of Evans' paintings, dated 1888, depicting a young woman standing before a painting.

[15] Powell, *op. cit.*, I, 252.

[16] W. Swift Wright, *Pastime Sketches.* . . . (Logansport, 1907), p. 215.

[17] The water colors are now owned by the Cass County Historical Society, Logansport.

[18] Biographical information from Joseph Lee Hewitt, North Sacramento, California. Her death occurred at Kansas City, February 7, 1901.

[19] *Lafayette Daily Journal*, November 16, 1849.

[20] Indianapolis *Indiana State Journal*, May 19, 1851.

[21] Jacob Piatt Dunn, *Greater Indianapolis* (Chicago, 1910), I, 478.

[22] Samuel Hays (ca. 1828–1916) painted portraits of some of the governors of North Dakota.

[23] Hays's portrait of his wife is owned by Jean Black, Indianapolis. Their daughter, Naomi Hays Hinshaw, Elmhurst, Illinois, has a number of her father's paintings, including a self-portrait.

[24] Lew Wallace, *An Autobiography* (Harper & Bros., New York, 1906), I, 49.

[25] John D. Forbes, "Lew Wallace, Romantic," *Indiana Magazine of History*, December, 1948, p. 390.

[26] Indianapolis *The Saturday Herald*, December 11, 1875.

[27] Frankfort *Tri-Weekly Yeoman*, Oct. 24, 1878.

[28] Charles Elliott, *The Life of the Rev. Robert R. Roberts* (Cincinnati, 1844), p. 349.

[29] *Goshen Daily News-Times*, January 29, 1925.

[30] *Goshen Daily News-Times*, April 6, 1909.

[31] South Bend, *St. Joseph Valley Register*, March 26, 1868. The term "kit-cat" refers to a canvas 36 x 28 inches in size, and derives from the portraits of uniform dimension in the Kit-cat Club, London.

[32] Owned by the Northern Indiana Historical Society, South Bend.

[33] Powell, *op. cit.*, I, 252.

[34] *LaPorte County Whig*, June 5, 1844.

[35] Charles Cist, *Cincinnati in 1841, Its Early Annals and Future Prospects* (Cincinnati, 1841), p. 137.

[36] Mary E. Baker, *Folklore of Springfield, [Vermont]* (Springfield, 1922), pp. 68–69.

CHAPTER 7

[1] *Indiana House Journal*, 1821, p. 25.

[2] Rooker's first known advertisement appeared in the *Indianapolis Gazette*, September 21, 1822, announcing himself as chairmaker and painter. Other announcements followed in the *Gazette* and *Indiana Journal*.

[3] John H. B. Nowland, *Early Reminiscences of Indianapolis* . . . . (Indianapolis, 1870), p. 83.

[4] *Portrait and Biographical Record of Madison and Hamilton Counties, Indiana* (Chicago, 1893), pp. 387–388.

[5] Indianapolis *Indiana Journal*, April 10, 1828.

[6] Indianapolis *Indiana Democrat*, February 19 — July 2, 1831. Indianapolis *Indiana Journal*, February 5 — July 3, 1831.

[7] *Terre Haute Western Register*, January 28, 1832: "Died in Indianapolis on 8th inst., Mr. Michael G. Rogers, portrait painter, formerly of Ohio, aged about 27 years."

[8] Indianapolis *Indiana Journal*, December 2, 1837.

[9] Louis H. Gibson, "Indiana Monographs," *Indianapolis News*, July 20, 1893.

[10] William R. Holloway, *Indianapolis, A Historical and Statistical Sketch* (Indianapolis, 1870), p. 74; Berry R. Sulgrove, *History of Indianapolis and Marion County, Indiana* (Philadelphia, 1884), p. 268.

[11] Hugh McCulloch, *Men and Measures of Half a Century* . . . . (New York, 1889), p. 71.

[12] Indianapolis *Indiana Journal*, March 16, 1833.

[13] Charles Cist, *Sketches and Statistics of Cincinnati in 1851* (Cincinnati, 1851), p. 126: eight owners of Cox's paintings are listed.

[14] Nowland, *op. cit.*, p. 301.

[15] The longest published list of Cox's paintings is in the catalogue of a retrospective exhibition, *Paintings by Jacob Cox*, held at the John Herron Art Museum, November 8–30, 1941.

[16] Indianapolis *Indiana Journal*, February 19, 1853. His uncle was Samuel B. Waugh, 1814–1885.

[17] Indianapolis *The Locomotive*, May 14, 1853.

[18] Indianapolis *The Locomotive*, September 24, 1853.

[19] Several easel paintings by Clark Gordon are owned by Mrs. Paul E. Newby, Indianapolis.

[20] Early in his career, the artist spelled his name "Whitridge," a form used by another branch of the family; but being admonished by his father for it, he changed back to "Whittredge."

[21] Quoted in Jacob Piatt Dunn, *Greater Indianapolis* (Chicago, 1910), I, 477. A similar account of Whittredge's sojourn in Indianapolis is found in "The Autobiography of Worthington Whittredge," edited by John I. H. Baur, *Brooklyn Museum Journal*, 1942 (Brooklyn Institute of Arts and Sciences, New York), p. 12.

[22] Indianapolis *Indiana State Journal*, January 27, 1843.

[23] Indianapolis *Indiana State Journal*, May 19, 1843.

[24] *Indianapolis News*, February 14, 1879.

[25] Indianapolis *Indiana State Sentinel*, December 6, 1845; the advertisement continued through June 10, 1846.

[26] Mary Q. Burnet, *Art and Artists of Indiana* (New York, 1921), p. 24.

[27] Although Mary Burnet states that Eaton was a pupil of Cox in 1846 and 1847, there is no reference to him in newspapers here after June 1846; Cist infers that he was in Cincinnati by 1846: Cist, *op. cit.*, p. 126.

[28] The only miniaturist known to have worked in Indianapolis before 1850 was Richard Verbrick, of Cincinnati. A portrait of Charles Cox, made by him here in 1836, is now in the Cincinnati Art Museum.

[29] Lew Wallace, *An Autobiography* (Harper & Bros., New York, 1906), I, 50.

[30] The names Elliott and Eaton may have been confused by early writers.

[31] The Moore portraits were formerly owned by Ida Fogleman, Mooresville; they are now in the John Herron Art Museum.

[32] Indianapolis *The Locomotive*, March 6, 1852.

[33] Dunn, *op. cit.*, I, 476. A pencil drawing by Dunlap of Hiram Moorehouse on trial for murder in 1850 is owned by the Indiana Historical Society Library.

[34] Laura N. Ream, "Letters and Art in Indianapolis," *Indianapolis Daily Journal*, March 12, 1867.

[35] Indianapolis *Indiana Saturday Herald*, February 20, 1875.

[36] *Ibid.*

[37] Indianapolis *Indiana Journal*, February 19, 1853.

CHAPTER 8

[1] William R. Holloway, *Indianapolis, A Historical and Statistical Sketch* (Indianapolis, 1870), p. 114.

[2] William T. Coggeshall, *Poets and Poetry of the West* (Columbus, 1860), p. 413.

[3] Mary Q. Burnet, *Art and Artists of Indiana* (New York, 1921), p. 106. Reed was one of the incorporators of the Chicago Academy of Design in 1866.

[4] Peter Fishe Reed, "The Importance of a More General Education in Literature and the Fine Arts," *Indiana School Journal* (1861), VI, 343.

[5] John H. B. Nowland, *Early Reminiscences of Indianapolis* . . . . (Indianapolis, 1870), p. 301; Dunn stated that Glessing arrived in 1861.

[6] Glessing was at Cincinnati about 1845–1848; a large oil painting by him, made before 1848, depicting *Shire's Garden,* is in the Ohio Historical and Philosophical Society library, Cincinnati.

[7] Jacob Piatt Dunn, *Greater Indianapolis* (Chicago, 1910), I, 482.

[8] *Indianapolis Daily Journal*, February 28, 1865.

[9] Burnet, *op. cit.*, p. 377.

[10] See especially. Katherine Metcalf Roof, *The Life and Art of William Merritt Chase* (New York, 1917), and the catalogue, *Chase Centennial Exhibition,* John Herron Art Museum, Indianapolis, November 1–December 11, 1949.

[11] *Indianapolis News*, December 5, 1916.

[12] Wallace Foster's account of the drawing appeared in the *Indianapolis Star,* January 31, 1910.

[13] Wilbur D. Peat, *Portraits and Painters of the Governors of Indiana, 1800–1943* (Indiana Historical Society Publications, XIV, no. 3, 1944), pp. 385–432.

[14] A portrait of John Gibson was acquired in 1941 and placed in the William Henry Harrison House, Vincennes.

[15] The Morse painting is owned by the Corcoran Gallery of Art, Washington, D.C.

[16] Indianapolis *Saturday Herald*, January 27, 1877.

[17] Dunn, *op. cit.*, I, 484.

[18] William Forsyth, *Art in Indiana* (Indianapolis, 1916), p. 12.

[19] *Ibid.*, p. 11.

[20] Indianapolis *Saturday Herald*, January 30, 1875.

[21] *Ibid.*, February 20, 1875.

[22] *Ibid.*, February 27, 1875.

[23] Dunn, *op. cit.*, I, 481.

[24] Forsyth, *op. cit.*, p. 8.

[25] *First Quarterly Exhibition of the Indiana Art Association*, Indianapolis, May 7, 1878. Some of Sinks's drawings were reproduced as woodcuts in early histories. In R. B. Sulgrove's *History of Indianapolis* (1884) are "Indianapolis in 1820" (imaginary) and "The Old National Bridge over White River."

[26] Indianapolis *Saturday Herald*, February 27, 1875.

[27] *American Art Annual* (Washington, D.C.), VI, 1907–1908, p. 106. Antrobus had a gallery with Douglas Volk in Chicago in 1862.

[28] Dunn, *op. cit.*, I, 481.

[29] *Ibid.* The present whereabouts of the bust is not known.

[30] Clara Erskine Clements and Laurence Hutton, *Artists of the Nineteenth Century and their Works* (Boston, 1879), I, 40.

[31] Indianapolis *Saturday Herald*, May 12, 1877.

[32] The journal is owned by Brandt Steele, Indianapolis.

[33] Indianapolis *Saturday Herald*, May 26, 1877.

[34] Forsyth, *op. cit.*, p. 12.

[35] Another art school was conducted in Circle Hall from 1891 to 1897 by Steele and Forsyth, known as the Indiana School of Art; the present art school of the John Herron Art Institute was organized in 1901.

Bibliographical Guide

Books referred to in the Roster of painters that follows.

AM ART ANN—American Art Annual, American Federation of Arts, Washington, D.C., vols. I–XXX, 1898–1933.

ART GUIDE—Art Guide to Indiana, compiled by Mrs. H. B. Burnet and Mrs. Robert E. Burke, Indiana University Extension Division Bulletin, XVI, no. 8, 1931.

BAKER—Baker, Mary E., Folklore of Springfield [Vermont], Springfield, 1922.

BARNHART—Barnhart, John D. (ed.), Henry Hamilton and George Rogers Clark in the American Revolution . . . , Crawfordsville, 1951.

BARTHOLOMEW—Bartholomew, Henry S. K., Pioneer History of Elkhart County, Indiana, Goshen, 1930.

BASH—Bash, Frank S., History of Huntington County, Indiana, Chicago, 1914.

BECKWITH—Beckwith, Hiram W., History of Montgomery County, [Indiana] . . . , Chicago, 1881.

BÉNÉZIT—Bénézit, Emmanuel, Dictionnaire critique et documentaire des peintres, sculpteurs, dessinateurs & graveurs . . . , Paris, 1924.

BIOG HISTORY—Biographical History of Eminent and Self-made Men of the State of Indiana, 2 vols., Cincinnati, 1880.

BROWN—Brown, Ignatius, History of Indianapolis, Logan's Indianapolis Directory, Indianapolis, 1868.

BROWN M—Brown, Sister Mary Borromeo, History of the Sisters of Providence, Saint Mary-of-the-Woods, New York, 1949.

BURNET—Burnet, Mary Q., Art and Artists of Indiana, New York, 1921.

BUTTS—Butts, Porter, Art in Wisconsin . . . , Madison, 1936.

CHASE—Chase Centennial Exhibition . . . , John Herron Art Museum, Indianapolis, 1949.

CIST 1—Cist, Charles, Cincinnati in 1841: Its Early Annals and Future Prospects, Cincinnati, 1841.

CIST 2—Cist, Charles, Sketches and Statistics of Cincinnati in 1859, Cincinnati, 1859.

CLARK—Clark, Edna M., Ohio Art and Artists, Richmond, 1932.

CLEMENT-H—Clement, Clara E. and Hutton, Laurence, Artists of the Nineteenth Century and their Works, Boston, 1885.

COGGESHALL—Coggeshall, William T., Poets and Poetry of the West . . . , Columbus, 1860.

COTTMAN—Cottman, George S., Forerunners of Indiana Art, Indiana Magazine of History, XV, 15–19, Indianapolis, March, 1919.

COX—Paintings by Jacob Cox: A Retrospective Exhibition of Work by an Early Indianapolis Artist, John Herron Art Museum, Indianapolis, 1941.

DAB—Dictionary of American Biography, 20 vols. and index, New York, 1928–1936.

DOCUMENTS—documents, letters, notes, and clippings on Indiana artists, collected by the author in compiling this volume, and deposited in the Library of the John Herron Art Institute, Indianapolis.

DUNN 1—Dunn, Jacob Piatt, Greater Indianapolis, vol. I, Chapt. XXXVII, "The Fine Arts," Chicago, 1910, 2 vols.

DUNN 2—Dunn, Jacob Piatt, Indiana and Indianans, Chicago, 1919.

FIELDING—Fielding, Mantle, Dictionary of American Painters, Sculptors and Engravers, Philadelphia, 1926.

FORSYTH—Forsyth, William, Art in Indiana, Indianapolis, 1916.

GIBSON—Gibson, Louis H., Indiana Art, Artists and Architecture, manuscript, Library of the John Herron Art Institute, Indianapolis, 1893.

GRISWOLD—Griswold, Bert J., Pictorial History of Fort Wayne, Indiana . . . , Chicago, 1917.

HOLLOWAY—Holloway, William R., Indianapolis, a Historical and Statistical Sketch . . . , Indianapolis, 1870.

IND ART—Indiana Art in the Permanent Collection of the John Herron Art Museum, 1951.

IND BIOG—Indiana Biography clippings, 38 vols., Indiana State Library, Indianapolis.

LOCKRIDGE—Lockridge, Ross F., The Old Fauntleroy House, New Harmony, 1939.

LOCKWOOD—Lockwood, George Browning, The New Harmony Communities, Marion, Ind., 1902.

McDERMOTT—McDermott, John Francis, Samuel Seymour: Pioneer Artist of Plains and Rockies, Smithsonian Institution Annual Report, Washington, D.C., 1950.

Morse—Morse, Abner, A Genealogical Register of the Descendants of Several Ancient Puritans, vol. IV., Boston, 1855–1864.

NCAB—National Cyclopedia of American Biography, 38 vols. and index, New York, 1898–1953.

Nowland—Nowland, John H. B., Early Reminiscences of Indianapolis . . . , Indianapolis, 1870.

Peat—Peat, Wilbur D., Portraits and Portrait Painters of the Governors of Indiana, 1800–1943, Indiana Historical Society, Indianapolis, 1944.

Powell—Powell, Jehu Z., History of Cass County, Indiana . . . , Chicago, 1913.

Reifel—Reifel, August J., History of Franklin County, Indiana, Indianapolis, 1915.

Roof—Roof, Katharine Metcalf, The Life and Art of William Merritt Chase . . . , New York, 1917.

Slocum-R—Slocum, Charles E. and Robertson, Robert S., History of the Maumee River Basin, Allen County, Indiana, 3 vols., Indianapolis & Toledo, 1905.

Steele—Theodore Clement Steele Memorial Exhibition, John Herron Art Museum, Indianapolis, 1926.

Sulgrove—Sulgrove, Berry R., History of Indianapolis and Marion County, Indiana, Philadelphia, 1884.

Thieme-B—Thieme-Becker, Allgemeines Lexikon der bildenden Künstler, Leipzig, 1908–1933.

Vail—Vail, Robert W. G., The American Sketchbooks of Charles Alexandre Lesueur, 1816–1837 . . . , Worcester, Mass., 1938.

Wallace—Wallace, Lew, An Autobiography, 2 vols., New York, 1906.

Wasmuth—Wasmuth, Edmund M., The Saga of a Hoosier Village, Huntington, Ind. [1946].

Weiss—Weiss, Harry B. and Ziegler, Grace M., Thomas Say, Springfield, Ill., 1931.

Winter—The Journals and Indian Paintings of George Winter, 1837–1839, Indiana Historical Society, Indianapolis, 1948.

Woollen—Woollen, William Wesley, Biographical and Historical Sketches of Early Indiana, Indianapolis, 1883.

Wright—Wright, W. Swift, Pastime Sketches . . . [Logansport, Ind.], 1907.

Roster

Painters active in Indiana from 1800 to 1885

ACKERMAN, JACOB
Portrait, landscape, and fresco painter, decorator, and teacher. Lafayette, 1873–1874; Logansport, ca. 1874–1880. Work: *Stanis Barnhart* and *Christine Barnhart*,* Mary Barnhart, Attica.†
References: Documents, Powell.‡

ADAMS, DAVID O.
Portrait painter (Adams and Mendenhall) Indianapolis, 1871–1872.
Reference: Documents.

ADAMS, GEORGE E.
Born, Harpers Ferry, W. Va., 1814; died, Logansport, Ind., 1885. Portrait and landscape painter. Logansport, 1836–1885. Work: *Self-Portrait* and landscapes, Sara D. Reed, Logansport.
Reference: Documents.

ADAMS, MRS. J. G.
Portrait painter. Indianapolis, 1858–1861.
Reference: Documents.

ADAMS, JOHN OTTIS
Born, Amity, Ind., July 8, 1851; died, Indianapolis, Jan. 28, 1927. Portrait and landscape painter. London, South Kensington Art School, 1872–1874; Martinsville and Seymour, 1874–1876; Muncie, 1876–1880; Munich, Royal Academy, 1880–1887; Muncie and Fort Wayne, 1888–1904; Indianapolis, 1904–1909; Brookville, 1909–1927. Work: (before 1885) *Sarah Heisohn*, Mrs. Robert H. Hartley, Muncie.
References: Bénézit, Burnet, Fielding, Forsyth, Gibson, Ind Art, Reifel, Thieme-B.

---

* Titles of paintings, in italics, are followed by names of owners.
† Unless otherwise indicated, all towns and cities named in this Roster are in Indiana.
‡ See Bibliographical Guide.

ADAMS, NELSON PERRY
Born, Henry County, Ind., June 29, 1861; died, Muncie, Ind., April 15, 1917. Animal, landscape, and portrait painter, and teacher. Muncie, ca. 1890–1917. Work: *Alvis Adams,* and *Aseneth Baldwin Adams,* Mrs. Adams N. Perry, Albany; *Cattle in Pasture,* John Nixon, Centerville; *Landscape with Cows,* Ball State Teachers College, Muncie.
References: Art Guide, Documents.

ALBERTINE, SISTER MARY (SONDERMANN)
Born, Pittsburgh, Pa., May 2, 1851; died, St. Louis, Mo., June 8, 1917. Landscape and figure painter. Indianapolis, 1877–1893; Saint Mary-of-the-Woods, 1870–1878; 1893–1917. Work: *Orphan Child,* St. Johns Academy, Indianapolis; *Francis Silas Chatard,* Saint Mary-of-the-Woods.
Reference: Documents.

ANASTASIE, MOTHER (JANE BROWN)
Born, near Paris, Ill., Oct. 13, 1825; died, Saint Mary-of-the-Woods, Ind., Aug. 10, 1918. Painter and teacher. Saint Mary-of-the-Woods, Terre Haute, Evansville, etc., 1843–1918. Work: Flower compositions, etc., Saint Mary-of-the-Woods.
References: Brown M, Documents.

ANTROBUS, JOHN
Died, Detroit, Mich., Oct. 18, 1907. Portrait and landscape painter. Savannah, Ga., 1853; Montgomery, Ala., 1856; Washington, D. C., Chicago, Ill., ca. 1863–1866; Indianapolis, 1874–1875. Work: *George J. Stilz* and *Anna Birkenmeyer Stilz,* Walter Bozell, Indianapolis.
References: Am Art Ann 1907–08, Documents.

ARCHER, SALLIE E.
Painter. Indianapolis, 1876.
Reference: Documents.

BALL, L. CLARENCE
Born, Mt. Vernon, O., July 4, 1858; died,
South Bend, Ind., Oct. 9, 1915. Landscape
painter. South Bend, 1882–1915.
References: Art Guide, Bénézit, Burnet,
Fielding, Forsyth, Thieme-B.

BANVARD, JOHN
Born, New York, N. Y., 1815; died, Water-
town, S. D., May 16, 1891. Panorama
painter. New Harmony, 1836.
References: Burnet, DAB, Documents,
Fielding, NCAB.

BARNES, ALBERT A.
Portrait painter. Indianapolis, 1867.
Reference: Documents.

BATES, DEWEY
Born, Philadelphia, Pa., 1851; died, Rye,
England, 1899. Genre and portrait painter.
Antwerp, Paris, London, and Philadelphia,
Pa.; Indianapolis, 1877–ca. 1880. Work:
Josephine Landis, Mrs. William M. Rock-
wood, Indianapolis; *John Love,* John Her-
ron Art Museum.
References: Bénézit, Burnet, Clement-H,
Documents, Fielding, Thieme-B.

BATES, ELIZA A.
Painter. Indianapolis, 1880–1895.
Reference: Documents.

BATMAN, ISABEL LOWRY (MRS.
    GEORGE BATMAN)
Born, New York, N. Y., Feb. 1, 1838; died,
Rushville, Ind., Dec. 30, 1925. Portrait and
landscape painter. Work: *Isaac Lowry,* Mrs.
Luther Overbeck, Rushville, and others.
Reference: Documents.

BATSON, MELVINA HOBSON (MRS.
    ANDREW BATSON)
Born, New Castle, Ind., 1826; died, New
Castle, February, 1853. Portrait painter.
Work: *James Peed* and *Elizabeth Elliott
Peed,* etc., Henry County Historical Mu-
seum, New Castle.
Reference: Documents.

BENNETT, J. WESLEY
Portrait painter. Indianapolis, 1881–1888.
Reference: Documents.

BERRY, WILSON (WILS) REED
Born, Adamsboro, Ind., April 22, 1851;
died, Logansport, April 28, 1928. Genre
and landscape painter, illustrator and
draughtsman. Logansport. Work: (before
1885) *Logansport Street Scene,* etc., Cass
County Historical Museum, Logansport;
Early Scene in Huntington, Women's
Club, Wabash.
References: Art Guide, Burnet, Documents.

BISHOP, GRANVILLE
Born, Fayette County, Ind., May 31, 1831;
died, Noblesville, Ind., Nov. 15, 1902.
Landscape painter, commercial artist, and
Spencerian penman. Cicero, Sheridan, and
Noblesville. Work: *Indianapolis in 1820*
(copy), etc., L. O. Bishop, Westfield; *Land-
scape,* Indiana State Museum, Indianapolis;
Landscape, Mrs. R. R. Williamson, Sheri-
dan.
Reference: Documents.

BLAIR, MARION M.
Born, Bloomington, Ind., Jan. 22, 1824;
died, near Bloomington, Feb. 22, 1901. Por-
trait painter. Bloomington and Indianapolis.
Work: *Oliver P. Morton,* Indiana State
Library, Indianapolis; *Austin Seward* and
Janet Irvin Seward, W. Austin Seward,
Bloomington; *Daily Voss,* Edgar R. Strong,
Bloomington.
Reference: Documents.

BODMER, CARL (KARL)
Born, Reisbach (Tiefenbrennen), Switzer-
land, Feb., 1809; died, Barbizon, France,
Oct. 30, 1893. Figure, animal, and land-
scape painter. North America, 1832–1834;
visited New Harmony and Vincennes.
Work: (executed in Indiana) *New Har-
mony on the Wabash,* etc., (engravings
published in "Illustrations to Maximilian
Prince of Wied's Travels in the Interior of
North America," 1844); *Vincennes, June
11, 1834,* etc., Karl Viktor Prinz zu Wied,
Munich.
References: Bénézit, Burnet, Clement-H,
Documents, Thieme-B.

BOWERS, T. J.
Portrait painter (Bowers & Purcell), Indi-
anapolis, 1855.
Reference: Documents.

BOYD, MONIMIA BUNNELL (MRS. SAMUEL S. BOYD)
Born, Greens Fork, Ind., July 3, 1824; died, Dublin, Ind., Jan. 7, 1862. Portrait and genre painter. Work: *Dr. William Bunnell*, and *The Hoosier's Nest*, Mrs. J. A. Bunnell, Hagerstown.
Reference: Documents.

BRANSON, MARY ELLEN HINSHAW (MRS. ELISHA BRANSON)
Born, Greensboro, Ind., Feb. 11, 1826; died, near Milton, Ind., June 15, 1911. Portrait painter. Knightstown. Work: *Seth Hinshaw, Benjamin Hinshaw*, etc., Henry County Historical Museum, New Castle.
Reference: Documents.

BRIGHT, C. E.
Painter. Indianapolis, 1863.
Reference: Documents.

BROWN, EPHRAIM K.
Portrait painter. Terre Haute and Indianapolis, ca. 1835–1840.
References: Burnet, Dunn 1, Gibson, Sulgrove.

BROWN, IMOGENE KEVIN
Born, Liberty, Ind., Feb. 15, 1853; died, Crawfordsville, Ind., Apr. 28, 1903. Painter and teacher. Liberty and Crawfordsville.
Reference: Burnet.

BROWN, JANE, see: ANASTASIE, MOTHER

BUNDY, JOHN ELWOOD
Born, Guilford Co., N. C., May 1, 1853; died, Cincinnati, O., Jan. 17, 1933. Portrait and landscape painter. Monrovia, 1858–1886; Indianapolis, 1873; Martinsville, 1886–1888; Richmond, 1890–1933. Work: (before 1885) *John Taylor*, H. H. Anderson, Indianapolis; *Rachael Marker Johnson and Daughter*, C. B. Showalter, Indianapolis; *Summer Landscape*, Jo C. Johnston, Greensburg.
References: Am Art Ann 1933, Bénézit, Burnet, Fielding, Forsyth, Gibson.

BURR, MRS. E. L.
Painter. Fort Wayne, 1864–1865.
Reference: Documents.

CAMERON, JAMES
Portrait painter. Indianapolis, 1839–ca. 1850; Philadelphia, Pa., 1850; Memphis, Tenn., 1860's.
Reference: Documents.

CAREY, HARRY
Philadelphia (?). Portrait painter. Rushville, 1877. Work: *James Wilson*, and *Mrs. James Wilson*, Rush County Historical Museum; *William W. Wilson*, Mrs. Charles F. Wilson, Rushville.
Reference: Documents.

CHAPPELSMITH, JOHN
English painter and engraver. New Harmony, 1826–1883.
References: Burnet, Lockwood, Documents.

CHASE, MARTHA OWEN (MRS. SAMUEL CHASE)
New Harmony after 1826. Painter and teacher of art and music.
Reference: Burnet.

CHASE, MARY M. POPE (MRS. TIMOTHY CHASE)
Born, Indianapolis, Ind., March 23, 1861; died, Indianapolis, June 25, 1921. Painter, craftsman and teacher. Chicago and Aurora, Ill., after 1880. Work: (Indiana) *Peninnah Mills Pope*, estate of Mrs. R. R. Shiel, Indianapolis.
References: Am Art Ann 1913, Burnet, Documents.

CHASE, WILLIAM MERRITT
Born, Williamsburg (Nineveh), Ind., Nov. 1, 1849; died, New York, N. Y., Oct. 25, 1916. Portrait, landscape, and still-life painter. Indianapolis, 1861–1868; New York, 1868–1869; St. Louis, 1869–1871; Munich, 1872–1878; New York, etc., 1878–1916. Work: (before 1870) *William Gurley Munson*, Mrs. Felix J. Wurzburg, California; *William Orbison*, Robert Orbison, Indianapolis; *Benjamin F. Love*, Prudence Douglas, Shelbyville.
References: Am Art Ann 1917, Burnet, Bénézit, Chase, Clement-H, Dunn 1, Forsyth, Fielding, Ind Art, Roof, Thieme-B.

CLARK, MORRIS W.
Portrait painter. Indianapolis, 1868; Kentucky, 1870's. Work: *Mrs. Morris W.*

Clark, Mrs. Arnold Mauk, Indianapolis.
Reference: Documents.

COLCORD, HARRY H.
Portrait painter. Indianapolis, 1878–1880.
Work: *James D. Williams,* Statehouse,
Indianapolis.
References: Documents, Dunn 1, Peat.

COMPERA (COMPARET), ALEXIS
Born, South Bend, Ind., April 15, 1856;
died, San Diego, Cal., July 29, 1906. Por-
trait and landscape painter. South Bend,
Denver, Colo., San Diego, Cal. Work: (be-
fore 1885) *Frances Comparet Coquillard,*
Notre Dame University.
References: Am Art Ann 1907–08, Burnet,
Documents, Thieme-B.

CONN, ALEX
Portrait painter. Evansville, 1863.
Reference: Documents.

CONNER, ALBERT CLINTON
Born, Fountain City, Ind., Sept. 5, 1848;
died, California, April 13, 1929. Painter.
References: Am Art Ann 1929, Burnet.

CONNER, CHARLES S.
Born, Richmond, Ind., Feb. 4, 1857; died,
Richmond, Feb. 15, 1905. Landscape
painter. Richmond and Fountain City.
California, 1887. Work: (before 1885) *In
the Parlor,* John Herron Art Museum.
References: Am Art Ann 1905–06, Burnet,
Fielding, Forsyth, Thieme-B.

COOK, C. D.
Painter. Vincennes, 1816. Work: *George
Rogers Clark,* Vincennes University (attri-
bution uncertain).
Reference: Documents.

CORY, LORETTA
Born, Shelbyville, Ind., June 24, 1859;
died, Shelbyville, April, 1917. Portrait, ani-
mal, and still-life painter. Work: *Alexander
Cory* and *Loretta Morrison Cory,* Elmer
Stout, Indianapolis.
Reference: Documents.

COSGROVE, B. G.
Portrait painter. Fort Wayne, ca. 1850.
Reference: Slocum-R.

COWGILL, ELISHA
Born, Kentucky. Portrait and landscape
painter. Greencastle and Indianapolis.

Work: *Oliver Rankin,* Soldiers' and Sailors' Monument, Indianapolis.
Reference: Documents.

COX, JACOB
Born, Burlington, N. J., Nov. 9, 1810; died,
Indianapolis, Jan. 2, 1892. Portrait, land-
scape and still-life painter. Indianapolis,
1833–1892. Work: *Henry S. Lane,* and
other governors, Statehouse, Indianapolis;
Charles G. McLean, etc., John Herron Art
Museum; *Thomas, John, and Eliza Spann,*
Anna H. Spann, Indianapolis and others.
References: Burnet, Cox, Dunn 1, Forsyth,
Gibson, Ind Art, Nowland, Peat, Sulgrove.

COX, JULIA MARY (MRS. ALBERT S.
  WHITE)
Born, Indianapolis. Portrait painter. Indi-
anapolis. Work: (before 1885) *Mrs. Abel
D. Streight,* Statehouse, Indianapolis.
Reference: Documents.

CRAFFT, R. B.
Portrait painter. Fort Wayne, 1839–1844.
Work: *Chief Francis LaFontaine,* etc., Mrs.
Howard Owens, Huntington; *Robert Fil-
son,* etc., Allen County-Fort Wayne His-
torical Museum, Fort Wayne.
References: Burnet, Griswold, Slocum-R.

CRANSTONE, LEFEVRE F.
English landscape and genre painter.
Visited United States, 1859–1860; Rich-
mond, winter 1859–1860. Work: (Indi-
ana) views of Richmond (pen and wash
drawings), Indiana University Library,
Bloomington; views of Richmond, water
colors, Indiana Historical Society Library,
Indianapolis.
References: Documents, Thieme-B.

CULBERTSON, MARY HILL (MRS.
  M. H. CULBERTSON)
Born, Richmond, Ind., 1846; died, Indi-
anapolis, Sept. 20, 1913. Landscape painter.
Indianapolis, 1878–1913.
References: Burnet, Dunn 1, Gibson.

DAVENPORT, PATRICK HENRY
Born, Danville, Ky., Nov. 3, 1803; died,
Sumner, Ill., May 13, 1890. Portrait
painter. Active in Kentucky, 1823–1837;
Sumner, Ill., 1840; Algiers, Mitchell,
Spencer, etc., 1850–1873. Work: *Robert
Logan* and *Elizabeth White Logan,* Fos-

ter T. Logan, Otwell; *Henry T. Hamer* and *Mary Ellen Lemon Hamer,* Spring Mill State Park, and others.
Reference: Documents.

DAVIES, THOMAS J.
Portrait painter. Indianapolis, 1865–1866. Work: *John Carlisle* and *Margaret Boyd Carlisle,* Mrs. Arthur Moore, Indianapolis. Reference: Documents.

DAVIS, MARY (MARIA ANN THE-RESA) CARTER (MRS. JOHN SAM-UEL DAVIS)
Born, Preston, England, July 10, 1827; died, Kansas City, Mo., Feb. 7, 1901. Portrait painter, photographer, and stained-glass craftsman. Philadelphia, Pa., 1848–1865; Logansport, 1865–1882; Cleveland, O., 1883–1890; St. Louis, Mo., etc., 1890–1898. Work: *George Bevan,* Winifred Bevan, Logansport; *Sophronia J. Murphy,* Louise Elliott, Logansport.
Reference: Documents.

DAVIS, W. R.
Cincinnati. Portrait painter; Gosport and Spencer, 1872.
Reference: Documents.

DE LA MATYR, MARIETTA OSBORN (MRS. GILBERT DE LA MATYR)
Painter. Indianapolis, 1874–1877.
Reference: Documents, Dunn 2.

DENNIS, JAMES M.
Born, Dublin, Ind., 1840; died, Detroit, Mich., May 6, 1918. Portrait and landscape painter. Cincinnati, O., ca. 1858–1865; Indianapolis, 1865–1883; Detroit, Mich., 1883–1918. Work: *James A. Mount,* State-house, Indianapolis; *Christian Park,* Edna Christian, Indianapolis, and others.
References: Burnet, Documents, Dunn 1, Forsyth, Peat.

DIETZ, JULIUS
Portrait painter. Evansville, Ind., 1872–1879.
Reference: Documents.

DILLE, JOSEPH H.
Born, near Cleveland, O., Aug. 29, 1832; died, Amelia, O., Oct. 19, 1918. Portrait, landscape, and still-life painter. Fort Wayne, ca. 1850–1856; Goshen, 1856–1865; Fort Wayne 1877–ca. 1910; Amelia, O., ca. 1910–1918. Work: *Mrs. John G. Olds,* and *Thomas W. Swinney,* Allen County-Fort Wayne Historical Museum, and others.
References: Bartholomew, Documents.

DODDS, J.
Portrait painter. Dublin, Ind., ca. 1869; New York, N. Y., ca. 1870.
Reference: Burnet.

DOUSA, HENRY
Born, Lafayette, Ind., ca. 1820; died, Lafayette. Portrait and animal painter. Lafayette; New Castle, 1879–ca. 1885. Work: *Solomon Denius* and *Cyrus Pence,* etc., Henry County Historical Museum, New Castle; *Residence of Thomas Fyffe,* Indiana Historical Society Library, Indianapolis.
Reference: Documents.

DUCLOS, PETER (PIERRE)
Born, Paris, France, 1815; died, New Harmony, Ind., Feb. 16, 1869. Scenery painter. New Harmony after 1826.
References: Burnet, Documents.

DUNLAP, JAMES BOLIVAR
Born, Indianapolis, Ind., May 7, 1825, died Indianapolis, Sept. 4, 1864. Painter, cartoonist, and engraver. Indianapolis, 1825–1864. Work: *Woodville Browning,* Mrs. George W. Pittman, Indianapolis; *Barnyard Scene,* Merrill B. Barkley, Indianapolis.
References: Burnet, Documents, Dunn 1, Nowland, Sulgrove.

DUNN, JOHN GIBSON
Born, Lawrenceburg, Ind., ca. 1826; died, New Orleans, La., ca. 1858. Genre painter. Indianapolis, 1840–1842, 1851; Cincinnati, O., 1843–1850; Lawrenceburg, 1852–1855; New Orleans, La., ca. 1856–1858. Work: *The Temperance Pledge,* John Herron Art Museum.
References: Burnet, Coggeshall, Cottman, Documents, Dunn 1.

DUPALAIS (DU PALAIS), VIRGINIA POULLARD (MRS. WILLIAM A. TWIGG)
Born, Philadelphia, Pa., Mar. 20, 1804; died, New Harmony, Ind., Jan. 8, 1864. Painter. New Harmony, 1826–1864.

Work: *Joseph Fauntleroy* (pencil), Old Fauntleroy House, New Harmony; *Maximilian, Prince of Wied* (pencil), Indiana Historical Society Library, Indianapolis. References: Burnet, Documents, Lockwood.

EAMES, LUCIA A.
Portrait painter. Evansville, 1863.
Reference: Documents.

EATON, JOSEPH ORIEL
Born, Newark, Ohio, Feb. 8, 1829; died, Yonkers, N. Y., Feb. 7, 1875. Portrait painter. Indianapolis, 1845–1848; Cincinnati, O., 1849–ca. 1863; New York, N. Y., 1863–1875. Work: (Indianapolis) *Joseph E. Pope,* W. K. Stewart, Louisville, Ky.; *Peninnah Mills Pope,* Mrs. Robert B. Moynahan, Indianapolis.
References: Bénézit, Burnet, Cist 2, Documents, Dunn 1, Forsyth, Thieme-B.

EDMONDSON, EDWARD
Born, Dayton, O.; died, California. Portrait and landscape painter. Visited Fort Wayne, 1863. Work: (Indiana) *Alice Belknap Torrence,* Dr. C. R. Dancer, Fort Wayne; *Landscape,* Mrs. Warren Sweet, Fort Wayne.
References: Clark, Documents.

EDWARDS, J. W.
Portrait painter and art teacher. Evansville, 1885.
Reference: Documents.

EVANS, DE SCOTT (DAVID SCOTT)
Born, Boston, Ind., Mar. 28, 1847; died at sea (on the *Bourgoyne*), July 4, 1898. Portrait and genre painter. Logansport (Smithson College), 1872–1874; Mount Union College, O., ca. 1875; Paris, France, 1877; Cleveland, O., 1878–1887; New York, N. Y., 1887–1898. Work: (Indiana) *Joshua Smithson,* Switzerland County Historical Society, Vevay; *George R. Chitwood,* William H. Chitwood, Indianapolis.
References: Am Art Ann 1898, Burnet, Clement-H, Documents, Powell, Thieme-B.

EVANS, LEWIS
Portrait painter (Massalon & Evans). Evansville, 1868–1869.
Reference: Documents.

FARRER, EDWIN
Born, London, England, May 3, 1851; died, Indianapolis, Ind., Nov. 21, 1921. Portrait and landscape painter. New York, 1861; Rushville, ca. 1870–1920. Work: *Ebenezer Smith,* Mrs. Wendell Willkie, Rushville; *Leven E. Wallace,* Rush County Historical Museum, Rushville.
Reference: Documents.

FERRY, MRS. ANNIE E.
Portrait painter and teacher. Indianapolis, 1883–1895; New York, N. Y., ca. 1900.
References: Burnet, Documents.

FETSCH (PFETSCH), CARL P.
Born, Blankenburg, Germany, 1817; died, Indianapolis, Ind., March 28, 1899. Portrait painter. New York, N. Y. ca. 1843–1855; Cincinnati, O., 1855; New Albany, 1856–1870; Indianapolis, 1870–1898. Work: *John Heitkam,* Mrs. Walter Heitkam, Indianapolis; *Grandmother and Child,* Carlton G. Weiss, Indianapolis.
References: Burnet, Documents.

FISCUS, CHARLES JOSEPH
Born, Indianapolis, Ind., May 26, 1861; died, Indianapolis, Feb. 6, 1884. Portrait and genre painter. Work: *Still Life,* John Herron Art Museum; *Self-portrait* (charcoal), Elmer Taflinger, Indianapolis.
References: Burnet, Documents.

FLETCHER, AARON DEAN
Born, Springfield, Vt., Sept. 15, 1817; died, Kuseville, N. Y. Portrait and landscape painter. La Porte, 1836. Work: (Indiana) *Jacob Replogle* and *Sinia Jones Replogle,* Lee W. Replogle, La Porte.
References: Baker, Documents.

FLETCHER, CALVIN I., M. D.
Born, Indianapolis, Ind., 1859; died, Glacier National Park, Mont., Aug. 19, 1913. Landscape painter. Indianapolis.
References: Documents, Ind Biog.

FORBES, JAMES G.
Born, Scotland, ca. 1800; died, Chicago, Ill. (?) ca. 1870. Portrait painter. Edinburgh, Scotland, London, England, 1852–1857; Chicago, Ill., 1860–1870; Evansville, and Indianapolis, 1869. Work: (Indiana) *John B. Baker,* Willard Library, Evansville;

Conrad Baker, Oliver P. Morton, etc., State-house, Indianapolis.
References: Documents, Peat.

FORGY, JOHN D.
Born, Logansport, Ind.; died, Des Moines, Ia. Landscape painter and illustrator. Logansport.
References: Burnet, Documents, Powell.

FORSYTH, WILLIAM J.
Born, Hamilton County, O., Oct. 15, 1854; died, Indianapolis, Ind., Mar. 29, 1935. Indianapolis ca. 1865–1881; Munich, Germany, 1882–1888; Indianapolis, etc., 1888–1935. Work: (before 1885) *Artist's Mother* and *Self-Portrait,* Mrs. William Forsyth, Indianapolis.
References: Burnet, Documents, Dunn 1, Forsyth, Gibson, Ind Art.

FOWLER, HARRY
Portrait painter. Indianapolis, 1877. Work: *Joseph E. Goss* and *Elizabeth Dittemore Goss,* George C. Goss, Indianapolis.
Reference: Documents.

FREEMAN, WILLIAM R.
Born, New York State, ca. 1820; died, St. Louis, Mo., ca. 1906. Portrait painter. New York, N. Y., 1844; Fort Wayne, ca. 1845; Vincennes, 1849–1850; Terre Haute, 1872–1873; Indianapolis, 1874–1875; San Francisco, Cal., 1875. Work: *Samuel P. Judah,* Reynolds Judah, Vincennes; *Preston Hussey,* Mrs. Warren Hussey, Terre Haute; *Thomas A. Hendricks,* Statehouse, Indianapolis; *Jacob Cox,* Cyril C. Spades, Saint Augustine, Fla., and others.
References: Burnet, Documents, Forsyth, Peat, Slocum-R.

GILLET, EDGAR P.
Painter. Madison, after 1852.
Reference: Documents.

GLESSING, THOMAS B.
Born, London, England, 1817; died, Boston, Mass., 1882. Landscape and scenic painter. Cincinnati, O., ca. 1845; Indianapolis, 1859–1873; Boston, Mass., and New York, N. Y., 1873–1882. Work: (Indianapolis) *Cold Springs, Riverside Park,* Benjamin Harrison Memorial Home, Indianapolis; *Landscape,* Herman L. Peck, Indianapolis.
References: Burnet, Documents, Dunn 1, Forsyth, Gibson, Holloway, Nowland.

GOODWIN, J. B.
Portrait painter. Brookville, 1844.
Reference: Documents.

GOOKINS, JAMES FARRINGTON
Born, Terre Haute, Ind., Dec. 30, 1840; died, New York, N. Y., May 23, 1904. Portrait and landscape painter. Terre Haute, etc., 1860–1865; Chicago, Ill., 1865–1869; Munich, Germany, 1870–1873; Indianapolis, 1873–1880; Terre Haute, 1880–1883; Chicago, 1883–1904; Indianapolis, 1887–1889. Work: *The Artist's Wife,* John Herron Art Museum; *Scene in Switzerland,* Elizabeth Claypool, Indianapolis; *Modisette Ferry,* etc., Sheldon Swope Art Gallery, Terre Haute, and others.
References: Burnet, Documents, Dunn 1, Gibson, Ind Art.

GORDON, THOMAS CLARKSON (CLARK)
Born, near Spiceland, Ind., Aug. 4, 1841; died, Spiceland, July 22, 1922. Panorama and decorative painter. Work: Panorama, *Battle Scenes of the Rebellion,* Mrs. Frank Davis, Spiceland; *Carl Millikan,* etc., Mrs. Paul E. Newby, Indianapolis.
Reference: Documents.

GORGAS, JOSEPH R.
Miniature and portrait painter (Gorgas & Bro.). Madison and Newburgh, 1854–1855.
Reference: Documents.

GREGORI, LUIGI
Born, Bologna, Italy, 1819; died, Florence, Italy, June 6, 1896. Mural and portrait painter. South Bend, 1874–1891. Work: (Indiana) Murals, Notre Dame University; *Thomas S. Stanfield,* Courthouse, South Bend, and others.
References: Bénézit, Documents, Fielding, Thieme-B.

GRENZARD, LOUIS S.
Landscape painter. Indianapolis, 1861–1870.
Reference: Directories.

GRUELLE, RICHARD BUCKNER
Born, Cynthiana, Ky., Feb. 22, 1851; died, Indianapolis, Ind., Nov. 8, 1914. Portrait, marine, and landscape painter. Arcola and Decatur, Ill., ca. 1875–1881; Indianapolis,

1882–1910; Norwalk, Conn., 1910–1914. Work: (before 1885) *Henry M. Socwell*, Indiana Historical Society Library; *Portrait of a Lady*, Cleo Degenford, Chenoa, Ill.; *The Canal, Morning*, John Herron Art Museum.
References: Am Art Ann, 1915, Burnet, Cottman, Documents, Dunn 1, Fielding, Forsyth, Gibson, Ind Art.

GUEZET, ALEXANDER
Historical painter. Indianapolis, 1863.
Reference: Documents.

GUFFIN, LOTTA (CHARLOTTE) HILLIS (MRS. HENRY CLAY GUFFIN)
Born, near Greensburg, Ind., 1844; died, Chicago, Ill., November, 1896. Portrait, animal, and landscape painter. Indianapolis, 1864–ca. 1885; New York, N. Y., and Chicago, Ill., ca. 1885–1896. Work: *Conrad Baker*, Thaddeus R. Baker, Indianapolis; *Addison C. Harris*, John W. Becker, Allisonville; *Dr. Thomas B. Harvey*, Indiana Medical School Library, and others.
References: Burnet, Documents, Dunn 1, Forsyth.

GULICH, SAMUEL W.
Scenic and panorama painter. Indianapolis, 1858–ca. 1863.
References: Burnet, Documents, Holloway.

HALL, BASIL
Born, Haddingtonshire, Scotland, Dec. 31, 1788; died, Gosport, England, Sept. 11, 1844. Naval officer and etcher. North America, 1827–1828; visited Indiana, May, 1828. Work: (Indiana) *House on the Banks of the Ohio River in the State of Indiana* and *Southwest end of Wabash Island*, Indiana University Library, Bloomington.
References: Documents, Thieme-B.

HANBECK, WILLIAM
Portrait painter. Madison, 1846.
Reference: Documents.

HARDING, HORACE
Born, Conway, Mass., 1794; died, Woodville, Miss., ca. 1857. Portrait painter. Paris, Ky., ca. 1816–1820; Vincennes, 1820; Cincinnati, O., Versailles, Ky., etc., 1820–1840; New York, N. Y., 1840; Little Rock,

Ark., etc., 1852–1857. Work: (Indiana) *Dr. Elias McNamee* (attributed), William Henry Harrison Mansion, Vincennes.
References: Documents, Morse.

HARRIS, JAMES F.
Portrait and genre painter. Madison, 1846; Indianapolis, 1853.
References: Burnet, Documents, Dunn 1.

HARRISON, CHRISTOPHER
Born, Cambridge, Md., 1775; died, Talbot County, Md., 1863. Amateur landscape painter. Fair Prospect, ca. 1805; Salem, 1815; Indianapolis, etc., 1820–1834.
References: Burnet, Nowland, Woollen.

HAYS, BARTON STONE
Born, Greenville, O., April 5, 1826; died, Minneapolis, Minn., Mar. 14, 1914. Portrait, animal, and still-life painter. Wingate, Attica, etc., ca. 1850–1858; Indianapolis, 1858–1870, 1874–1883; Cincinnati, O., 1871–1873; Minneapolis, Minn., 1883–1914. Work: (Indiana) *Dr. Lewis D. Lyons* and *Mary A. Alford*, John Herron Art Museum; *Lewis Hanes*, Mrs. John B. Martin, Covington; *Joseph Dumont Shipp*, May Louise Shipp, Indianapolis; *George F. Adams* and *Rebecca Raymond Adams*, Bertha Ellis, Indianapolis; *Melons and Peaches*, Carl B. Shafer, Indianapolis.
References: Burnet, Documents, Dunn 1, Forsyth, Gibson, Peat.

HEATON, CHARLES M., JR.
Born, South Bend, Ind., Dec. 17, 1840; died, Tacoma Park, D. C., Aug. 19, 1921. Portrait painter. South Bend until ca. 1870; Washington and Tacoma Park, D. C., ca. 1870–1921. Work: (Indiana) *Mrs. Charles Heaton, Sr.*, Northern Indiana Historical Museum, South Bend.
Reference: Documents.

HEGLER (HAEGLER), JOHN JACOB
Born, Bretzwil, Switzerland, Jan. 21, 1812; died, Attica, Ind., May 2, 1856. Portrait painter. Came to U. S. A., 1831; Fort Wayne, 1845; Lafayette, 1849–1853; Attica, 1853–1856. Work: *Dr. Turner Welch*, etc., Tippecanoe County Historical Museum, Lafayette; *Alice Lyons*, John Herron Art Museum; *William Johnson and Daughter Belle*, etc., W. J. Sheetz, Fowler;

Harriet and Nancy Johnson, Mrs. W. E. Tubbs, Fowler.
References: Documents, Slocum-R.

HILL, JOHN BAYLESS
Born, Indianapolis, Ind., 1849; died, Indianapolis, Nov. 19, 1874. Portrait painter. Indianapolis, 1869–1874. Work: *Abram A. Hammond,* Statehouse, Indianapolis; *Maude Hill,* Mrs. Paul Weer, Indianapolis.
References: Burnet, Documents, Dunn 1, Peat.

HILLIARD, WILLIAM HENRY
   (HARRY)
Born, Auburn, N. Y., 1836; died, Washington, D. C. April, 1905. Portrait, landscape, and still-life painter. Madison, Ind., ca. 1860–ca. 1870; Indianapolis, ca. 1870–1880; Boston, Mass., etc., 1880–1905. Work: *Landscape,* water color, Estate of Lucetta Ohr, Indianapolis; *Italian Roses,* Carl B. Shafer, Indianapolis.
References: Am Art Ann 1905–06, Burnet, Clement-H, Documents, Fielding.

HOLBRUNER, CHARLES EDWIN
Born, Woodsboro, Md., Jan. 11, 1855; died, Brooksville, Fla., 1930. Landscape painter. Logansport, 1880–ca. 1910. Work: Landscapes owned by Mrs. Florence Pennington and Earl Guthrie, Logansport.
Reference: Documents.

HUEY, M. S.
Portrait painter, Indianapolis, 1867.
Reference: Documents.

HYDE, EMILY GRIFFIN
Born, Lake County, Ind., 1859; died, Spiceland, Ind., Sept. 13, 1919. Painter.
Reference: Burnet.

INGRAHAM, CHARLES B.
Portrait painter. Indianapolis, 1882–1890.
Reference: Documents.

INGRAHAM, ELLEN M., (MRS.
   CHARLES B. INGRAHAM)
Born, New Haven, Conn., Aug. 12, 1832; died, Indianapolis, Ind., June 2, 1919. Portrait painter. Indianapolis after 1865. Work: *Bishop Joseph C. Talbott,* Hewitt Talbot, Indianapolis; *Florence and Oren Coffin,* Florence Coffin, Beverly Hills, Calif.
References: Burnet, Documents.

JENISON, EMILY
Portrait painter. Fort Wayne, 1859–1861.
Reference: Documents.

JUDAH, HARRIET BRANDON
Born, Piqua, O., July 4, 1808; died, Vincennes, Ind., June, 1884. Painter. Vincennes.
Reference: Burnet.

KELLOGG, MINER KILBOURNE
Born, Menlius Square, N. Y., Aug. 22, 1814; died, Toledo, O., Feb. 17, 1889. Portrait, figure, and landscape painter. New Harmony, Ind., 1826–1827 and 1860; Europe, 1841–1858; Toledo, O., ca. 1860–1889. Work: (Indiana) *Robert Dale Owen,* Kenneth Dale Owen, New Harmony.
References: Documents,   Fielding, Thieme-B.

KENDALL, BROOK
Portrait painter. Cambridge City, 1865.
Reference: Documents.

KENDRICK, JAMES ROBERT
Painter. Indianapolis, 1869–1884.
Reference: Documents.

KERSEY, PLINY EARLE
Born, North Carolina, Jan. 13, 1850; died, San Diego, Cal., 1873. Painter and teacher. Richmond, 1861–1869; California, 1869–1873. Work: Views of Richmond, watercolor sketches, Emily Kersey, Pasadena, California.
Reference: Documents.

KETCHAM, SUSAN M.
Born, Indianapolis, Ind., 1841; died, Indianapolis, Feb. 1, 1930. Landscape painter and teacher. Indianapolis until 1886; Europe, 1886–1889; New York, N. Y., 1889–1930.
References: Burnet, Dunn 1, Forsyth.

KIRKLAND, INDIA UNDERHILL
   (MRS.)
Born, Indianapolis, Ind.; died, Indianapolis. Painter and sculptor. Indianapolis in the 1870's.
References: Burnet, Dunn 1.

KLEPPER, MAX FRANCIS
Born, Zeitz, Germany, Mar. 1, 1861; died, Brooklyn, N. Y., May 5, 1907. Landscape

painter and illustrator. Toledo, O., 1876; Logansport, 1877–1879; New York, N. Y., etc., 1880–1907. Work: (Indiana) *On the Wabash,* Mrs. Charlotte Van Doorn, Flora, Ind.
References: Am Art Ann 1905–06, Bénézit, Burnet, Fielding, Powell, Wright.

KOTZ, DANIEL
Born, near South Bend, Ind., March 21, 1848; died, Park Ridge, N. J., Sept. 14, 1933. Landscape painter. South Bend, 1848–ca. 1890; New York, N. Y., 1891.
References: Am Art Ann 1933, Burnet.

LANG, PH. (PHILIP ?)
Portrait painter. Cincinnati, O., ca. 1850; Rockport, 1852. Work: *James Proctor,* Mrs. C. W. Halbruge, Rockport; *Samuel Park,* Mrs. Melba Bullock, Rockport; *Matthias Sharp,* Mrs. Samuel I. Hill, Rockport.
Reference: Documents.

LE FER DE LA MOTTE, see: ST. FRANCIS XAVIER, SISTER

LESUEUR, CHARLES ALEXANDRE
Born, Le Havre, France, Jan. 1, 1778; died, Ste. Adresse, France, Dec. 14(?) 1846. Landscape and portrait painter, and naturalist. Philadelphia, Pa., 1815–1826; New Harmony, 1826–1837; Le Havre, France, 1837–1846. Work (Indiana): Pencil and water-color sketches, Purdue University Library, W. Lafayette; *A Shrike,* water color, Library, New Harmony.
References: Burnet, DAB, Fielding, Lockwood, Vail.

LEWIS, JAMES OTTO
Born, Philadelphia, Pa., 1799; died, New York, N. Y., 1858. Engraver, portrait and genre painter, chiefly American Indian subjects. New York, 1816–1823, Fort Wayne, 1827; Detroit, Mich., etc., 1833. Philadelphia, Pa., 1835.
References: Butts, Fielding, Thieme-B.

LIETZ, THEOBALD
Born in Germany; died in Indianapolis, Ind. Portrait painter. Indianapolis, ca. 1870–1884.
References: Burnet, Documents.

LINEN, GEORGE
Born, Greenlaw, Scotland, 1802; died, New York, N. Y., 1888. Portrait painter. New York, N. Y., 1843–1888; Terre Haute, ca. 1860. Work: (Indiana) *Chauncey Warren,* Mrs. John C. Warren, Terre Haute; *Caleb Mills,* Helen Condit, Terre Haute; *Chauncey Rose,* Rose Polytechnic Institute, Terre Haute, and others.
References: Burnet, Documents, Fielding, Thieme-B.

LOVE, JOHN WASHINGTON
Born, Napoleon, Ind., Aug. 10, 1850; died, Indianapolis, Ind., June 24, 1880. Portrait and landscape painter. New York, N. Y. 1871; Paris, France, 1872–1876; Indianapolis, 1876–1880. Work: *Louis A. Kiefer, The Sycamores,* etc., John Herron Art Museum; *Henry L. Sielken,* H. L. Sielken, Indianapolis.
References: Biog History, Burnet, Documents, Dunn 1, Forsyth, Gibson, Ind Art.

LUDINGTON, JULIA (MRS. W. H. H. LUDINGTON)
Landscape painter. Indianapolis, ca. 1873–1890.
References: Burnet, Documents.

LUMBERT, HORACE
Painter. Indianapolis, 1882.
Reference: Documents

MacDONALD, MARY CATHERINE
Born, Camden, Ind., 1852; died, Baltimore, Md., Jan. 8, 1897. Painter, illustrator, and teacher. Logansport, 1883–1896.
References: Burnet, Documents, Powell, Wright.

McDOWELL, LUCINDA BOWERS (MRS. JOSEPH McDOWELL)
Born, New Castle, Ind., Sept. 29, 1827; died, New Castle, Nov. 29, 1909. Portrait painter. Work: *Samuel Graham,* Henry County Historical Museum, New Castle.
Reference: Documents.

McEVOY, HENRY N.
Landscape painter. Indianapolis, 1860–1861.
Reference: Documents.

McLEAN, JEROME
Portrait painter. Logansport, 1873–1875. Work: *Joseph Seiter,* Victor E. Seiter, Logansport.
Reference: Powell.

MAENTEL, JACOB
Born, Cassel, Germany, June 15, 1763; died, New Harmony, Ind., Apr. 28, 1863. Portrait painter. Stewartsville and New Harmony, ca. 1840–1863. Work: *Jonathan Jaquess* and *Rebecca Jaquess,* Arthur E. Jaquess, Poseyville; *James Overton and Son,* Library, New Harmony; *John Cooper,* and others, Charles H. Ray, Terre Haute, etc.
Reference: Documents.

MASON, JOSEPH
Portrait painter. Cincinnati, O., 1822–ca. 1840; Michigan, 1840; La Porte, ca. 1841. Work: (Indiana) *Marie Jane Andrew,* Charles F. Cochran, La Porte.
References: Cist 1, Documents.

MASSALON, JAMES
Portrait painter (Massalon & Evans). Evansville, 1866–1870.
Reference: Documents.

MATHEWS, RETTA T.
Born, Arlington, Ind., Apr. 7, 1856; died, Arlington, Feb. 24, 1899. Landscape and still-life painter. Work: *Flowers,* Rush County Historical Museum, Rushville; *Landscape,* Clark Offutt, Arlington.
Reference: Documents.

MAURICE, SISTER (MADELEINE SCHNELL)
Born, Inspach, Germany, Oct. 27, 1830; died, Saint Mary-of-the-Woods, Ind., Jan. 13, 1902. Painter and teacher. Saint Mary-of-the-Woods, 1847–1902. Work: *Refugee from Alsace-Lorraine,* Saint Mary-of-the-Woods.
References: Brown M, Documents.

MENDENHALL, JOB B.
Portrait painter (Adams & Mendenhall). Indianapolis, 1871–1872.
Reference: Documents.

MERINE, A.
Portrait painter. South Bend, 1841.
Reference: Documents.

MILLER, GUSTAV (AUGUST)
Born, Rugersdorf, Germany, Feb. 11, 1851; died, Evansville, Ind. (?) Landscape painter and decorator. Evansville ca. 1880–ca. 1900. Work: *Landscape,* Evansville Public Museum.
Reference: Burnet.

MILLISON, ROYAL HILL
Born, Batavia, O., 1849; died, Evanston, Ill., Dec. 18, 1936. Landscape painter. Indianapolis, 1878–1895; Boston, Mass., ca. 1895–ca. 1900; Chicago, Ill., after 1900.
References: Burnet, Documents, Fielding, Thieme-B.

MILLIKAN, RHODA HOUGHTON
Born, Marlboro, Vt., Dec. 1838; died, Indianapolis, Ind., Oct. 2, 1903. Painter and teacher. Piqua, O., Greenfield, Ind.
Reference: Burnet.

MILLS, HENRY ALBERT
Born, Bankers, Mich., July 24, 1848; died, Mt. Vernon, Iowa, Sept. 23, 1921. Painter and teacher. Greencastle, 1885–1894; Mt. Vernon, Iowa, 1896–1921.
Reference: Documents.

MOMBERGER, WILLIAM
Born, Frankfort am Main, Germany, 1829. Landscape painter and illustrator. North America, 1848–1860; visited Fort Wayne, Vincennes, and Evansville ca. 1860. Work: (Indiana) *Wabash River near Vincennes, Indiana,* etc., (engravings published in "National Gallery of American Landscape," 1869).
References: Documents, Fielding, Thieme-B.

MORRISON, GEORGE W.
Born, Baltimore, Md., 1820; died, New Albany, Ind., Dec. 24, 1893. Portrait and landscape painter. New Albany, 1840–1893. Work: *Ashbel P. Willard,* Statehouse, Indianapolis; *William A. Scribner,* etc., Scribner House, New Albany, *Potomac River,* T. M. Gardner, Indianapolis; *Harry and Mary Emma Woodward,* Katharine Woodward, Middleburg, Va.
References: Burnet, Cottman, Documents, Dunn 1, Peat.

MOTE, W. ALDEN
Born, West Milton, O., Aug. 27, 1840; died, Richmond, Ind., Jan. 13, 1917. Portrait and landscape painter. Richmond, ca. 1880–1917. Work: *Daniel A. Reid,* Reid Memorial Hospital, Richmond.
References: Burnet, Clark, Documents.

MOTE, MARCUS
Born, West Milton, O., June 19, 1817; died, Richmond, Ind., Feb. 26, 1898. Por-

trait and genre painter, and teacher. Miamisburg and Lebanon, O., 1859–1862; Richmond, 1863–1898. Work: *Daniel Wiggins,* etc., Wayne County Historical Museum, Richmond; *Elizabeth Chalfont Gilbert,* Harry W. Gilbert, Richmond; *Indiana Yearly Meeting of Friends,* etc., Earlham College, Richmond, and others.
References: Burnet, Clark, Documents.

NEW, JAMES R.
Died, Salem, Ind. (?) ca. 1828. Portrait painter. Salem, ca. 1826. Work: *Joseph Bartholomew,* Bartholomew County Courthouse, Columbus.
Reference: Documents.

NEWPORT, JAMES HERSCHEL
Portrait and landscape painter. Logansport, 1874–1890; Richmond, 1883–1884.
Reference: Documents.

NICHOLSON, ELIZABETH
Born, Clinton County, O., Dec. 10, 1833; died, Indianapolis, Ind., Apr. 26, 1926. Portrait and landscape painter. Indianapolis, 1868–1926.
References: Am Art Ann 1926, Burnet, Documents.

NICHOLSON, JOHN
Born, Jefferson County, Ind., July 12, 1825; died, Crawfordsville, Ind., 1893. Portrait painter. Franklin, 1850–1870; Kokomo, 1870–1879; Crawfordsville, 1879–1893. Work: *Royal Singleton Hicks,* Mrs. Bess Ehrmann, Rockport.
References: Beckwith, Documents.

NIEMEYER, JOHN HENRY
Born, Bremen, Germany, June 25, 1839; died, New Haven, Conn., Dec. 7, 1932. Portrait and figure painter. Cincinnati, 1843–ca. 1850; Indianapolis, ca. 1850–1860; New York, N. Y., 1860; Paris, France, 1866; New Haven, Conn., 1871–1932.
References: Am Art Ann 1932, Burnet, Clement-H, DAB, Fielding, Thieme-B.

OBEONESSER, BALTHAZAR
Swiss painter. New Harmony, 1826–1827.
References: Burnet, Documents.

O'BYRNE, ROSE
Landscape painter. Evansville.
Reference: Documents.

OWEN, DAVID DALE
Born, New Lanark, Scotland, June 24, 1807; died, New Harmony, Ind., Nov. 13, 1860. Landscape and portrait painter, and geologist. New Harmony, 1825–1827; Europe, 1827–1833; Cincinnati, O., 1835–1837; New Harmony, etc., 1837–1860. Work: *Joseph Neef,* Library, New Harmony; *Richard Owen,* Kenneth Dale Owen, New Harmony.
References: DAB, Documents, Lockridge, Lockwood.

PECKHAM, LEWIS
Born, Newport, R. I., Sept. 19, 1788; died, Vincennes, Ind., Sept. 8., 1822. Portrait painter. Boston, Mass., 1810; Vincennes, 1815–1822. Work: *Hyacinthe Lasselle,* Indiana State Library, Indianapolis; *Self Portrait* and *Paul Peckham,* miniatures, John Herron Art Museum, Indianapolis.
References: Burnet, Documents, Ind Art.

PERING, CORNELIUS
Born, England, Nov. 5, 1806; died, Louisville, Ky., Nov. 28, 1881. Portrait and landscape painter, and teacher. Bloomington, 1832–1846; Louisville, Ky., 1846–1881. Work: *Seminary Campus, Bloomington,* Indiana University Library, Bloomington.
Reference: Documents.

POINDEXTER, JAMES THOMAS
Born, Christian County, Ky., June 6, 1832; died, Eddyville, Ky., June 10, 1891. Portrait painter. Evansville, 1852–ca. 1860; 1871–1882; Kentucky, etc., 1883–1891. Work: (Indiana) *Charles Hallett White,* Library, New Harmony; *Mrs. Charles Mason* and *Madison J. Bray,* Evansville Museum of Arts and Sciences; *Charles Parke Bacon,* Mrs. C. H. Hinkle, Evansville, and others.
References: Burnet, Documents.

POPE, MARY M., see: CHASE, MARY M.

POTTER, WILLIAM J.
Landscape painter. Logansport, 1868.
Reference: Documents.

PULLMAN, MARGARET MacDONALD (MRS. GEORGE M. PULLMAN)
Born, Camden, Ind. (?); died, Baltimore, Md., May 19, 1892. Landscape painter.

Camden and Logansport, ca. 1880–1881; Chicago, Ill., 1881–1892.
References: Burnet, Documents, Powell, Wright.

PURCELL, C. W.
Painter. (Bowers and Purcell). Indianapolis, 1855.
Reference: Documents.

READ, THOMAS BUCHANAN
Born, Chester County, Pa., Mar. 12, 1822; died, New York, N. Y., May 11, 1872. Painter, sculptor, architect, and poet. Cincinnati, O., 1839–1841; Madison, ca. 1840; New York, N. Y., 1841–1850; Rome, Italy etc., 1850–1870; Indianapolis, 1865. Work: (Indiana) *James F. D. Lanier,* Mrs. Charles Davidson, Madison; *Oliver P. Morton,* City Hall, Cincinnati, O.
References: Bénézit, Burnet, Cist 1 & 2, DAB, Documents, Fielding, NCAB, Thieme-B.

REED, LOUIS (LEWIS) HENRI
Born, Cincinnati, O., 1847; died, Indianapolis, Ind., Apr. 6, 1910. Painter and sculptor. Indianapolis, 1875–1910.
References: Burnet, Documents, Dunn 1.

REED, PETER FISHE
Born, Boston, Mass., May 5, 1817; died, Burlington, Ia., 1887. Portrait, landscape, and genre painter. Cincinnati, O., 1844–1846; Indianapolis, 1860–1863; Centerville, 1861; Chicago, Ill. 1865–ca. 1875; San Francisco, Cal., 1878.
References: Brown, Burnet, Coggeshall, Cottman, Documents, Dunn 1, Holloway.

REID, JOHN
Portrait painter of New York. Terre Haute, ca. 1875–1880. Work: *Lucien W. Berry,* DePauw University; *Molly Edwards Connelly,* Mrs. John N. Ott, Indianapolis.
Reference: Documents.

RICHARDS, J. R.
Portrait painter. Logansport, 1837–1844; La Porte, 1844.
References: Burnet, Documents, Powell.

RICHARDS, SAMUEL G.
Born, Spencer, Ind., Apr. 22, 1853; died, Denver, Colo., Nov. 30, 1893. Portrait, landscape, and genre painter. Spencer, 1870–1872; Franklin, 1873–1877; Anderson, 1877–1880; Munich, Germany, and Switzerland, 1880–1891; Anderson, 1891; Denver, Colo., 1892–1893. Work: (Indiana) *Harlan Richards,* Harlan Richards Logan, Tampa, Fla.; *James L. Mitchell,* Library, Indiana University, Bloomington; *John Fothergill and Son,* Mary M. Hunt, Franklin, and others.
References: Burnet, Documents, Forsyth, Gibson, Ind Art.

RIESS, WILLIAM J.
Born, Berlin, Germany, 1856; died, Chicago, Ill., Mar. 30, 1919. Landscape and figure painter. Indianapolis, 1884. Work: *Dr. Thomas A. Wagner,* Mrs. Herbert T. Wagner, Indianapolis.
References: Am Art Ann 1919, Burnet.

ROCKWELL, HORACE
Born, Philadelphia, Pa. (?) July 6, 1811; died, Roanoke, Ind., Jan. 9, 1877. Portrait painter. Philadelphia, Pa., and New York, N. Y., 1835; Fort Wayne and Roanoke, 1836–1877. Work: *Edward Stopelford,* etc., Allen County-Fort Wayne Historical Museum, Fort Wayne; *Samuel Hanna Family,* Fort Wayne Art Museum.
References: Bash, Documents, Griswold, Slocum-R, Wasmuth.

ROGERS, MICHAEL G.
Born, Ohio, ca. 1805; died, Indianapolis, Ind., Jan. 28, 1832. Portrait painter. Indianapolis, 1831. Work: *Isaac Dunn* and *Frances Piatt Dunn,* Caroline Dunn and Eleanor Dunn Moore, Indianapolis.
References: Brown, Burnet, Documents, Dunn 1, Sulgrove.

ROOKER, SAMUEL SAFFEL
Born, Tennessee, ca. 1800; died, Indiana, ca. 1875. Portrait painter. Indianapolis, 1821–ca. 1865.
References: Brown, Burnet, Documents, Dunn 1, Nowland.

ROWLEY, FAYETTE R.
Portrait painter. Indianapolis, 1875–1876.
References: Burnet, Documents.

RUDISILL, MARGARET
Born, Montgomery County, Ind., July 2, 1857; died, Indianapolis, Ind., June 29, 1933. Landscape and figure painter. Indian-

apolis, 1876–1888; Paris, France, 1889–1892; Indianapolis, 1893–1933.
References: Am Art Ann 1930, Burnet, Documents, Dunn 1.

ST. FRANCIS XAVIER, SISTER (IRMA LE FER DE LA MOTTE)

Born, Saint-Servan, France; died, Saint Mary-of-the-Woods, Dec. 31, 1855. Painter and teacher. Saint Mary-of-the-Woods 1841–1855. Work: Flower studies and outdoor sketches, Saint Mary-of-the-Woods.
References: Brown M, Documents.

SAY, LUCY SISTAIRE (MRS. THOMAS SAY)

Born, New London, Conn., Oct. 14, 1801; died, Lexington, Mass., Nov. 15, 1886. Painter and scientific draughtsman. New Harmony, 1826–1834; New York, N. Y., 1834. Drew plates for *American Conchology* (Thomas Say), etc.
References: Burnet, Lockridge, Weiss.

SCHOFIELD, LAURA GIFFORD (MRS. FRANK SCHOFIELD)

Born, Fayette County, Ind., Sept. 25, 1841; died Rushville, Ind., May 27, 1918. Portrait painter. Work: *Jesse Peters,* Herschel Peters, Rushville.
Reference: Documents.

SCHNELL, MADELEINE see: MAURICE, SISTER

SCOTT, FRANK EDWIN

Born, Buffalo, N. Y., 1863; died, Paris, France, Dec. 24, 1929. Figure and landscape painter. Indianapolis, ca. 1877–1880; New York, N. Y., 1880–1882; France, etc., 1882–1890; New York, N. Y., etc., 1891–1892; Paris after 1895.
References: Am Art Ann 1930, Burnet, Dunn 1.

SEGAR, WILLIAM S.

Born, New England, Feb. 16, 1823; died, Covington, Ind., Aug. 14, 1887. Portrait painter. Boston, Mass., 1844; Albany, N.Y., ca. 1850; Covington, ca. 1878–1887; Chicago, Ill., 1882. Work: *Michael Mayer,* Michael Mayer II, Covington.
Reference: Documents.

SEYMOUR, SAMUEL

Born, England (?); died, Philadelphia, Pa. (?). Figure and landscape painter (principally western scenes and Indians). Philadelphia, Pa., 1818; western trips 1819–1824; Fort Wayne, 1823.
References: Dunlap, Fielding, McDermott.

SIES, WALTER

Born, York County, N.Y.; died, Terre Haute, Ind (?). Landscape and carriage painter. Crawfordsville, ca. 1870–1879; Terre Haute, 1880–ca. 1885; Paducah, Ky., ca. 1885–1890; Terre Haute, after 1890. Work: *Steamboats on the Wabash,* Fairbanks Memorial Library, Terre Haute; *Landscape,* Delphine Bradley, Terre Haute; *Landscape,* Sheldon Swope Art Gallery, Terre Haute.
References: Burnet, Documents.

SINKS, ALOIS E.

Born, Dayton, O., Oct. 1848; died, Indianapolis, Ind., July 3, 1881. Painter, poet, and critic. Indianapolis, 1875–1881. Work: *Pioneer School House,* Mrs. F. E. Wickard, Indianapolis, etc.
References: Burnet, Documents, Dunn 1, Forsyth.

SMALLWOOD, WILLIAM

Painter. Indianapolis, 1860–1861.
Reference: Documents.

SNYDER, WILLIAM McKENDREE

Born, Liberty, Ind., Dec. 20, 1849; died, Madison, Ind., Sept. 7, 1930. Portrait, figure, and landscape painter. Cincinnati, O., ca. 1868–1870; Columbus, 1870–1872; Philadelphia, Pa., and New York, N.Y., ca. 1872–1875; Madison, 1875–1930. Work (before 1885): *Rev. W. W. Snyder,* Frank R. Snyder, Oxford, O., *Madison on the Ohio,* Paul N. North, Columbus, O., and others.
References: Burnet, Documents.

SONDERMANN, MARY see: ALBERTINE, SISTER MARY

SPREAD, HENRY FENTON

Born, Kinsale, Ireland, 1844; died, Chicago, Ill., Sept. 3, 1890. Figure painter and teacher. Chicago, Ill., 1871–1875; Indianapolis, 1875; Chicago, Ill., 1876–1890. Work: (Indiana) *Elijah B. Martindale,* Elijah B. Martindale, Indianapolis.
References: Burnet, Clement-H, Documents, Fielding.

STARLING, MRS. S. S.
Painter and teacher. Indianapolis, 1863–1872.
Reference: Documents.

STEELE, THEODORE CLEMENT
Born, Owen County, Ind., Sept. 11, 1847; died, Brown County, Ind., July 24, 1926. Portrait and landscape painter. Battle Creek, Mich., 1870–1873; Indianapolis, 1873–1880; Munich, Germany, 1880–1885; Indianapolis, Brookville, etc., 1885–1910; Brown County, 1910–1926. Work: (before 1885) *Mary Larkin Steele*, Brandt Steele, Indianapolis; *William T. Royse*, Benjamin F. Royse, Bloomington, *James Whitcomb Riley*, Lesley Payne, Indianapolis; *A. S. Bryan*, Mrs. Elizabeth B. Hamrick, Greencastle; *Pleasant Run*, Carl B. Shafer, Indianapolis, and others.
References: Am Art Ann 1926, Biog History, Burnet, Documents, Dunn 1 & 2, Forsyth, Gibson, Ind Art, Steele.

STEPHENS, JOSIAH W.
Portrait and sign painter. Logansport, 1835–1880. Work: *John P. Dillon*, Indiana State Library, Indianapolis.
References: Burnet, Cottman, Documents.

STEVENSON, ELIZABETH (MRS. THOMAS H.)
Portrait painter. Indianapolis, 1883–ca. 1890.
Reference: Documents.

STILLWAGON, G. B.
Painter and teacher. Indianapolis, 1845; Bowling Green, 1868.
Reference: Documents.

SUFFRINS, MRS. N. M.
Portrait painter. Indianapolis, 1865–1866; Muncie, 1868.
Reference: Documents.

SWAIM, CURRAN
Born, Randolph, N.C., Feb. 3, 1826; died, Jasper County, Mo., Sept. 1, 1897. Portrait painter. South Bend, 1856–1869; McHenry County, Ill., 1869–1878; Jasper County, Mo., 1878–1897. Work: (Indiana) *Reynolds Dunn, Robert Sample*, etc., Northern Indiana Historical Museum, South Bend; *Thomas S. Stanfield*, Anna H. Stanfield, South Bend, and others.
Reference: Documents.

SWAIM, ROBERT
Portrait painter. Logansport, 1875–1881; Chicago, Ill., 1882–1886. Work: (Indiana) *Joseph Gammon Barron*, Mrs. H. H. Walker, Shelbyville.
References: Documents, Powell.

SWING, JENNIE (MRS.)
Portrait painter. Richmond, 1865.
Reference: Documents.

TALBOTT, ANNA MATILDA WARES (MRS. JOSEPH C. TALBOTT)
Born, Kentucky, ca. 1810; died, Indianapolis, Ind., Aug. 7, 1882. Painter and teacher. Louisville, Ky., 1838; Indianapolis, 1853–1882.
References: Cottman, Documents, Dunn 1.

TERRELL (TERRYLL), RICHARD (RICHARDSON)
Portrait painter. Lexington, Ky., 1795; Madison, ca. 1825; Indianapolis, 1828; Jefferson County, 1830. Work: *La Fayette*, Masonic Lodge, Madison; *Rebecca Cook Coe*, Evelyn R. Sickels, Indianapolis; *James Mitchell Ray*, Mrs. Louis M. Howe, Fall River, Mass.
References: Burnet, Documents, Dunn 1.

TESTER, PETER
Born, Graubünden canton (Grisons canton), Switzerland, Sept. 11, 1810/19; died, Freelandville, Ind., March 14, 1882. Portrait painter. Freelandville and Vincennes, ca. 1860–1882. Work: *H. L. Bergeman* and *Amanda Piety Bergeman*, Mrs. Flora M. Robbins, Oaktown; *Marcellas Lacroix* and *Adele Bayard Lacroix*, Mrs. T. M. Shircliff, Vincennes.
References: Burnet, Documents.

THRALL, A. N.
Artist. New Harmony, 1850.
Reference: Documents.

THYSSENS, FRANCIS
Artist, Evansville, 1860–1861.
Reference: Documents.

TROWBRIDGE, MRS. M. O.
Portrait painter. Indianapolis, 1879–1883.
Reference: Documents.

UNTHANK, WILLIAM S.
Born, Richmond, Ind., 1813; died, Council Bluffs, Iowa, July 22, 1892. Portrait painter.

Indianapolis, 1840–1841; Richmond, 1857; Indianapolis, 1859–1860; Council Bluffs, Iowa, 1891–1892. Work: *Henry Wishard* and *Harriet Moreland Wishard,* Presbyterian Church, Greenwood; *Edward McGuire,* William M. McGuire, Lima, O.; *Samuel Moore,* John Herron Art Museum, Indianapolis.
Reference: Documents.

VAN FAVOREN, J. H.
Portrait painter. South Bend, 1847. Work: *Alexis Coquillard,* Notre Dame University.
Reference: Documents.

VAN SICKLE, ADOLPHUS
Portrait painter. Goshen, 1848; La Porte, 1849; South Bend, 1849–1874. Work: *Frederick C. King,* Historical Museum, La Porte; *Sarah Thomas,* Mrs. George A. Riley, South Bend, and others.
References: Bartholomew, Documents.

VON SMITH, AUGUSTUS A.
Born, Germany. Portrait painter. Vincennes, 1836–1843. Work: *Francis Vigo,* Vincennes University; *Robert R. Roberts,* De Pauw University, Greencastle.
References: Burnet, Documents.

WAKEMAN, JACOB
Painter. Lafayette, 1873–1874.
Reference: Documents.

WALKER, FERDINAND GRAHAM
Born, Mitchell, Ind., Feb. 16, 1859; died, New Albany, Ind., June 13, 1927. Portrait and landscape painter. New Albany, and Louisville, Ky., 1883–1927. Paris, France, 1885 and 1902–1908. Work: (before 1885) *Silas C. Day,* Mary Scribner, New Albany.
References: Am Art Ann 1927, Burnet, Documents.

WALKER, SAMUEL SWAN
Born, Butler County, O., Feb. 17, 1806; died, Cincinnati, O., May 15, 1848. Portrait painter. Dayton, O., Cincinnati, O., etc., 1836–1848; Richmond, 1841.
Reference: Documents.

WALLACE, LEWIS (LEW)
Born, Brookville, Ind., Apr. 10, 1827; died, Crawfordsville, Ind., Feb. 15, 1905. Portrait and figure painter; soldier, author, and lawyer. Work: *Henry S. Lane,* Lane Place, Crawfordsville; *Isaac C. Elston,* Isaac C. Elston, Jr., Crawfordsville, *The Conspirators,* etc., Lew Wallace Study, Crawfordsville.
References: Burnet, DAB, Documents, Forsyth, Wallace.

WAUGH, HENRY W.
Born, ca. 1835; died, England. Actor and painter. Indianapolis, 1853–ca. 1855; Rome, Italy, ca. 1860–1865. Work: *Landscape,* Eleanor Whitcomb, Indianapolis.
References: Brown, Burnet, Documents, Dunn 1, Gibson.

WHITLOCK, W.
Portrait painter. La Porte, 1876–1877.
Reference: Documents.

WHITTREDGE (WHITRIDGE) THOMAS WORTHINGTON
Born, Springfield, O., 1820; died, Summit, N.Y., Feb. 25, 1910. Portrait and landscape painter. Indianapolis, 1842; Cincinnati, O., 1842–1849; Europe, 1849–1859; New York, N.Y., 1859–1910.
References: Am Art Ann 1910–11, Burnet, Cist 1, Documents, Dunn 1, Fielding, Ind Art, NCAB.

WILLIAMS, JOHN INSCO
Born, Oldtown, O., May 3, 1813; died, Dayton, O., June 26, 1873. Portait painter. Richmond, New Castle, and Indianapolis, 1835. Cincinnati, O., 1835–1840; Richmond, 1840–1841; Cincinnati, O., etc., 1842–1870. Work: (Indiana) *Miles Murphy,* etc., Helen Goodwin, New Castle; *Lewis Crowell Freeman,* and *Susan H. Freeman,* Mrs. William E. Gavin, Indianapolis; *Benjamin Conklin,* Mrs. Robert Montgomery, Cambridge City.
References: Burnet, Clark, Documents, Forsyth, Gibson.

WILSON, VIRGINIA ROHM (MRS. CLAYTON H. TODD)
Born, Beallsville, Pa., Sept. 30, 1851; died, Urbana, Ill., Jan. 10, 1930. Portrait painter. Attica. Work: *Artist's Grandmother,* Will B. Schermerhorn, Attica.
Reference: Documents.

WINTER, GEORGE
Born, Portsea, England, June 10, 1810; died, Lafayette, Ind., Feb. 1, 1876. Portrait

and landscape painter. London, England, 1826–1830; New York, N.Y., 1830–1835; Logansport, 1836–1851; Lafayette, 1851–1876. Work: *Joseph Barron*, etc., Cable G. Ball, Lafayette; *Mary Galpin Cole*, Mrs. Kate Cole Porter, Peru; *Gathering of Indians*, Eli Lilly, Indianapolis; *William Digby*, Wells Memorial Library, Lafayette; *Scene on the Wabash River*, John Herron Art Museum, Indianapolis, and others.
References: Burnet, Cottman, Documents, Dunn 1, Forsyth, Ind Art, Winter.

WITT, JOHN HARRISON
Born, Dublin, Ind., May 18, 1840; died, New York, N.Y., Oct. 22, 1901. Portrait painter. Dublin, 1860–1862; Columbus, O., 1862–1878; New York, N.Y., 1879–1901. Work: (Indiana) *Samuel Dillon*, Florence Stewart, Dublin; *Julia Stanton*, H. Edgar French, New Castle.
References: Am Art Ann 1903–04, Burnet, Clark, Documents, Fielding.

WITTIG, CHARLES
Painter. Indianapolis, 1878–1879.
Reference: Documents.

WOLF, ANNE L.
Painter. Indianapolis, 1881–1884.
Reference: Documents.

WOODWARD, WILBUR WINFIELD
Born, St. Omer, Ind., Jan. 8, 1851; died, Lawrenceburg, Ind., Mar. 19, 1882. Portrait and figure painter. Greensburg, 1867; Indianapolis, 1868; Cincinnati, O., 1869–1871; Antwerp, Belgium, 1871–1873; Paris, France, 1874–1880; Cincinnati, O., 1880–1881. Work: (Indiana) *Adaline Tomlinson McFadden*, Mrs. Everett F. McCoy, Indianapolis, and others.
References: Burnet, Documents, Ind Art.

WOODY, SOLOMON
Born, near Fountain City, Ind., Mar. 11, 1828; died, Fountain City, Nov. 30, 1901. Portrait and landscape painter. Cincinnati, O., 1849; Fountain City, 1852–1868; Cincinnati, O., 1868–1870; Fountain City, 1870–1901. Work: *Paul Way* and *Achsa Moorman Way*, Wayne County Historical Museum, Richmond; *Self-Portrait*, Mrs. Earl F. Smith, Fountain City.
Reference: Documents.

WRIGHT, JAMES D.
Portrait painter. Terre Haute, 1857–1861.
Reference: Documents.

WYETH, P. C.
Portrait painter. New York, N.Y., 1846; Brooklyn, N.Y., 1858; Cincinnati, O., 1849–1851; Madison, Ind., 1851. Work: *Mrs. Charles Shrewsbury and Daughter*, *Five Shrewsbury Sons*, Shrewsbury House, Madison.
Reference: Documents.

WYLIE, THEOPHILUS ADAM
Born, Oct. 8, 1810; died, Bloomington, Ind., June 9, 1895. Professor of natural sciences, and painter. Indiana University, Bloomington, 1837–1852; Miami University, Oxford, O., 1852–1855; Bloomington, 1855–1895. Work: *Political Gathering*, Indiana University, Bloomington.
Reference: Documents.

YONGE, WILLIAM ZEBULON
Born, Aurora, Ind., 1851; died, Vevay, Ind., 1931. Portrait painter. Vevay, 1871–1907; Chicago, Ill., 1907–1930. Work: *Lucille Morerod Detraz*, Switzerland County Historical Society, Vevay; *Julia Morerod Le Clerc*, Mrs. Julie LeClerc Knox, Vevay, and others.
Reference: Documents.

Index

Academie Gérôme, 197
Academy of Design, Chicago, 43, 196, 218
Academy of Design, Cincinnati, 40, 101, 118
Academy of Fine Arts, Cleveland, 119
Academy of Natural Sciences, Philadelphia, 38
Ackerman, Jacob, 118, 120, 125, 225
   Stanis Barnhart, Mary Barnhart, 120, 125
Adams, David, O., 188, 225
Adams, George E., 117, 120, 225
   Self-Portrait, 117
Adams, Mrs. J. G., 171, 225
Adams J. Ottis, 70, 77, 105, 106–107, 204, 206, 225
   Hazel Anderson, 70; *Julius A. Heinsohn,* 106; *Sarah Heinsohn,* 106, pl. 48; *Mrs. W. C. Willard,* 106
Adams, Nelson P., 107–108, 225
   Alvis Adams, Aseneth Baldwin Adams, 108; *Landscape with Cows,* 107, pl. 49
Adams, Wayman, 107
Adams, Winifred Brady, 107
Albertine, Sister Mary (Sondermann), 40, 225
   Orphan Child, 40
Allen County-Fort Wayne Historical Museum, 110, pl. 51, pl. 52
American Art Union, 154, 169
Anastasie, Sister, 40, 225
Anonymous
   Richard Blake, Franceska Blake, 39; *Ratliff Boon,* 52; *Lucien Davenport, Mary Lauer Davenport,* 112; *Miles Cary Eggleston,* 56–57; *Robert M. Evans,* 46; *John Finley,* 87; *John Gibson,* 218; *Jacob Julian, Rebecca Hoover Julian,* 98; *James Lanier,* 60–61; *A. A. Louden,* 147; *Antoinette Dufour Morerod,* 65; *Dennis Pennington,* 52; *Thomas Posey,* 52; *James Ridgway,* 145; *E. H. Shirk, Mary Shirk,* 112; *Catherine Eliza Tate,* 66; *John L. Van Trees,* 18.

Antrobus, John, 188, 192, 219, 225
   James Mitchell, 193; *George J. Stilz,* 193
Archer, Sallie, 177, 225
Art Association of Indianapolis, 40, 134, 182, 199
Art Institute of Chicago, 40, 43, 196
Art Students League, New York, 197, 204, 207
Artists Fund Society, New York, 110
Audubon, John James, 23

Baker, Conrad, 50, 180
Baker, George, 96
Baker, S. Burtis, 181
   William Hendricks, 181
Ball, L. Clarence, 226
Ball State Teachers College, Muncie, 107, pl. 49
Banvard, John, 35–36, 158, 226
   Panorama Royal of the Mississippi and Ohio Rivers, 36
Barker, Mrs. William R., 50
Bartholomew County Courthouse, Columbus, 70
Barnes, Albert A., 226
Bates, Dewey, 183, 188, 197–198, 226
   Ella Bates, 198; *Dutch Comfort,* 198; *Little Jannetje,* 198; *Josephine Landis,* 198, pl. 80; *John Love,* 198
Bates, Eliza, 177, 226
Bates, William O., 205
Batman, Isabel Lowry, 226
Batson, Melvina Hobson, 102, 103, 226
   Amenda Elliott Bundy, 103; *Abraham Elliott,* 103; *Elizabeth Elliott Peed,* 102, pl. 44
Beard, James H., 43
Benjamin Harrison Memorial Home, Indianapolis, 174
Bennett, J. Wesley, 226
Berry, Wilson (Wils) Reed, 17, 118, 122–123, 226
   Logansport Street Scene, 122, pl. 56, *Early Scene in Huntington,* 226

Bierstadt, Albert, 40, 63, 118
Bishop, Granville, 135–136, 226
Blair, Marion, 76–77, 226
   Abraham Lincoln, 77; *Oliver P. Morton*, 77; *Austin Seward, Janet Seward*, 77; *Daily Voss*, 77, pl. 31
Bodmer, Carl, 11–12, 226
   Cut-Off River: Branch of the Wabash, 12; *A Lynx*, 12; *Mouth of the Fox River*, 12; *New Harmony on the Wabash*, 12; *Vincennes*, 12, pl. 3; *White-tail Deer*, 12
Bohe Club, 205
Bowers, T. J., 226
Boyd, Monimia Bunnell, 96–98, 227
   William Bunnell, 98; *George W. Julian*, 98, *The Hoosier's Nest*, 96, pl. 41; *The Lord's Supper*, 98
Branson, Mary Ellen, 103, 227
Bright, C. E., 227
British Institute, London, 49
Brown County, 64, 80, 172
Brown, Ephraim, 150–151, 227
   A. L. Chamberlain, 151; *Bazil Brown*, 151; *Thomas Dowling*, 151; *James Whitcomb*, 151
Brown, Imogene K., 227
Bruening, E. & J., 171
Buckley, R. H., 181
Bundy, John E., 77–79, 94–95, 227
   Rachel Marker Johnson and Daughter, 79; *Thompson Hendricks*, 79; *Summer Landscape*, pl. 33
Burr, Mrs. E. L., 114, 227
Bush, Joseph H., 22

Cameron, James, 151, 227
Carey, Harry, 83–84, 227
   James Wilson, 84
Cass County Historical Museum, Logansport, 116, 216, pl. 56
Chandler, Henry C., 184
Chappelsmith, John, 29, 227
Chase, Martha Owen, 30, 227
Chase, Mary M. Pope, 227
Chase, William M., 40, 81, 167, 177–179, 185, 205, 207, 227
   Mary Elizabeth Browning, 179; *Emma S. Carpenter*, 179; *Benjamin F. Love*, 81, 179; *Wallace Foster*, 179; *William Gurley Munson*, 179, pl. 74; *James B. McFadden*, 81; *William Orbison*, 179
Chicago Historical Society, 137
Chicago World's Fair (Columbian Exposition), 83, 177

Children's Museum, Indianapolis, 128
Cincinnati Art Museum, 217
City Art Museum, St Louis, 20
Clark, Morris W., 227
Clawson, Charles, 96
Colcord, Harry M., 181, 200, 228
   W. McRea, 200; *James D. Williams*, 200
Comparet (Compera), Alexis, 142, 228
   Mrs. Alexis Coquillard, 142
Conn, Alex, 50, 228
Conner, Albert C., 228
Conner, Charles, 95, 228
   In the Parlor, 95, pl. 40; *Wet Night in February*, 95
Conner Prairie Homestead, Noblesville, 155, 175
Cook, C. D., 15–16, 23–24, 228
   George Rogers Clark, 22, pl. 9
Corcoran Gallery of Art, Washington, 218
Cory, Loretta, 228
Cosgrove, B. G., 113, 228
Costigan, Francis, 60
Cottman, George, 205
Cowgill, Elisha, 228
Cox, Jacob, 62, 66, 67, 107, 129, 151, 152–158, 160, 161, 162–165, 171, 180–181, 186, 188, 192, 194, 195, 203, 204, 208, 228
   William Conner, 155; *James Bigger*, 154, 181; *Jesse Fletcher*, 155; *George M. Lockerbie*, 155; *Henry S. Lane*, 181; *Achsa McCollough*, 155; *Charles G. McLean*, 155; *Samuel Merrill*, 155; *Noah Noble*, 181; *James B. Ray*, 181; *Alexander W. Russell*, 155; *John L. Spann*, 155; *Thomas, John, and Eliza Spann*, 155, pl. 67; *Oliver H. Smith*, 154; *William Sullivan*, 153; *David Wallace*, 154, 181, pl. 65; *Joseph A. Wright*, 181; *Morris Morris Farm*, 155, pl. 66; *Mountain Lake*, 154; *Political Banner*, 153; *Temperance Panorama*, 156
Cox, Julia M., 177, 195, 228
Crafft, R. B., 111–112, 113, 228
   Chief Francis LaFontaine, 112; *Catherine Richardville LaFontaine*, 112; *John LaFontaine*, 112; *Jean Baptiste Richardville*, 112; *Robert Filson, Eliza Filson*, 111, pl. 51
Cranstone, Lefevre F., 12–13, 91, 228
   Street Scene in Richmond, 13, pl. 4
Culbertson, Mary Hill, 177, 188, 195–196, 228

Davenport, Patrick H., 71–72, 186, 228
  Abner Alexander, 71; *Brutus J. Clay,* 72;
  George Dunn, 71; *William Franklin,*
  Mary Franklin, 71; *Thomas Jameson,*
  Anna Jameson, 72; *George Hamer, Wil-*
  liam Hamer, Henry Hamer, Mary Ellen
  Hamer, 71, pl. 28; *Jacob Lemon, Mary*
  Lemon, 71; *Robert Logan, Elizabeth*
  Logan, 71
Davies, Thomas J., 175, 229
  John Carlisle, Margaret Boyd Carlisle,
  175; *Fabius M. Finch,* 175; *Mary John-*
  son Tutewiler, 175
Davis, H. A., 125
Davis, Mary Carter, 121–122, 229
  George Bevan, 122; *Sophronia Murphy,*
  122; *Stations of the Cross,* 122
Davis, W. R., 74, 229
De la Matyr, Mrs. Gilbert, 193, 229
Dennis, James M., 99, 174–175, 186, 188,
  192, 204, 229
  Christian Park, 175; *Jefferson Davis,*
  175; *J. W. Gordon,* 175; *James A.*
  Mount, 175; *John C. New,* 175
DePauw University, 24, 134
Detroit Institute of Arts, 106
Dietz, Julius, 50, 229
Dille, Joseph H. 114, 137–138, 229
  James Barnes, 138; *Mrs. John C. Olds,*
  114; *Thomas W. Swinney,* 114, pl. 52;
  Political Banner, 138
Dille, Ralph, 114
Dodds, J., 101, 229
Dousa, Henry, 104, 125, 229
  Solomon Dennis, Elizabeth T. Dennis,
  104; *Cyrus Pence, Catherine Pence,* 104;
  Kate Elliott, 104; *Residence of Thomas*
  Fyffe, 104, pl. 46
Duclos, Peter, 30, 32, 33, 229
Dunlap, James B., 165–167, 171, 229
  Woodville Browning, 166, pl. 70; *Mrs.*
  James Dignan, 166; *Livingston Dunlap,*
  166; *John A. Sutter* (sculpture), 166;
  Barnyard Scene, 166; *Hiram Moore-*
  house on Trial, 218
Dunn, John Gibson, 66–67, 153, 159, 164,
  165, 229
  Christ's Descent from the Cross, 66–67;
  The Temperance Pledge, 66–67, pl.
  26
Dupalais, Virginia Poullard (Twigg), 30,
  229
  Joseph Fauntleroy, 30, pl. 14

Eakins, Thomas, 40
Eames, Lucia A., 50, 230
Earlham College, 78, 91, 93, 94, pl. 39
Eaton, Joseph O., 99, 159, 160–162, 174,
  230
  Charles Good, Margaret Schofield Good,
  162; *Joseph E. Pope,* 162; *Peninnah*
  Mills Pope, 162, pl. 68
Ecole des Beaux-Arts, Paris, 67, 185, 197
Edmondson, Edward, 113, 230
  George Torrence, Alice B. Torrence,
  113; *George W. Wood,* 113; *Landscape,*
  113
Edwards, J. W., 230
Elkhart County Courthouse, Goshen, 138
Emmet, Leslie, 60
  James F. D. Lanier, 60
Evans, D. Scott (DeScott), 118–119, 122,
  230
  George R. Chitwood, 119, pl. 55; *Francis*
  Harwood, Margaret Harwood, 119; *Jo-*
  siah Smithson, 119
Evans, Lewis, 50, 230
Evansville Museum of Arts and Science,
  48, pl. 20
Eyden, William, 96

Fairbanks Public Library, Terre Haute, 45
Farrer, Edwin, 82, 230
  Ebenezer Smith, 82; *Leven E. Wallace,*
  82, pl. 34
Farrer, Henry, 82
Farrer, Thomas, 82
Ferry, Annie E., 230
Fetsch Carl P., 53–54, 183, 186–187, 204,
  208, 230
  John Heitkam, 187; *Grandmother and*
  the Bath, 54, 187
Filson Club, Louisville, 22
First Quarterly Exhibition, Indianapolis,
  184, 197
Fiscus, Charles, 204, 230
  John Stern, 204; *Self-Portrait,* 204;
  Studio Still Life, 204
Fletcher, Aaron Deane, 144–145
  Jacob Replogle, Sinia Replogle, 145
Fletcher, Calvin I., 230
Fluhart, Harry D. (Williams), 91
Forbes, James G., 49, 180, 230
  Conrad Baker, 180, pl. 75; *John B.*
  Baker, 49; *Ratliff Boon,* 180; *Paris C.*
  Dunning, 180; *Jonathan Jennings,* 180;
  Oliver P. Morton, 180; *James Whitcomb,*
  180

Forgy, John D., 118, 120, 231
Forkner, Edgar, 96
Forsyth, Clarence, 205
Forsyth, William, 91, 184, 185, 191, 203, 205–206, 231
   Artist's Mother, 205, pl. 82; *Self-Portrait*, 205
Fort Wayne Art Museum, 100, pl. 50
Fowler, Harry, 200, 231
   Curtis G. H. Goss, Angelica Goss, 200; *Joseph E. Goss, Elizabeth Goss*, 200
Francis Vigo Chapter, D. A. R., Vincennes, pl. 8
Franklin College, 73, 80
Frederickson, William, 188
Freeman, William R., 24–25, 41–42, 59, 181, 186, 188–190, 231
   Tousant C. Buntin, 42; *Blackford Condit*, 42; *Jacob Cox*, 188, pl. 78; *Preston Hussey*, 42; *Samuel P. Judah*, 25, pl. 11; *David F. Vinton, Almus E. Vinton*, 188; *Thomas A. Hendricks*, 181, 188; *François C. Van der Burgh and Josaphine Somes*, 25; *Andrew Weisert, Eleanor Weisert*, 25

German-American Art Club, New York, 53, 187
Gillet, Edgar P., 62, 231
Girardin, Frank J., 96
Glessing, Thomas B., 171, 173–174, 186, 231
   Cold Springs, Riverside Park, 174, pl. 73; *History of Indianapolis*, 174
Goodwin, J. B., 85, 231
Gookins, James F., 41, 42–44, 184, 185, 204, 207, 231
   The Artist's Wife, 44; *Modisette Ferry on the Wabash*, 44, pl. 19
Gordon, Thomas Clark, 158, 231
   Battle Scenes of the Republic (panorama), 158
Gorgas, Joseph R., 47, 231
Greenwood Presbyterian Church, 164, pl. 69
Gregori, Luigi, 231
Grenzard, Louis S., 231
Gruelle, Richard, 206–207, 231
   The Canal, Morning, 207, pl. 84; *Henry M. Socwell*, 207
Guezet, Alexander, 232
Guffin, Lotta, 82, 121, 177, 183, 188, 193–194, 204, 232

Conrad Baker, 194; Horace P. Biddle, 121, 194; Ben F. Davis, 193; John Froelking, Charlotte W. Froelking, 194; Annie Guffin, 193; Addison C. Harris, 194, pl. 79; Thomas C. Harvey, Elizabeth B. Harvey, 194
Gulich, Samuel, 171, 232

Hakelier, Oscar, 50
Hall, Basil, 11, 12, 232
   House on the Banks of the Ohio River, 11, pl. 2; *End of Wabash Island*, 11
Hallock, Minnie, 50
Hamilton, Henry, 3–5, 109
   Burying Place of the Ottawa Indians, 4; *Falls of the Passaic*, 5; *Niagara Falls*, 5; *Ship Rock, Wabash River*, 4, pl. 1
Hanbeck, William, 58–59, 232
Hankins, Samantha Ann, 92–93
Hanover College, 56
Harding, Chester, 18, 19, 20
   Daniel Boone, 18; *Horace Harding*, 20
Harding, Dexter, 19–20
   Wm. A. Chatfield, 19, pl. 7
Harding, Horace, 17–21, 232
   Robert Hamilton Bishop, 20, 21; *Joseph C. Carter*, 20, 21; *Chester Harding*, 20; *Dexter Harding*, 20; *Elias McNamee*, 20 pl. 8
Harding, Spencer, 19
Harris, James F., 58–59, 157, 167, 232
   Evils of Intemperance, Mirror of Intemperance (panoramas), 157; *Indiana Banner*, 158
Harrison, Christopher, 28, 55, 69, 146, 232
Hart, Mary E., 50
Hays, Barton S., 78, 81, 94, 106, 107, 125–128, 129, 167–169, 171, 178–180, 183, 185, 186, 204, 205, 232
   George F. Adams, Rebecca R. Adams, 167, pl. 71; *Mary A. Alford*, 167; *James M. Dougherty*, 127; *James Hays*, 126; *William Henry Harrison*, 168, 180; *Daniel K. Hays*, 126; *Lewis D. Lyons*, 126, pl. 57; *Eleanor M. McKinney*, 127; *James McClure, Phoebe D. McClure*, 127; *William Sandunsky*, 127; *America E. Sewell*, 127; *James Sconce*, 127; *Lewis Haines, Angelica R. Haines*, 127; *W. C. Willard*, 106; *Amy Jane Woodmansee*, 167; *Hays's Homestead, Greenville*, 126; *Uncle Tom's Cabin* (panorama), 126; *Melon and Peaches*, pl. 72

Hays, Samuel, 126, 216
Healy, George P. A., 192
Heart, Jonathan, 7
  Fort Finney, 7
Heaton, Charles M., 142, 232
  Artist's Mother, 142
Heed, J., 137
  Purchasing Sacksee from the Indians, 136–137
Hegler, Jacob, 112–113, 123, 125, 128–129
  Julia Ann Richards Hegler, 128; *Elisha Hitchens, Mary Kent Hitchens*, 128; *William Kent with William and Mary*, 128; *Mary Alice Lyons*, 128, pl. 58; *William Johnson and daughter Belle*, 128; *Nancy and Harriet Johnson*, 128; *Margaret F. Johnson and son James*, 128; *Robert Milford*, 128; *Charles A. Munson*, 113; *Turner Welch*, 123; *Raft on the Ohio*, 128
Henry County Historical Museum, New Castle, 93, 102, 104, pl. 44, pl. 45
Hetherington, Fred A., 205
Hibben, Thomas E., 205
Hill, John B., 180, 195, 233
  Abram A. Hammond, 180; *Thomas Posey*, 180
Hilliard, William Henry (Harry), 62–63, 94, 233
  Anna Webber Dold, 62; *Italian Roses*, 62; *Mountain Scene*, 63; *Prairie Fire*, 62; *Stags with Locked Horns*, 62
Holbruner, Charles E., 122, 233
Holder, J. A., 50
Houghton Library, Harvard University, 5, 211, pl. 1
Howell, Frank J., 178, 179
Huey, M. S., 233
Hunt, William M., 63
Hyde, Emily G., 233

Indiana Art Association, 131, 135, 173, 175, 183
Indiana Department of Conservation, pl. 28
Indiana Historical Society, 124, 174
Indiana Historical Society Library, 7, 13, 29, 30, 33, 104, 131, 207, 218, pl. 4, pl. 46
Indiana Medical School Library, Indianapolis, 194
Indiana School of Art, 43, 183, 204, 205, 207, 219
Indiana Soldiers' & Sailors' Monument, 43

Indiana State Fair, 42, 169, 187
Indiana State Library, 17, 77, 87, 118, pl. 6
Indiana University, 73, 74
Indiana University Library, 11, 13, 73, pl. 2, pl. 30, pl. 32
Indianapolis Art Association, 182
Indianapolis Art Society, 44
Ingraham, Charles B., 176–177, 233
Ingraham, Ellen M., 176–177, 204, 233
  Florence Coffin, Minnie Coffin, 177; *Thomas A. Hendricks*, 177; *Joseph Talbot*, 177
Inness, George, 63

Jarvis, John Wesley, 22
Jenison, Emily, 114, 233
John Herron Art Museum, 17, 44, 67, 106, 126, 128, 155, 167, 179, 198, 199, 204, 218, pl. 5, pl. 26, pl. 40, pl. 57, pl. 58, pl. 66, pl. 76, pl. 84
Jouett, Matthew H., 22
Judah, Harriet B., 233
Julien Academy, Paris, 197

Karolik, Maxim collection, Boston, 13
Kellogg, Miner K., 30, 33–35, 233
  Robert Dale Owen, 35, pl. 16
Kendall, Brook, 233
Kendrick, James R., 233
Kersey, Pliny E., 96, 233
Ketcham, Susan, 206, 207–208, 233
Kirkland, India Underhill, 195, 233
  Oliver P. Morton (sculpture), 195
Klepper, Max, 118, 120–121, 233
Kotz, Daniel, 142, 234

Lane Place, Crawfordsville, 131
Lang, Philip, 51, 234
  Matthias Sharp, 51, pl. 21; *Mary Morgan*, 51; *Samuel J. Park*, 51; *James Proctor*, 51
La Porte County Historical Society, pl. 62
Le Dru, Pierre, 8
  Tecumseh, 8; *The Prophet*, 8
Lesueur, Charles A., 11, 27–29, 30, 31, 34, 234
  John Badollet, 29; *Francis Vigo*, 29; *A Snipe*, 29; *Major Phillips seated on a Box of Potatoes*, pl. 13
Lewis, James O., 9–10, 109, 234
  Chief Francis Godfroy, 10
Lewis, Mrs. M. E., 188
Lew Wallace Study, Crawfordsville, 131

Library of the Workingmen's Institute, New Harmony, 28, 29, 31, 37, 48
Lieber's Art Emporium, Indianapolis, 131, 170, 176, 200, 206
Lietz, Theobald, 72, 74, 108, 183, 186-187, 204, 234
Linen, George, 41, 234
  Henry Clay, 41; *Lucia and Fannie Craft*, 41; *Caleb Mills*, 41, pl. 18; *Chauncey Rose*, 41; *Chauncey Warren, Frances M. Warren*, 41; *Levi Warren*, 41; *Daniel Webster*, 41
Love, John W., 103, 183, 184, 185-186, 191, 201, 205, 207, 234
  Louis Kiefer, 186; *Fontainebleau Forest*, 186; *Henry L. Sielken*, 186, pl. 77; *The Sycamores*, 186, pl. 76
Ludington, Julia, 177, 234
Lumbert, Horace, 234
Lutz, Lewis Cass, 101
  Thomas S. Noble, 101
Luxembourg Gallery, Paris, 62
Lyon, Lyman, 30

McDonald, Charles L., 205, 206, 207
MacDonald, Mary, 122, 234
McDowell, Lucinda Bowers, 103, 104, 234
  Samuel Graham, 103, pl. 45
McEvoy, Henry N., 171, 234
McLean Female Seminary, 168
McLean, Jerome, 118, 120, 234
  Joseph Seiter, 120
McMicken School of Design, Cincinnati, 67, 101
McNiff, P., 211
McQuigg, Lizzie, 50
Maentel, Jacob, 35, 36-37, 235
  John Cooper, 37; *Jonathan Jaquess, Rebecca Jaquess*, 37, pl. 17; *James and Emory Overton*, 37; *Thomas and James Rabb*, 37
Mason, Joseph, 144, 235
  Maria Jane Andrew, 144
Massalon, James, 50, 235
Mathews, Retta, 83, 235
  Still Life, 83
Mattes, Joseph, 122
Maurice, Sister, 40, 235
Maximilian, Prince of Wied, 12, 30
Mayfield, James, 137
  Self-Portrait, 137
Mendenhall, J. B., 188, 235
Merine, A., 139, 235

Mersmann, Ferdinand, 184
Metropolitan Museum of Art, New York, 78
Metropolitan Theater, Indianapolis, 173
Metzner, August, 204, 206
Miami County Historical Museum, Peru, 105, 116, pl. 47
Miami University, 20, 75, 119
Miller, Gustav, 235
Miller, William, 159, 162, 177
Millison, Royal H., 188, 235
Millikan, Rhoda H., 235
Mills, Henry A., 134, 235
  Reuben Andrus, 134; *John P. D. John*, 134; *Alexander Martin*, 134
Mitchell, Harvey, 44-45
  Warren Davis, Amelia Davis, 45; *John H. O'Boyle*, 45
Momberger, William, 12, 13, 235
  Evansville on the Ohio, 13; *St. Mary, St. Joseph & Maumee Rivers near Fort Wayne*, 13; *Wabash River near Vincennes*, 13
Montgomery County Historical Society, Crawfordsville, pl. 59
Morgan, Louis, 57
Morgan, T. W., 57
Morret, E. L., 50
Morrison, George W., 45, 52-53, 181, 235
  Jessie Austin, 53; *Edward Bindley, Aimee Bindley*, 46; *Thomas Collins, Margaret Collins*, 53; *Charles Hale*, 52; *John Reily*, 53; *Eliza Reddick Stillson*, 53; *William A. Scribner, Harriet Hale Scribner*, 52; *Mary Stewart Shields*, 53; *Self-Portrait*, 53; *Ashbel P. Willard*, 53; 181; *Mary Emma and Harry Woodward*, 53, pl. 22
Morse, Samuel F. B., 181
  House of Representatives, 181
Mosler, Henry, 96, 185
Mote, Alden, 94, 235
  Daniel Reid, 94; *James M. Starr*, 94; *Edna Stubbs Cathell*, 94
Mote, Marcus, 87, 92-94, 102, 103, 105, 235
  Jehu Elliott, Hannah B. Elliott, 93, 102; *James Garr*, 93; *Elizabeth C. Gilbert*, 93, pl. 38; *Lavina Hunt Morris*, 93; *Jonathan Roberts, Mary Roberts*, 93; *Self-Portrait*, 93; *John Shroyer, Elizabeth Shroyer*, 93, 102; *John Smith*, 93; *Josiah White*, 87; *Indiana Yearly Meeting of Friends*, 93, pl. 39; *Course of Creation*

(panorama), 94; *Uncle Tom's Cabin*, 94; *Paradise Lost and Regained*, 94
Munsey, David, 178

National Academy of Design, New York, 61, 100, 115, 155, 178, 185
New Albany Public Library, 53
New Harmony Thespian Society, 28, 32
New, James R., 69–70, 79, 236
    Joseph Bartholomew, 70, 79
Newman, E. P., 70
    Home of John H. Farnum, 70
New Orleans Exposition, 177
Newport, James H., 122, 236
Nicholson, Elizabeth, 177, 236
Nicholson, John, 79–80, 81, 133, 236
    Royal S. Hicks, 80; *Benjamin P. Irwin*, 80
Nicolai, Charles, 205
Niemeyer, John H., 169, 171, 236
Northcote, James, 38
Northern Indiana Historical Society, South Bend, 216, pl. 61

Obeonesser, Balthazar, 236
O'Byrne, Rose, 50
    Evansville Waterfront, 50
Odd Fellow's Lodge, Rushville, 82
Ohio Historical and Philosophical Society Library, Cincinnati, 218
Owen, David Dale, 30, 31, 32, 33, 38, 236
    Hot Springs of Arkansas, 31; *Joseph Neef*, 31; *Richard Owen*, 31, pl. 15
Owen, Richard, 30, 31, 32

Panoramas, 35–36, 90, 94, 126, 156, 157, 158, 171
Park, Asa, 72
Pattison, James W., 179
Peckham, Lewis, 14–17, 23, 28, 236
    Hyacinthe Lasselle, 17, pl. 6; *Thomas Peckham and Self-Portrait*, 17, pl. 5
Pennsylvania Academy of Fine Arts, 87
Pentzer, Orrin, 81
Pering, Cornelius, 74–75, 236
    Andrew Wylie, 75; *Seminary Campus, Bloomington*, 75, pl. 30
Pering, Cornelia, 75
Philadelphia Centennial Exhibition, 187, 198–199
Poindexter, James T., 38, 47–49, 50–51, 236
    Madison J. Bray, 48; *Samuel G. Brown, Marie Louisa Brown*, 51; *James P. Ben-*

nett, 38, 48; *Willard Carpenter*, 48; *Mrs. Charles Mason*, 48, pl. 20; *Sarah Nelson*, 48; *Charles H. White*, 38, 48; *The Tribute Money*, 49
Potter, William J., 118, 236
Pullman, Margaret MacDonald, 122, 236
Purcell, C. W., 237
Purdue University, 29, 124, pl. 13

Quick, Isaac, 81
    Mary Ewing, 81

Raleigh, Eldora, 50
Read, Thomas Buchanan, 59–60, 175–176, 237
    Milton Dictating Paradise Lost to his Daughters, 59; *James F. D. Lanier*, 60; *Oliver P. Morton*, 175–176
Reed, Louis H., 237
Reed, Peter F., 81, 99, 154, 171–173, 237
    In the Adirondacks, 173; *On the Susquehanna*, 173
Reid, John, 237
Richards, J. R., 117, 143–144, 237
Richards, Samuel, 72–74, 81, 105–106, 187, 204, 206, 237
    Silas Bailey, 73; *John Fothergill and Son*, 73; *James L. Mitchell*, 73; *Harlan Richards*, 72, pl. 29; *Guy Robinson*, 73; *Evangeline*, 106
Richmond Art Association, 216
Riley, James Whitcomb, 105
    Making Hay while the Sun Shines, 105, pl. 47
Riess, William J., 237
Roberts, Daniel, 135
Rockwell, Horace, 109–111, 113, 237
    Frances Comparet, 110; *Charlotte Griffith Ewing*, 110; *Samuel Hanna Family*, 110, pl. 50; *Resurrection of Christ and the Virgin Mary*, 110
Rogers, Michael G., 149–150, 237
    Isaac Dunn, Frances Dunn, 149, 150, pl. 64
Rooker, Samuel S., 28, 146–148, 237
    John H. B. Nowland, 147
Rose Polytechnic Institute, Terre Haute, 41
Rowley, Fayette R., 237
Royal Academy, Antwerp, 197
Royal Academy, London, 12, 49, 75, 115
Royal Academy, Munich, 40, 43, 74, 106, 107
Royal Scottish Academy, Edinburgh, 41, 49
Rudisill, Margaret, 177, 193, 195, 204, 237

Rush County Historical Museum, Rushville, 82, 83, 84, pl. 34
Ryan, George W., 85
Ryan, Linda Jenkins, 108
    Susan Ryan, 108

St. Francis Xavier, Sister, 40, 238
St. John's Academy, Indianapolis, 40
St. Louis Exposition, 95
Saint Mary-of-the-Woods, 40
Salon, Paris, 12, 62, 185
Say, Lucy Sistaire, 30, 238
Scantlin, Bertha, 50
Schofield, Laura Gifford, 83, 238
    Jesse Peters, 83
Scott, Frank Edwin, 204, 205, 238
Segar, William S., 129, 238
    Michael Mayer, 129
Seymour, Samuel, 8–9, 109, 238
    Cave-in-Rock, 9
Shackleford, William S., 134
    George Whitfield Reed, 134; *Isaac Reed*, 134
Sheldon Swope Art Gallery, Terre Haute, 24, 44, 45, pl. 19
Shirlaw, Walter, 43
Sies, Walter, 44, 45, 133, 238
    Fort Harrison, 45; *Steamboat on the Wabash*, 45
Sinks, Alois, 131–133, 168, 188, 189–196, 200, 238
    Battlefield of Stone River, 191; *Country Schoolhouse*, 191; *Study of Beech Trees*, 191; *View of Indianapolis from the Union Stock Yards*, 191
Smallwood, William, 171, 238
Smith, Russell, 87
Smithsonian Institution, Washington, 9
Smithson College, Logansport, 118, 119, 122
Snyder, R. W., 64
Snyder, William McK. (Will), 56, 63–64, 65, 80–81, 238
    Artist's Mother-in-law, 63; *John F. Crowe*, 56; *Madison on the Ohio*, pl. 24; *Battle of Shiloh*, 64; *Nymph of the Lillies*, 64; *Ophelia*, 64; *Phythias at the Block*, 64
Society of British Artists, London, 198
South Kensington School of Art, London, 70
Spread's Art Academy, Chicago, 196
Spread, Henry F., 44, 45, 142, 196, 238
    Elijah B. Martindale, 196; *Sad News, Chicago Arising from her Ashes*, 197

Spring Mill State Park, 71
Stark, Otto, 197
Starling, Mrs. S. S., 177, 239
Statehouse, Indianapolis, 50, 53, 97, 155, 166, 168, 175, 188
State Museum, Indianapolis, 136
Steele, Brandt, 219
Steele, Theodore C., 107, 135, 182, 183, 192, 200–203, 206, 239
    Alexander Bryan, Susan Bryan, 135; *A. S. Farrow*, 135; *Doctor Fletcher*, 202; *Major Gordon*, 202; *Andrew Lockridge, Elizabeth Lockridge*, 135; *Albert G. Porter*, 182; *James Whitcomb Riley*, pl. 81; *Christ Church*, 202; *Wabash Alley from Canal*, 202; *Pleasant Run*, pl. 83
Stem, Hartsel, 205
Stephens, Josiah M., 117–118, 239
    John E. Dillon, 117–118
Sternback, Joseph, 188
Stevenson, Elizabeth, 239
Stigleman, Flora, 99
    Paul O. Jones, 99; *Henry Stigleman, Caroline Stigleman*, 99
Stillwagon, G. B., 239
Stillwell, W. D., 134
Stuart, Gilbert, 15
Suffrins, Mrs. N. M., 108, 117, 239
Sully, Thomas, 87
Swaim and Clark, 141
Swaim, Curran, 140–141, 239
    Thelus Bissell, Ellen Bissell, 141; *Reynolds Dunn, Phoebe T. Dunn*, 141; *Samuel Sample*, 141, pl. 61; *Thomas S. Stanfield*, 141
Swaim, Robert, 118, 120, 239
    Joseph Gammon Barron, 120
Swing, Jennie, 239
Switzerland County Historical Society, Vevay, 65, 119

Talbott, Mrs. M. A., 195, 239
Terrell, Richard, 28, 57–58, 148–149, 239
    Marquis de Lafayette, 57–58; *Rebecca Cook Coe*, 149, pl. 63; *Ruth Parker Hobbs*, 149, *James Mitchell Ray, Marie Coe Ray*, 149
Tester, Peter, 24, 26, 239
    H. L. Bergeman, Amenda Bergeman, 26; *Henry S. Cauthorn*, 26; *Andrew Gardner*, 26; *Marcellas Lacroix, Adele Bayard Lacroix* 26, pl. 12
Tiebout, Cornelius, 30
Thrall, A. N., 239
Thyssens, Francis, 239

Tinsley, Harriet Hillis, 82
  David Hollis, 82
Tippecanoe County Historical Museum, Lafayette, 116, 123, 124
Trowbridge, Mrs. M. O., 239
Tyrrell, Grace, 50

University Art Galleries, University of Notre Dame, 139, 142, pl. 60
Unthank, William S., 164, 239
  Edward McGuire, 164; *Samuel Moore, Eliza Moore*, 164; *William A. Reddish, Sarah S. Reddish*, 165; *Henry Wishard, Harriet Moreland Wishard*, 164, pl. 69
Upchurch, Mary, 50

Van Favoren, J. H., 139, 240
  Alexis Coquillard, 139, pl. 60
Vanneman, Hiram B., 104–105
Van Sickle, Adolphus, 137, 140, 144, 240
  Mrs. Joseph H. Defrees, 137; *Frederick C. King*, 144, pl. 62; *Mrs. Sarah Thomas*, 137; *Thomas Webber, Emaline P. Webber*, 144; *Leroy Webber, Sarah D. Webber*, 144
Verbrick, Richard, 217
  Charles Cox, 217
Vincennes University, 22, 24, pl. 9, pl. 10
Volk, Douglas, 219
Von Smith, Augustus A., 24, 135, 240
  Robert R. Roberts, 24, 134; *Francis Vigo*, 22, 24, pl. 10

Wabash College, 42, 70, 130, 133
Wakeman, Jacob, 125, 240
Waldo and Jewett, 60
Walker, Ferdinand G., 53, 54, 240
  Silas C. Day, 54
Walker, James, 30
Walker, Samuel S., 88, 89, 90, 91, 240
  Elizabeth Rohrer, Josaphine Rohrer, 91
Wallace, Lew, 42, 130–133, 159, 163–164, 181, 189, 240
  Isaac C. Elston, 130; *Henry Smith Lane*, 130, pl. 59; *The Conspiracy*, 131; *Over the Dead Line*, 131; *Reluctant Love*, 131–132; *Kankakee River*, 131
Walters, William T., collection, Baltimore, 207
Warder, John H., 184
Warren, George, 32, 33
Warren, Josiah, 33
  Head of a Girl, 33
Waugh, Henry W., 156–157, 167, 240
Wayne County Historical Museum, Richmond, 93, pl. 42

Wells Memorial Library, Lafayette, 124
Welby, Adlard, 10
  Log Tavern, 10; *Rappite Church*, 10
West, Benjamin, 46, 92
West, John Benjamin, 46
West Point Military Academy, 6, 34
West, William E., 46
Whistler, George Washington, 6, 109
Whistler, James Abbott McNeill, 7
Whistler, John, 6, 109
  Fort Dearborn, 6; *Fort Wayne*, 6
White, George, 81
  Marie Louise Chitwood, 81
Whitewater College, Centerville, 99, 172, 173
Whitlock, W., 145, 240
Whittredge, Thomas Worthington, 159–160, 240
  Tilghman Howard, 159; *Henry Ward Beecher*, 159; *Harriet Beecher Stowe*, 159
Wiley's Auction Room, Indianapolis, 154, 160
Willard Library, Evansville, 48, 50
William Henry Harrison Mansion, Vincennes, 20, 218
Williams, J. Insco, 63, 86–91, 93, 101–103, 150, 158, 240
  William Buford, 89; *Benjamin Conklin, Alice Harris Conklin*, 89, 101, pl. 37; *Lewis Crowell Freeman, Susan Harris Freeman*, 150, pl. 36; *George McCullough, Eliza Jane McCullough*, 89; *Miles Murphy, Elizabeth Murphy*, 87, pl. 35; *Joseph Tarkington, Maria S. Tarkington*, 87; *Grand Moving Panorama of the Bible*, 90
Williams, Harry D. Fluhart, 91
Williams, John N., 91
Williams, Margaret, 91
Wilson, Virginia R. (Todd), 129, 240
  Artist's Grandmother, 129
Winter, George, 7, 81, 88, 115–117, 120, 123–124, 240
  Joseph Barron, 116, pl. 53; *Daniel Bearss, Emma Cole Bearss*, 116; *Albert Cole, Mary Galpin Cole*, 116; *Chief Francis Godfroy*, 116; *William Digby*, 123, 124, frontispiece; *John Purdue*, 124; *David D. Pratt*, 116; *George Proffit*, 116; *Frances Slocum*, 116; *Rebecca T. Squire*, 124; *Edward Reynolds, Sarah Reynolds*, 124; *Mary C. Wagstaff*, 124; *Simon Wilkinson*, 116; *Jordan Vigus, Cyrus Vigus*, 116; *Gathering of Indians*, 116, pl. 54;

Tippecanoe Battleground, 124; *Views of Biddle's Island*, 121
Witt, John H., 99–100, 241
  Samuel Dillon, 100; *Julia Stanton*, 100, pl. 43; *The Old Crossing*, 100
Wittig, Charles, 241
Wolf, Annie L., 241
Wolff, Carrie, 204
Woodward, Wilbur, 67–68, 241
  America, 68; *Ossian*, 68; *Springtime*, 68; *Adeline Tomlinson McFadden*, 68, pl. 27
Woody, Soloman, 95–96, 241
  Paul Way, Achsa Moorman Way, 95, pl. 42

Wright, James D., 41, 42, 241
Wyant, Alexander, 63, 100, 138, 174
Wyeth, P. C., 61, 241
  Mrs. Charles Shrewsbury and Daughter, 61; *Sons of Charles L. Shrewsbury*, 61, pl. 23
Wylie, Richard D., 76
  Andrew Wylie, 76
Wylie, Theophilus A., 75, 241
  Political Rally, 75, pl. 32

Yonge, William Z., 65, 241
  Lucille Morerod Detraz, 65, pl. 25; *Julia Morerod LeClerc*, 65; *John E. Williams*, 65

PRIVATE OWNERS OF PAINTINGS MENTIONED
IN THIS BOOK

Institutional owners are listed in the above section of the Index

Austin, Harry, 214
Bailey, Mrs. Cicero, 103
Baker, Thaddeus R., 194
Ball, Cable G., 124, pl. 53
Barnard, Mrs. Belle, 98
Bass, Mamie L., 191
Baum, Mrs. Harry, 122
Becker, John W., pl. 79
Berkley, Merrill, 166
Bevan, Winifred, 122
Bindley, Delphine, 45, 46
Bishop, L. O., 136
Black, Jean, 167, 216
Bloomfield, May, 215
Bozell, Walter, 193
Bray, Mrs. E. C., 99
Browning, Elizabeth, 166
Browning, Mrs. R. H., 179
Brumenshenkel, Mrs. A. G., 179
Bullock, Mrs. Melba, 51
Bunnell, Mrs. V. A., 98, pl. 41
Bushman, Emma, 194
Buttolph, Mrs. Henry W., 165
Carr, James W., 63

Cauthorn, Clotilde, 26
Chitwood, William H., 119, pl. 55
Christian, Mrs. Edna, 175
Claypool, Elizabeth, 44
Cochran, Charles F., 144
Coe, Mrs. Demus S., 89
Collins, Lloyd, 214
Comstock, Elizabeth, 91
Condit, Helen, pl. 18
Conner, Paul, 78
Cooper, Mrs. Perry, 73
Corrington, Knox, 46
Cox, Linton, 194
Crampton, Mrs. Charles C., 89
Dakin, Mrs. Esse Bissell, 141
Dancer, C. R., 113
Davidson, Mrs. Charles, 60
Davis, Mrs. Frank, 158
Defrees, Donald, 137
DeVal, W. J., 129
Donnell, Arthur, 81
Dougherty, Maud, 127
Douglas, Mrs. Prudence, 81, 179
Drummond, Mrs. James, 72

Dunn, Caroline, 149, 214, pl. 64
Edwards, Mrs. Richard E., 215
Ehrmann, Mrs. Bess, 80
Eldridge, Mrs. Addie, 122
Elliott, Louise, 119, 122
Ellis, Bertha, 167, 175, pl. 71
Elston, Isaac C., Jr., 130
Englehart, Mrs. Ira H., 126
Everhart, Oscar C., 212, pl. 7
Ewbank, Mrs. Howard, 82
Farley, Mrs. Daniel A., 63
Fee, Bert, 81
Fogleman, Ida, 164, 218
Forsyth, Mrs. William, 205, pl. 82
French, H. Edgar, 100, pl. 43
Garber, Michael E., 57
Gavin, Mrs. William E., 150, pl. 36
Gilbert, Harry W., 93, pl. 38
Goode, Harriet, 57
Goodwin, Helen M., 87, pl. 35
Goss, George C., 200
Gray, Anna L., 200
Halbridge, C. W., 51
Hall, Fannie H., 26
Hamrick, Mrs. Elizabeth, 135
Hartley, Mrs. Robert H., 106, pl. 48
Hegler, Willoughby R., 128
Heitkam, Walter, 187
Hill, Mrs. Samuel I., 51, pl. 21
Hinshaw, Naomi Hays, 167, 216
Hobbs, Carrie, 149
Holloway, Mrs. Alice Good, 162
Howe, Mrs. Louis McHenry, 149
Hunt, Mary M., 73
Hyatt, Harry V., 18
Irwin, Howard, 80
Jaquess, Arthur E., 37, pl. 17
Johnson, Mrs. Roscoe, 44
Johnston, Isabelle, 175
Johnston Jo C., pl. 33
Jones, Mrs. Addie, 99
Judah, Reynolds S., 25, pl. 11
Karl Viktor Prince zu Wied, 12, pl. 3
Kersey, Emily, 215
Knox, Julie Le Clerc, 65, pl. 25
Krull, Mrs. Frederic, 188
Landis, Mrs. M. M., 198
Lewis, Mrs. Frank, 167, 175
Lilly, Eli, pl. 54
Lilly, Josiah K., 215
Lindsay, H. W., 103
Logan, C. E., 71
Logan, Harlan Richards, pl. 29
McClure, Arthur, 127
McCoy, Mrs. Everett F., 68, pl. 27

McGuire, William M., 164
Madigan, Mrs. Gertrude, 127
Manlove, Mrs. Edd A., 33
Martin, Catherine, 126
Martindale, Elijah B., 196
Matson, Clifford, 110
Mayer, Michael, 129
Miller, Milford, 50
Montgomery, Pauline Woodward, 215, pl. 37
Moore, Arthur, 175
Moore, Eleanor Dunn, pl. 64
Moore, Mrs. George, 71
Moynahan, Mrs. Robert B., 162, pl. 68
Newby, Mrs. Paul E., 217
Nixon, John, 95
North, Paul H., pl. 24
Oaks, Mrs. L. R., 77
Offutt, Clark, 83
Owen, Howard, 112
Owen, Kenneth Dale, 31, pl. 15, pl. 16
Parker, Minnie, 126, 128
Payne, Lesley, pl. 81
Peck, Herman L., 174
Peckham, Mary W., 17
Pierce, Douglas, 188
Pittman, Netta B., 166, pl. 70
Porter, Elmer, 93
Rabb, Winfield W., 37
Ray, Charles, 37
Reed, Mrs. Sarah D., 117
Reed, Mrs. William B., 126
Reily, E. A., 214
Replogle, L. W., 145
Reynolds, Eva Peters, 121
Ridgway, John A., 145
Riley, Mrs. George A., 137
Robbins, Mrs. Earl, 26
Robinson, Jesse, 73
Rockwood, Mrs. William M., 198, pl. 80
Rose, Mrs. George, 44
Ross, Mrs. John C., 39
Schermerhorn, Will B., 129
Scott, Mrs. Emmet, 144
Scribner, Mary, 54
Seiter, Victor E., 120
Seward, W. Austin, 77
Shafer, Carl B., 62, pl. 72, pl. 83
Sheetz, W. J., 128
Shircliff, Mrs. Thomas M., 26, pl. 12
Showalter, C. B., 79
Sickels, Evelyn R., 149, pl. 63
Sielken, Harry L., pl. 77
Simpson, Mrs. Edward, 51
Smith, Mrs. Earl T., 95

Smith, Mrs. Edna, 79
Smith, Rodney D., 214
Smith, S. Edwin, 77
Snyder, Frank R., 63
Somes, Harry, 25
Spades, Cyril C., pl. 78
Spann, Anna H., pl. 67
Spinning, Mrs. Julia, 127
Stahl, Mrs. J. H., 127
Stanfield, Anna H., 141
Stanfill, Mrs. Allen, 20
Stewart, Mrs. Florence, 100
Stewart, W. K., 162
Stewart, Mrs. W. V., 124
Stillson, Blanche, 214
Stitt, Samuel Forrest, 48
Strong, Edgar R., 77, pl. 31
Sullivan, William George, 153
Sweet, Mrs. Warren, 113
Taflinger, Elmer, 204
Talbott, Harriet, 177

Terrell, Mrs. Maud E., 49
Thompson, George B., 124
Todd, Elizabeth, 129
Tubbs, Mrs. W. E., 128
Turner, Mrs. William, 125
Walker, Mrs. H. H., 120
Weaser, Hilda, 64
Webster, Mrs. Hayden, 174
Weisert, Clementine, 25
Weiss, Carlton, 187
White, Esther Griffin, 87
White, Mrs. Floyd E., 148
Wickard, Mrs. F. E., 191
Williams, Albert E., 134
Williamson, Mrs. R. R., 136
Willkie, Mrs. Wendell, 82
Wood, Eleanor Shrewsbury, pl. 23
Woodward, Katherine, 214, pl. 22
Wurzburg, Mrs. Felix, 179, pl. 74
Wylie, Thana L., 76